Migration and Ethnicity in Chinese History

MIGRATION AND ETHNICITY IN CHINESE HISTORY

Hakkas, Pengmin, and Their Neighbors

SOW-THENG LEONG

Edited by TIM WRIGHT
with an Introduction and Maps by G. WILLIAM SKINNER

STANFORD UNIVERSITY PRESS
STANFORD, CALIFORNIA
1997

Stanford University Press
Stanford, California

Printed and bound by CPI Group (UK) Ltd,
Croydon, CR0 4YY
CIP data appear at the end of the book

For Tania

Editor's Preface

This book has unfortunately had to be completed by Sow-Theng Leong's friends after his untimely death in 1987. He left extensive writings on the Hakkas and Pengmin, in three major papers, which Mrs. Vickie Leong asked me to help edit for publication. This book is the result.

Sow-Theng Leong was born in 1939 in Malaysia, where he received his secondary education. He then went to university in the United States, graduating with a B.A. magna cum laude in history from Brandeis and with an M.A. and Ph.D. (in 1969) from Harvard.

Apart from a brief period teaching in Malaysia before embarking on his Ph.D., Professor Leong began his career with a post at the International Christian University in Tokyo. From there he went in 1971 to a research fellowship in the Department of Far Eastern History at the Australian National University. After teaching in the Department of History at Melbourne University from 1974 through 1984, he moved to Western Australia in 1985 to take up the chair of Asian Studies at Murdoch University. As a colleague, Professor Leong combined tact with quiet effectiveness, playing an active part in university life while also promoting Asian Studies in the wider community. He was widely popular with both staff and students.

Sow-Theng Leong's scholarship entitles him to a prominent position in the field of Chinese history. His first major interest was Sino-Soviet relations, to which he brought outstanding talents both as a historian and as a linguist. He used published and archival materials in English, Japanese, Russian, and Chinese, especially the Waijiao bu archives at the Institute of Modern History,

Academia Sinica in Taibei. The two full-length works that resulted from this research, his monograph *Sino-Soviet Relations: The First Phase, 1917–1920* and his book *Sino-Soviet Diplomatic Relations, 1917–1926*, remain the standard works in the field. He contributed also to many other aspects of the study of Sino-Russian relations, ranging from the Czarist presence in the northeast to contemporary foreign policy. He retained this interest throughout his career, most recently writing before his death an excellent paper on Sun Yat-sen's Bolshevik alliance. Later in his career, Professor Leong turned to social history and began to work on the history of the Hakka people, to which he himself belonged.

Those of us who were fortunate enough to know Sow-Theng Leong will miss him for his personal qualities, perhaps even more than for his scholarly and professional achievements. Everyone valued his unselfishness, kindness, and quiet sense of humor, and many can cite stories of those little things he unstintingly did to help others—the little things through which a person's real character emerges.

This volume stands as a tribute to Sow-Theng Leong both as a scholar and as a person.

It remains to say what I have done as the book's editor. All the primary research, ideas, and intellectual input are from Sow-Theng Leong. Nevertheless, after some thought, I decided that this work would be most useful to readers if it included at least some reference to that literature published since Professor Leong's death. Thus, although I have neither tried nor thought it appropriate to do extra substantive work on the topics, I have in places supplemented the analysis using recently produced secondary materials from China and Taiwan (the major examples are indicated by notes enclosed in brackets). The most important substantive additions to the original manuscript are the maps, which have been prepared by G. William Skinner. As editor I have also attempted to draw out some of the inferences that emerge from these maps.

The author's intention had been to supplement the analysis of the Hakkas and Pengmin with one of the She minority, whom the Hakkas displaced. Unfortunately, this project was never completed.

Thus, the intellectual content of the work is entirely the contribution of the original author, but I must take responsibility for much of the actual form the present work takes. Professor Leong left three large, though partially overlapping, papers: on ethnicity and migration, on the Hakkas in Lingnan in modern times (the only one that has been previously published), and on the Pengmin. I have reworked these into their present form, so that much of the chapter structure and therefore some of the introductory and concluding paragraphs are my work, though I never did more than to try to contextualize the author's ideas. It has not been possible to check all the references against the original sources, many of which are rare gazetteers, and I would be very grateful for any corrections that could be included in a second printing.

I have no doubt that if Sow-Theng Leong had lived to see the publication of this book, his first acknowledgment would be to Professor G. William Skinner, whose immense contributions to the study of China are visible on every page. In the editing, too, Professor Skinner's support and intellectual contribution have been invaluable. Not only has Professor Skinner written the Introduction and been the force behind producing the maps, which are an important contribution to the field in their own right, but he has made numerous other contributions to the manuscript both before and after I took it over.

Mary Erbaugh, Danny Kane, Harry Lamley, Lo Hui-min, Susan Mann, Susan Naquin, Evelyn Rawski, Jon Unger, Wang Gung-wu, and many others have been helpful in the course of editing this work, and they encouraged me to continue. The editors of Stanford University Press—Muriel Bell, Richard Gunde, and Nathan MacBrien—have also been of great help in making a complex manuscript more clear, concise, and accessible.

The maps were produced by G. William Skinner, who also generously contributed much of the necessary funding. With consummate skill, Chessy Qi Si helped in carrying out the GIS (geographic information systems) work and map production. William Lavely, director of CITAS (China in Time and Space), was kind enough to share data and provide technical assistance. From his China GIS Project at Griffith University, Australia, Lawrence Crissman very generously made available the basic hydrology coverage used in our 1:1 million map and computerized maps from the *Language Atlas of China*. The elevation contours were taken from the *Digital Chart of the World*.

Some funding for the production of the maps came from a Special Research Grant from Murdoch University, for which I would like to express my thanks.

I also thank the School of Humanities, Murdoch University, for funding some research assistance in the final stages of the project, Wang Yi for help in translating some difficult passages, and Anna Clark-Doyle and Anne-Marie Brady for assistance in checking the manuscript. Professor Leong's original research also benefited from an Australian Research Council grant.

Finally, I would like to acknowledge the permission of the University Press of America to publish as Chapters 3 and 4 of this book a revised version of "The Hakka Chinese in Lingnan: Ethnicity and Social Change in Modern China," in David Pong and Edmund Fung, eds., *Ideal and Reality: Social and Political Change in Modern China, 1860–1949* (Lanham, Md.: University Press of America, 1985), pp. 287–326.

Above all, from Mrs. Vickie Leong came the original impetus for this project to be completed after Professor Leong's tragic death. Since then Vickie Leong has given patient and steadfast support to a project that has taken all too long. Through this and her interest in the S.-T. Leong Memorial Scholarship Fund, she has ensured that Professor Leong's memory lives on both in his own university and in the broader scholarly world.

Tim Wright
Murdoch University

Contents

Illustrations

FIGURE

MAPS

Tables

A Note on Conventions in the Text, Tables, and Maps

PLACE NAMES

The conventions for place names used in this book are largely pinyinized versions of those in G. William Skinner, *Modern Chinese Society: An Analytical Bibliography* (Stanford: Stanford University Press, 1973).

The generic designation *xian* (county) is omitted except where the name would otherwise have only one syllable. Conversely, two-syllable place names with no generic designation are *xian*.

For higher-level administrative units and one-syllable *xian*, a distinction is made between the administrative unit and the settlement that was the capital of that unit. In the former case, the generic designation is given as a separate word; for example, "Wei xian" refers to the county Wei xian in Shandong, and "Guangzhou fu," to the prefecture of Guangzhou fu in Guangdong. In the latter case, the generic part of the name is hyphenated, and thus "Wei-xian" and "Guangzhou-fu" denote the capitals of the two units mentioned above.

TABLES

The following conventions are used in Tables 2.1, 2.2, 6.1, 8.1, and 9.1:

Names are as of 1893; names in 1940, where different, are given in parentheses.

Where a county name appears in parentheses, the parentheses indicate that although data exist for that administrative unit, it was not established as a county-level unit in 1820 (the base date for the maps).

All units were *xian* in 1940; units that were not *xian* in 1893 are specified.

Province is specified following the name of the county unit.

Macroregions

GY	Gan Yangzi
LN	Lingnan
LY	Lower Yangzi
MY	Middle Yangzi
N	North China
NW	Northwest China
SEC	Southeast Coast
UY	Upper Yangzi

Provinces

AN	Anhui
FJ	Fujian
GD	Guangdong
GS	Gansu
GX	Guangxi
HB	Hubei
HN	Hunan
JS	Jiangsu
JX	Jiangxi
SA	Shaanxi
SC	Sichuan
ZJ	Zhejiang

Time of Migration

SZ	Shunzhi, 1644–62
KX	Kangxi, 1662–1723
YZ	Yongzheng, 1723–36
QL	Qianlong, 1736–96
JQ	Jiaqing, 1796–1821
DG	Daoguang, 1821–51
XF	Xianfeng, 1851–62
TZ	Tongzhi, 1862–75
GX	Guangxu, 1875–1908

References to Sources

Cao (1)	Cao Shuji, "Ming-Qing shiqi de liumin he Gan-nan shanqu de kaifa"
Cao (2)	Cao Shuji, "Ming-Qing shiqi de liumin he Gan-bei shanqu de kaifa"
Chen Yundong	Chen Yundong, *Taiwan de kejiaren*
FZ	fu zhi
SZ	shi zhi
TZ	ting zhi
XCZ	xian ci zhi
XJZY	*Xijiang zhengyao*
XTZ	xiangtu zhi
XXZ	xian xu zhi
XZ	xian zhi (of the relevant county unless otherwise specified)
ZPYZ	*Zhupi yizhi*
ZZ	zhou zhi (of the relevant department unless otherwise specified)

Entries citing Cao (1) and Cao (2) as sources have been added by the editor. Although the two works by Cao are secondary sources, they are fully referenced, and primary sources can be ascertained by consulting them.

These abbreviations are also used in the Notes.

MAPS (CONTRIBUTED BY G. WILLIAM SKINNER)

All maps for this volume were designed to depict administrative arrangements and hydrology as of 1820. Beginning with a large-scale computerized map of modern China and using GIS (geographic information systems) technology, we modified the coastline and river systems as necessary to reflect the situation in the early nineteenth century, and we plotted administrative capitals and prefectural boundaries as they were at the end of the Jiaqing reign. Our source for constructing the 1820 base map was *Zhongguo lishi dituji* (The historical atlas of China), produced under the general editorship of Professor Tan Qixiang (Beijing: Ditu chubanshe, 1987). The language data shown in Maps 2.3 and 6.2 were adapted from the *Language Atlas of China* (Hong Kong: Longman, 1987).

Caveats and technical comments for particular maps accompany their presentation in the text.

Migration and Ethnicity in Chinese History

Introduction

BY G. WILLIAM SKINNER

The administrative hierarchy of provinces, prefectures, and counties enjoys great cognitive salience both within Chinese society and among China specialists outside China. In late imperial times, one's native place, a critical element of personal identity, was invariably identified in terms of administrative units. Because of their close association with the bureaucratic apparatus, the Chinese literati quite naturally took the state's system for organizing the empire's territory as the sole spatial framework for scholarly description and analysis. And in learning the language and the classics from Chinese mentors, Western sinologues absorbed the same cognitive map.

The very salience of the administrative conceptualization of China's territory has hindered recognition of another encompassing spatial hierarchy, structured quite differently, namely, the hierarchy of economic central places and their hinterlands. For the most part, social and economic phenomena were more strongly shaped by position in the hierarchy of local and regional economies than by administrative arrangements. In this book, Sow-Theng Leong nails this point for both ethnicity and migration. Moreover, he shows that the overall historical patterning of Hakka and Pengmin expansion and ethnic relations becomes intelligible only when analyzed within the dynamic structure of China's regional systems. This monograph is important not only for its bold sweep, novel findings, and insightful interpretations, but also for its historiographic vision. The potential of regional-systems analysis for social and economic history is here made manifest for the first time.

A few years ago a historian writing on the Pengmin (with no little sophistication, let it be said) described their migration in the usual fashion: They "moved inland into the mountains of western Fujian and northwestern Guangdong. From there they moved over the mountain passes into Jiangxi, southern Anhui, and western Zhejiang."[1] Leong describes those same migrations in terms of the western periphery of the Southeast Coast macroregion, the northern periphery of Lingnan, the Xiang-Gan frontier, and the southern periphery of the Lower Yangzi where it abuts the Gan Yangzi and Southeast Coast macroregions. It makes a difference. What is most distinctive about Hakka and Pengmin migrations is precisely the combination of regional peripherality with strategic destinations near major commercial centers. But even to enunciate these features requires reference to China's regional systems and their internal core-periphery structures.

I take as my first task in this introduction to elucidate the structure of regional systems in the areas of South-Central China where the Hakka and Pengmin stories unfold. It was generally the case in Eurasian agrarian (peasant-based) civilizations that high-order regional economies took shape within the major physiographic regions associated with drainage basins. In China by the sixteenth century, the four major basins of the Yangzi drainage each supported a macroregional economy, as did the drainage basin of the rivers flowing to the Pearl River delta in Lingnan (see Map 1.1, p. 22). While the Southeast Coast macroregional economy was reasonably well integrated by the sea routes linking its major ports, its internal structure was distinctive in that each of its four physiographically defined subregions boasted a discrete core area.

The core-periphery structure that characterized each of these regional systems was manifest in myriad ways. Such key resources as arable land, population, and capital investment were concentrated in the lowland riverine cores of drainage basins, thinning out toward their mountainous peripheries. Agriculture was more intensive and productivity high in core areas, owing to fertility migration through deforestation, erosion, and deposition, and to the greater potential for irrigation and reclamation in lowlands as compared to uplands. In addition, regional cores enjoyed major transport advantages vis-à-vis peripheral areas. Both the efficiency of transport and the density of the transport network varied from high in the inner core to low in the far periphery. Regional systems of cities also reflected and reinforced core-periphery differentiation, with high-order cities concentrated in core areas and urbanization levels low in the peripheries. It follows from these contingencies that local economies in core areas were consistently more commercialized than those in peripheral areas. In virtually all respects, then, the macroregional economy climaxed in the urbanized inner core, where the density of economic transactions was highest, where markets of all kinds were most developed, where financial and wholesaling services were concentrated, and where industrial production was greatest.

For the most part, each of the major speech groups of southeastern China dominated one macroregional or subregional core. In the Lower Yangzi, it was Wu speakers of the Taihu subgroup. In the Ou-Ling subregion of the Southeast Coast macroregion, it was Wu speakers of the Oujiang subgroup. The core areas of the other three subregions of the Southeast Coast were each dominated by a distinct Min-speaking group: Hokchius in the Min basin, Hokkiens in the Zhang-Quan subregion, and Teochius (Hoklos) in the Hanjiang basin. For the rest, Cantonese dominated the regional core of Lingnan, Gan speakers that of the Gan Yangzi, and Xiang speakers that of the Xiang basin subregion of the Middle Yangzi. Of all the major cultural/linguistic groups of South-Central China, only the Hakkas had no substantial drainage basin of their own.

In the mid-sixteenth century, when economic growth resumed in South China, the Hakka heartland straddled three macroregional economies and extended into a fourth (see Map 1.2, p. 24). To the east, in the Southeast Coast macroregion, Hakkas occupied the upstream drainages of the Hanjiang basin, the southernmost subregional economy. To the south, in the Lingnan macroregion, Hakkas were settled in the middle and upper reaches of the East River (Dongjiang) basin and in less extensive areas within the North River (Beijiang) basin. To the north, in the Gan Yangzi macroregion, the Hakka heartland encompassed most of the drainage basins of three tributaries of the Gan River (see Map 1.2). Hakkaland also included a small portion of the upper drainage of the Lei River, a tributary of the Xiang, in the Middle Yangzi macroregion.

The geographic position of the Hakkas, then, was highly anomalous, not to say unique, among Chinese speech groups. Each of their neighbors—Min-speaking Hokchius and Hokkiens to the east, Teochius to the southeast, Cantonese to the south, Xiang speakers to the northwest, and Gan speakers to the north—dominated the lowland core of a macroregional or subregional economic system. By contrast, the Hakka heartland had no particular economic integrity and lacked even one city at the regional-city level in the economic hierarchy. Its various sectors were economically oriented to downriver regional cities in all directions: in the east to Yanping-fu and Quanzhou-fu (Maps 1.1 and 1.2 depict the situation in the nineteenth century, by which time Xiamen [Amoy] had displaced Quanzhou as the regional city), in the southeast to Chaozhou-fu (displaced by Shantou in the late nineteenth century), in the south to Huizhou-fu, in the southwest to Shaozhou-fu, in the west to Chenzhou, and in the north to Ganzhou-fu. The Hakka homeland was even more remote from the metropolises of the macroregional economies in question: Fuzhou-fu in the Southeast Coast, Guangzhou-fu (Canton) in Lingnan, Changsha-fu and Hankou in the Middle Yangzi, and Nanchang-fu in the Gan Yangzi.

It is against this backdrop that Leong recounts the saga of the Hakkas—a revisionist account that eschews chauvinism and leaves little of received wisdom intact. The ancestors of the Chinese who were residing in the Hakka heartland as of the early fourteenth century had for the most part migrated there during the Southern Song. The descendants of these migrants, who originally spoke a northern dialect, assimilated to the Hakka language that was already spoken in much of the Hakka homeland. For nearly two centuries, ending ca. 1520, this peripheral area was largely isolated from downriver economies, and Leong shows that it was during this long "incubation" that the adaptation of Hakka livelihood to an upland environment was completed and Hakka culture stabilized. Of particular interest is Leong's account of the role played in this process by the She, an aboriginal group long settled in the same mountainous terrain.

A key to the historical dynamics of Hakka migrations and ethnic mobilization lies in the developmental cycles associated with the various regional economies. These long waves of prosperity and depression shaped the temporal structure of migration and ethnic conflict. When a regional economy was on the upswing, with economic growth paced by a flourishing trade, Hakkas emigrated to take advantage of new opportunities. During the subsequent downswing of the regional cycle, however, competition in a stagnant or shrinking economy sparked conflict with the natives and promoted ethnic mobilization. As it happened, the developmental cycles of Lingnan, the Southeast Coast, the Gan Yangzi, and the Middle Yangzi were more or less in synchrony from the late Yuan to the early Qing. The prolonged depression during the fourteenth and fifteenth centuries in the regional economies on all sides of the Hakka heartland accounts for the absence of any significant Hakka out-migration during the incubation period already mentioned, while the sixteenth-century economic revival that affected these same regional economies prompted major migrations in all directions (see Map 2.1, p. 44). During most of the Qing, however, the developmental cycles of southerly macroregions were out of sync, so that, for instance, Hakka migrations during the early seventeenth century largely avoided the Southeast Coast, which remained depressed even as its neighbors were experiencing rapid economic growth. This spatially grounded temporal model, which is, of course, applied by Leong with far greater subtlety and historical specificity than can be suggested here, enables him to account, inter alia, for the timing and the location of major ethnic strife during the waning decades of the Ming and again in the mid-nineteenth century.

The sheer magnitude of the Hakka migration during the period 1550–1850 is noteworthy. The descendants of Hakkas outside their original homeland today far outnumber those still residing there. As Leong shows, virtually all of the Hakka migration to Taiwan came from the Hanjiang basin, which also supplied most of the migrants to the Upper Yangzi and Southeast Asia. Hakka descendants today number over 3 million each in Taiwan, in the Upper Yangzi, and in Southeast Asia, whereas the present (1990) population of Hakka areas in the Hanjiang basin is only 6.2 million. Population growth in the heartland must have been sustained at a remarkably high level to have supported such substantial out-migrations. Since this issue is not pursued in Leong's analysis, let me point to some of the relevant considerations.

It was generally the case, I believe, that in premodern agrarian societies mortality was lower and fertility higher in the rural far peripheries of regional systems than in their urbanized inner cores. China was no exception. Mortality was almost certainly lower in the peripheral Hakka homeland than in the cores of the surrounding regional systems on three counts. The first is a direct function of occupance density. In cities and other densely populated areas, interpersonal contact was frequent and living conditions were crowded. Extensive contact guaranteed a higher level of exposure to airborne pathogens, while crowding facilitated the spread of waterborne and filth-borne pathogens. The second reason follows from the fact that regional systems were nested in drainage basins. The risk of infection from polluted water increased as one moved from uplands to the plains. The third reason follows from the usual direction of migration flows from rural periphery toward urbanized core. The migrants attracted to core areas brought with them a fresh supply of new pathogens and had little resistance to those already present. Thus, Hakkas must have enjoyed a significantly healthier environment than did their neighbors in the lowlands.

On the side of fertility, the generic proposition is that the "demand" for children among agriculturalists is higher in peripheral areas. Not only is the importance of child labor enhanced where labor markets are poorly developed, but the "return" to child labor is higher where agriculture is less intensive. In particular, the concern of peasants in densely populated lowlands that too many sons would fractionate their smallholdings at the time of family division is obviated where slash-and-burn agriculture prevails, as it did in the Hakka homeland throughout the period of incubation.

To these generally applicable reasons for expecting relatively rapid population growth in peripheral areas must be added another that is peculiar to the Hakka, namely, their surprisingly egalitarian gender system. Since women were more highly valued than in other Chinese ethnic groups, female infanticide was much less widely practiced. Among the Chinese populations of southeastern China, Hakkas aside, excess mortality of female infants and children typically yielded ratios of 120 men for every 100 women of marriageable age. To cull a fifth or sixth of all females in a given generation is to reduce the number of mothers in the next by the same proportion, thereby radically slowing population growth. But, with their preference for gender-balanced as opposed to male-heavy offspring sets, the Hakkas effectively sidestepped this growth-suppressing feature of the usual Chinese demographic regime. In short, it is quite plausible that population growth was extraordinarily high in Hakkaland, providing a major push to the out-migration that began in the sixteenth century.

In Leong's analysis, the economic specialties that gave Hakkas a comparative advantage in their diaspora were largely related to the exploitation of upland resources. The particular ecological niche to which they adapted during their period of incubation was characteristic of regional peripheries throughout southeastern China. What appeared as hilly "wasteland" of little value to downstream paddy farmers could in Hakka hands be made to yield a bounty. The Hakkas had become expert prospectors and miners, and a major motivation for the earliest Ming migrations was to locate and exploit mineral deposits in other upland areas. By the sixteenth century, iron, tin, lead, zinc, and gold were all being mined and smelted by Hakka out-migrants, who also opened quarries for limestone and building stone. Quarrying and smelting fostered related artisan specialties, and Hakkas became noted as expert stone cutters, blacksmiths, and tinsmiths. Mountain forests along the regional divides were also made to yield, and by the seventeenth century lumbering, charcoal burning, papermaking, and mushrooming were all well developed as Hakka specialties.

As for subsistence, the lifestyle of Hakka migrants, especially in the first generation after opening new territory, was quite simple. Sheds or shacks made of rough-hewn timber and thatch were in sharp contrast with the more substantial farmhouses of lowland peasants. Clothes were cut from rough homespun, typically hemp or ramie rather than cotton. While Hakka pioneers had pigs and chickens and the usual Chinese vegetables, they did not rely on wet rice as their staple. During the incubation period they subsisted on coarse grains, including some borrowed from the She, and dry rice, to which sweet potatoes and maize, both New World crops, were added by the early sixteenth century. Leong identifies this critical expansion of the crop inventory as greatly facilitating the subsequent expansion of Hakka agriculturalists. The most distinctive feature of Hakka agriculture in the early centuries was widespread recourse to the slash-and-burn techniques that, as Leong establishes, had been learned from the She. In penetrating new territory, either sweet potato or maize, usually the former, was the first crop planted in the fields that had been newly carved out of the forest.

For the majority of Hakka migrants, however, subsistence agriculture was a means rather than the end: the ultimate objective was production for the market. This was true not only of the miners, charcoal burners, lumberjacks, and papermakers already mentioned, but also of many farmers. Hemp, ramie, and indigo were the cash crops most widely cultivated by the Hakka, and in many parts of southeastern China their production was virtually a Hakka monopoly. Tea, sugarcane, and tobacco were also important commercial crops in many Hakka settlements.

Leong identifies, confronts, and resolves the basic paradox posed by the Hakka diaspora: How could the products of upland mines, forests, and dry fields, all situated around the periphery of regional economies, find a market? Why, in an era when transport was unmechanized and costly, were these commodities not priced out of marketing networks that were centered for the most part in lowland regional cities? Part of the answer lies in straightforward economic geography. Waterborne transport was, of course, much more efficient and less expensive than overland transport, and in consequence Hakkas sited their productive activities near the tributaries of major river systems. Logs were floated downstream, so that only those timber stands near streams were exploited, and the same principle held a fortiori for quarries. As for smelted metals, their high value per unit of weight made it possible to exploit some mines that were less favorably situated in relation to the river systems. But it is with respect to cash crops that locational strategizing is most readily apparent. The topography of southeastern China is such that navigable tributaries often flow through hilly terrain and many river ports and seaports are nestled near the foothills of mountains. The most striking feature of Hakka migrations is that their destinations were precisely those upland areas that were close to major commercial centers or near the heads of navigation on the major river systems. Hakka strategizing in this respect was already apparent in the late Ming migrations (see Map 2.1). By the early seventeenth century, Hakka agriculturalists producing indigo, hemp, and other cash crops had settled, inter alia, near the Ou River upstream from Wenzhou, near the Min River upstream from Fuzhou, near the Jin River upstream from Quanzhou, in the western foothills of the Jiuling Mountains within striking distance of Changsha, in the eastern foothills of the same range near Nanchang, in the hills near the river ports of Guixian and Xunzhou-fu upstream on the West River system, and in the uplands north of Lianzhou-fu (Hepu), China's major port on the Gulf of Tonkin.

The paradox is thus partly resolved by evidence that Hakka producers deliberately sought out unexploited uplands whose location minimized cost-distance to markets. But only partly: the rest of the story has to do with exceptionally low production costs. Compared to lowland competitors, Hakka commercial farmers paid lower rents and fewer taxes. Given the shifting nature of their agriculture and the ebb and flow of seasonal migrants, they were a moving target for tax collectors; and in any case, the Chinese land-tax system consistently underappraised dry fields in relation to paddy. Rents were initially set low because the lowland landowners had no appreciation of the productive potential of the uplands they claimed but never knew how to exploit. Leong provides delicious accounts of the wicked schemes whereby Hakka tenants manipulated or bilked their landlords. In addition, Hakka farmers avoided much of the capital investment associated with lowland agriculture, e.g., in draft animals, plows and other heavy implements, and in the infrastructure of irrigation.

But the strong competitive position of Hakka farmers rested more than anything else on their womenfolk, whose role in production set them apart from other Chinese women. Families were normally units of production among all Chinese groups, but in most of them cultural ideals of female seclusion enforced a gender division in which field labor was mainly or strictly men's work. Only among the Hakkas did women regularly and routinely engage in all kinds of agricultural labor, excluding only the most physically demanding. The comparative advantage was twofold: on the one hand an increase in agricultural productivity and on the other the liberation of men to pursue nonagricultural economic strategies. With regard to the first advantage, a nineteenth-century gazetteer for Xunzhou prefecture in Guangxi noted, with only a bit of hyperbole, that "men and women all engage in farming, not shrinking from hardship, and are consequently able to double the yield from the land, compared to others." As to the second advantage, it was precisely because wives and adolescent children of both sexes could keep the family farm going that men were able to work for a season or longer as miners or lumberjacks or to pursue sojourning strategies as blacksmiths, stone cutters, and barbers in lowland market towns.

In Leong's analysis, indeed, the distinctive gender system of the Hakkas developed in response to male itinerancy and sojourning. While he is almost certainly correct, it would be useful to problematize the historical development of the Hakka gender system. Its distinctive features in the nineteenth century are clear enough: Hakka women did not bind their feet; they engaged in physical labor outside the home (construction work as well as farm labor) as a normative expectation and without community stigma; they went to market as vendors and buyers with the same freedom as men; their economic power vis-à-vis husbands was significantly greater than in other Chinese groups; Hakka mothers typically played the decisive role in determining marriage strategies for their offspring; and youths who had not been betrothed in childhood (and, one suspects, some who had) engaged in courtship rituals and played a significant role in selecting their spouses. In the Chinese context, this was a distinctly attenuated patriarchy.

On the face of it, then, the Hakka gender system is a textbook case for Engels:

productive labor enhances women's power and status. But, in historical fact, did the causal flow go straight from absent menfolk to farming women to women's enhanced power and status, or did female power and status also derive directly from the absence of men? Were all elements of the Hakka gender system in place at the end of the incubation period in the sixteenth century, or was the system still evolving into the eighteenth century? Leong argues that one critical element, the "large"—i.e., normal—feet of Hakka women, which enhanced their productivity as farmworkers, was an innovation of the mid-seventeenth century. When the Qing government banned footbinding, the Hakkas conformed, whereas neighboring Chinese groups resisted. This suggests that footbinding was rejected in response to the felt "demand" for female field labor that had built up during the late Ming heyday when Hakka men were taking advantage of opportunities away from home. On the other hand, pre-Qing footbinding may well have been limited to the Hakka elite, in which case field labor may indeed have become normative for the women of farming families during the incubation period. Noting that "the active participation of woman in manual labour" was characteristic of the She as well as the Hakka, Segawa raises the pointed question of who influenced whom.[2]

Two additional features of Hakka family and kinship—lineage organization and marriage systems—are arguably implicated in the evolution of gender relations. Anthropologists studying Hakka communities have noted that, in comparison with other southeastern Chinese groups, their lineages are genealogically shallow (or else based on spurious agnatic links), small, and weak. Strong lineages, the argument goes, backstopped family patriarchs; weak lineages were unable to interfere in the affairs of individual families or provide moral support for weak husbands.[3]

The marriage form at issue is the exotic custom of little daughter-in-law marriage. In the usual form of Chinese marriage, the match was arranged by the parents of the young couple, bride-price passed from the groom's family to that of the bride, the bride was dowered, and on the day of the wedding the adult bride moved into the family of the groom. In the alternative little daughter-in-law form, the bride-to-be moved in with her new family as an infant or young girl; there was no dowry, only a token bride-price, and no wedding feast. The girl was reared by her mother-in-law along with her "husband"—for she was technically married from the time of transfer. At an appropriate age, the marriage was consummated without public ceremony. An advantage of this alternative marriage form is that it avoids the great expense associated with the preferred form, particularly for the groom's family. As older women informants have carefully explained to anthropologists, however, the greatest virtue of the alternative form is that it completely obviates the discord and conflict that typically marks the preferred form of marriage, in which the adult daughter-in-law enters the groom's family as a total stranger. The little daughter-in-law is seldom at odds with her mother-in-law, for the latter has already socialized her to the family ways and trained her to do the precise chores that will be her lot as an adult daughter-in-law. Moreover, the custom enables the mother to maintain her son's filial devotion after marriage and facilitates her control of the joint family.

On first principles, then, this form of marriage may be taken as a female strategy, its high incidence indicating enhanced power for women within the family system.[4] Mothers preferred little daughter-in-law marriage, and when sufficiently empowered within the family system they acted on that preference. It is particularly intriguing, then, to learn that in the nineteenth century little daughter-in-law marriage was common among Hakkas throughout the mainland.[5] The functional link between marriage form and lineage strength should be apparent. Strong lineages buttressed the authority of husbands and favored the preferred form of marriage for reasons of status. When lineages were weak, families were on their own, domestic harmony took precedence over agnatic privilege, men confronted their wives without agnatic support, and wives held out for little daughter-in-law marriages for their sons. In the New Territories of Hong Kong, little daughter-in-law marriage was rare among the dominant Cantonese lineages but commonplace among the small Hakka lineages of the eastern peninsulas.

Returning now to the historical development of the Hakka gender system, we must ask, first, if Hakka lineages had always been small and weak and, second, when little daughter-in-law marriage became customary in Hakkaland. On the first question, it seems reasonable to expect that massive outmigration of men would have weakened patrilineages in the Hakka heartland, even as the very nature of emigrant frontier society would have slowed the development of strong lineages in diaspora settlements. In that case, weak lineages should be seen as the historical consequence of the diaspora itself, and lineages may well have been strong in, say, the Mei River valley at the end of the incubation period. On the second question, we confront the telling fact that little daughter-in-law marriage, widely practiced among mainland Hakkas in the nineteenth century, was eschewed by contemporaneous Hakka communities in Taiwan.[6] The main influx of Hakkas to southern Taiwan occurred at the end of the seventeenth century. Did the migrants to Taiwan lose one of the most characteristic customs of their native places within a few generations, or did the alternative form of marriage become common on the mainland only in the eighteenth century, after their departure? I incline toward the latter scenario, while recognizing that an either/or question may steer us away from the actual historical process. It may have been that little daughter-in-law marriage was already a viable, albeit uncommon, alternative on the mainland at the time of the Hakka out-migration to Taiwan and that the custom atrophied in the one setting while growing ever more popular in the other. It is pertinent to note that while male itinerancy, sojourning, and migration continued unabated on the mainland during the eighteenth century, all such mobility strategies were precluded in Taiwan by intense ethnic hostility. Not only would the absence of husbands give greater scope to the marriage strategy preferred by their wives, but the absence of married sons would enhance the value to mothers of compliant, congenial, and cooperative daughters-in-law. In Taiwan, where the husbands and sons of Hakka women were not going anywhere, these considerations would have lost all force.

In Part Two, Leong extends his analysis from the Hakka to the Pengmin, a much more inclusive and less precise category. Of the in-migrant groups identified as Pengmin in local gazetteers, some were wholly Hakka in origin, others partly Hakka, and still others entirely non-Hakka. However, Leong establishes clearly enough the major regional differences in this regard. Irrespective of the nomenclature used in the gazetteers, virtually all Chinese migrants in Lingnan were Hakka, as were the great majority of those moving into the Xiang-Gan frontier. Hakkas were also generally prominent, though by no means always a majority, among the Pengmin who settled in the Southeast Coast and its immediate frontier with the Gan Yangzi and Lower Yangzi (see Map 8.1, p. 152). However, in the southern mountainous zone of the Lower Yangzi (Tianmushan and Huangshan), extending across the macroregional border into the Gan Yangzi, Hakkas were a distinct minority among Pengmin settlers. Finally, there were few if any Hakkas among the Pengmin who settled in the upper Hanshui basin.

Regardless of the extent of Hakka participation, however, Pengmin migrations conformed to the general geographic pattern that Leong describes for the Hakkas in Part One. Migration routes followed the foothills of mountain ranges; settlements were in the upland peripheries of regional systems; and commercial production was concentrated in locales that minimized the cost of transport to markets. In the Lower Yangzi, for instance, Pengmin grew cash crops within striking distance of all three of the macroregion's metropolises: Suzhou, Nanjing, and Hangzhou (see Map 8.1).

In general, Hakka migrants relied more heavily on sweet potatoes than on maize, whereas the reverse was true of non-Hakka Pengmin. The settlement patterns of Hakkas and non-Hakka Pengmin alike positioned them upstream from lowland agriculturalists, thus ensuring disputes centered on erosion and water diversion. But erosion was significantly more severe in the Lower Yangzi and the upper Hanshui than elsewhere, and Leong points to the Pengmin mode of maize cultivation as a major culprit. Moreover, in the high mountains of the upper Hanshui, where maize could not be grown, the Pengmin planted Irish potatoes, all too often on steeply sloping fields. Though one must guard against romanticizing aborigines as ecologically correct, it is worth pondering that Hakkas learned the techniques of upland agriculture from the She and passed them on to non-Hakka Pengmin; some ecological tricks may have been lost in transmission.

Leong also argues that for non-Hakka Pengmin as well as for the Hakkas, and for the Lower Yangzi and upper Hanshui as well as for Lingnan and the Xiang-Gan frontier, the dynamics of migration, economic activity, and ethnic conflict were shaped by the rhythm of regional developmental cycles. In general, Pengmin entered a given frontier for the first time during the upswing of an economic cycle. The subsequent contraction of the regional economy typically saw a partial shift from cash crops to subsistence agriculture, return migration for some, increased competition with natives, and the onset of ethnic conflict. The eventual revival of trade and the resumption of economic growth stimulated renewed production for the market, new migration from the homeland, reduced competition with natives, and easing of ethnic hostility. The evidence painstakingly assembled in Part Two largely accords with this general model, with some intriguing exceptions that one may hope will stimulate further research.

If Hakka/Pengmin migration and settlement were shaped by the structure of regional economies, they also served in turn to transform the internal structure of those same economies. It is common knowledge that traditional Chinese agriculture and technology were geared to plains and valleys, and prior to the late Ming the productive potential of upland areas was largely unrealized throughout Central and South China. In consequence, the lowland cores of economic regions were sharply distinguished from their underdeveloped peripheries. The net effect of Hakka/Pengmin settlement and exploitation of the near periphery of regional systems was to transform a dichotomy into a continuum. The economy of hilly areas surrounding plains and valleys was significantly more advanced in 1850 than in 1550, and not only in absolute terms: with respect to level of commercialization as well as productivity, these areas of the near periphery had been brought relatively closer to the more developed regional cores.

I have dwelled on two of Leong's major themes: Hakka exceptionalism and the regional-systems logic of Hakka/Pengmin migration and settlement. Of the many other important topics with which Leong's rich history grapples, I limit myself to a brief mention of four.

Ethnic mobilization. Following Barth and Patterson, Leong argues that Hakkas, Cantonese, Hokkiens, and other southeastern Chinese sociolinguistic groups, while indubitably sharing a common culture and tradition, take on the character of ethnic groups only in certain contact situations. A cultural group "becomes 'ethnic' only when, in competition with another, these shared markers are consciously chosen to promote solidarity and mobilization, with a view to enhancing the group's share of societal resources or simply minimizing the threats to its survival." Moreover, when a segment of a cultural group goes ethnic, as it were, this does not imply that the whole cultural group thereby becomes an ethnic group. This theoretical orientation serves Leong well as he analyzes throughout this book the ethnic boundaries that developed between immigrants and natives. One significant finding is that at no time (prior to the twentieth century at least) did Hakkas unite in ethnic solidarity across macroregions. Ethnic mobilization occurred repeatedly along the Hakka-Gan isogloss in the western periphery of the Gan Yangzi and in mixed Hakka-Cantonese areas all around the regional core of Lingnan, but neither had any impact in the portions of Hakkaland that lie in neighboring regional systems.

Peripherality and rebellion. Migrations took Hakkas and Pengmin to the mountainous regional peripheries that had typically been the breeding grounds of rebellion throughout imperial history. And, indeed, some of the major rebellions of the Qing period were mounted in Hakka or Pengmin immigrant areas. Leong gives a judicious account of the four uprisings by Hakka-cum-Pengmin in the western Gan Yangzi during the first three Qing reigns (1644–1723). Despite the uncanny coincidence of these revolts with other anti-Qing struggles and the usual interpretation of them as antistate, he sees them as primarily native-immigrant conflicts. The rebels "may be viewed as capitalizing on the weakness of outside authority, whose policies invariably favored natives over immigrants, and seizing upon the vulnerability of their native exploiters, who had grown more rapacious at a time of shrinking commercial opportunities." By contrast, the White Lotus Rebellion of 1798–1806, centered on the Dabashan frontier of the upper Hanshui where Pengmin were a majority of the population, involved little or no ethnic conflict. Ironically, it was an oppressive and extortionist local administration that provoked an eschatological turn within the sect and directed both religious fervor and socioeconomic discontent against the state. In the Taiping Rebellion, which originated in the western periphery of Lingnan, it was Hakka-Cantonese tensions that set the scene for the religious mobilization of the Godworshippers. Its Hakka origins are no less significant for the fact that the Taiping movement increasingly emphasized universalistic themes after the northern march from Lingnan into the Middle Yangzi.

Hakkas in nationalist movements. One of Leong's most insightful analyses argues that Hakkas threw themselves into nationalist movements as a means of achieving full acceptance and upward mobility within Chinese society. He shows how they worked simultaneously toward acceptance of Hakkas as rightfully and fully Chinese and toward the establishment of a new political order in which they intended to have a place. Of the 112 Guangdong members of the Tongmenghui in Tokyo in 1905–6, no less than 50 were Hakkas from the Mei River valley. The significance of that statement does not lie solely in the numbers, for it tells us that this, the first modern revolutionary movement in Chinese history, had organized itself in accordance with the state's system for subdividing imperial territory. The relevant arena was Guangdong province, not Lingnan, and for the first time Hakkas in that portion of the Hanjiang basin (a subregion of the Southeast Coast macroregion) that fell in Guangdong found themselves in a position to cooperate with ethnic brethren across the macroregional border. The die was cast. From the Tongmenghui to the Guomindang and from the first decade of the century through to the end of the Republican era, Mei River valley natives were the acknowledged leaders of Guangdong Hakkas. As Leong argues, their ethnicity may be viewed as mobilization in a competition with Cantonese and Hoklos for power. The story of their dramatic success is beautifully documented in Chapter 4.

Meanwhile, farther north, the Communist movement was proceeding in the framework of regional systems and in accordance with the logic of traditional antistate movements. After the failed Nanchang Uprising in 1927, some Communist units headed for the hills in the Xiang-Gan frontier, while the main force moved south along the Gan-Min divide. When the movement finally assumed a rural character in the early 1930s, most soviets came to be based in heavily Hakka-populated areas. (One of these, the Western Fujian Revolutionary Base, incorporated the northernmost portion of the Hanjiang basin, which fell in Fujian province; immediately to the south was the Mei River valley, the home of many of the most prominent Hakkas in the Guomindang.) As Leong observes, the strategic considerations that drove the Communists out of urbanized regional cores into the peripheries and upland areas "mirrored closely the logic of the Hakka migration and settlement strategies." Interestingly, another Communist base area was established in the predominantly Pengmin area of the Dabashan that had been involved in the White Lotus Rebellion.

Assimilation. Prevailing opinion holds that the descendants of Hakka migrants fiercely resist assimilation to the language and culture of the receiving society, a view that my own field experience did nothing to undermine. In the upland areas to the east of Chengdu in the Upper Yangzi, where I conducted field research in 1949–50, most of the farming population was descended from Hakka migrants who had arrived more than two centuries earlier during the Yongzheng reign. In public arenas everyone spoke flawless Sichuanese Mandarin, and I could detect nothing distinctive about their behavior, but in the privacy of their homes, as I discovered to my astonishment, they spoke Hakka and performed a few distinctively Hakka rituals. (This pattern of bilingualism and residual biculturalism is, I suspect, the rule among Hakka descendants in many areas that are shown in the *Language Atlas of China* as wholly non-Hakka in speech [cf. Map 6.2].) In some of the areas settled by Hakkas in the sixteenth-century diaspora (and not, apparently, reinforced by subsequent migration), assimilation was still not complete three centuries later, though it is today. In Yongfu (now Yongtai), a county in Fujian near Fuzhou-fu where Hakka settlement dates to the early sixteenth century, an American missionary reported in 1873 that nearly one-third of the women had unbound feet, a sign that the Hakkas had remained unassimilated.[7] One reason, then, why Hakka assimilation may have speeded up since the 1930s is that what had been an obvious and stigmatizing ethnic marker simply disappeared with the end of footbinding.

While recognizing that instances of extraordinary cultural and linguistic persistence are not uncommon among Hakka populations, Leong takes a situational approach and nicely complicates the picture with examples of acculturation both ways. In some cases, whole Hakka lineages "became" Hokkien or Cantonese, as the case may be, within a few generations. I am moved to cite yet another example from the anthropological literature: in his ethnography of Sheung Shui, Hugh Baker mentions that the founding ancestor of the Liao lineage, one of the Five Great [Cantonese] Clans of the Hong Kong New Territories, was a Hakka tinker from Tingzhou.[8] A particularly intriguing example of cross-cultural influence and assimilation concerns the descendants of Hakka and She in the Southeast Coast. As Leong shows, She and Hakkas often traveled together in the course of the "Pengmin" migrations to Southeast Coast destinations. As of the 1953 census, there were virtually no self-identified She within the solidly Hakka areas of the upper Hanjiang basin, whereas She enclaves were recorded throughout the uplands elsewhere in the Southeast Coast. The *Language Atlas* shows far more She than Hakka enclaves in these same areas. Fieldworkers have reported that the language spoken by the She minority, whether in southern Zhejiang, Fujian, or the Teochiu portion of the Hanjiang basin of Guangdong, is a slightly creolized dialect of Hakka. She informants, significantly, were not aware that "their" language was related to Hakka.[9] It appears likely, then, that the already Hakkacized She had by mid-century lost their separate identity when residing in solidly Hakka areas, while retaining it when surrounded by Wu- or Min-speaking Chinese. The descendants of Hakkas who originally migrated with the She must have completely assimilated, either becoming She or merging with the local Wu- or Min-speaking population.

Leong was among the first China historians to enrich their analyses through on-the-ground ethnography. His interviews and observations in Ninggang, a county in southwestern Jiangxi, have fleshed out and strengthened several of the analyses set out below. He expected and planned to do more historical ethnography before completing this work, and it is our loss that he did not live to do so. Leong was particularly interested in Hakka-She interrelations, and he would have relished—and pursued in the field—the intriguing findings described above, which came too late for him to incorporate in his analysis.

This book as a whole is testimony to Sow-Theng Leong's well-honed sense of problem and his sweeping analytical vision. The chapters that follow attest to his virtues as a practicing scholar: shrewd in judgment, respectful of evidence, skilled at synthesis, and ever alert to the contingencies and ironies of history. The writing, too, is revealing: the carefully reasoned exposition reflects clearly the lucidity of Leong's mind, just as the understated style of argumentation suggests the gentleness of his character. But this work in itself cannot speak to the essence of the man: his deep-seated humanity. In this introduction I mean to honor the person as well as the scholar; the loss of both is hard to bear.

1. The Origins and Historiography of the Hakkas

This book examines two insufficiently studied phenomena in late imperial and modern China: ethnicity and internal migration. It does so through an extended analysis of the modes of migration and the formation of an ethnic consciousness among the Hakka people and among a broader though still predominantly Hakka group, the Pengmin (shack people). Among Han Chinese, the Hakkas were unmatched in the extent of their cultural deviance, geographical mobility, stubborn resistance to assimilation, and ethnic self-consciousness. From a resource-poor base in the border highlands of Guangdong, Fujian, and Jiangxi provinces, they have migrated in all directions at various times between the sixteenth and twentieth centuries, interacting with other Chinese in a rhythm of ethnic assertiveness.

Three questions inform the analysis in this book. What determined the temporal and geographical pattern of Hakka and Pengmin migration in late imperial China? In what circumstances and over what issues did ethnic or subethnic conflict emerge? And how did the Chinese agrarian state react to the phenomena of migration and ethnic conflict?

To answer these questions a model must be developed that can encompass and make sense of what would otherwise appear to be disparate data. The model presented here brings together three ideas and types of data: the analytical concept of ethnicity; the history of internal migration in China; and the regional systems methodology of G. William Skinner, which has been a breakthrough in the study of Chinese society as well as an approach of broad social scientific application.[1]

Two key aspects of the conceptualization of ethnicity are most relevant here.

First, it is important to distinguish between a "cultural" and an "ethnic" group. As Orlando Patterson argues, a group that shares, consciously or unconsciously, a common culture and tradition can only be designated as "cultural." It becomes "ethnic" only when, in competition with another, these shared markers are consciously chosen to promote solidarity and mobilization, with a view to enhancing the group's share of societal resources or simply minimizing the threats to its survival.[2] Ethnicity is thus "essentially a form of interaction between cultural groups operating within common social contexts."[3] Frederik Barth makes a similar point when he proposes the notion of the ethnic group not as a sociocultural "isolate," but only as one group in interaction with another. The we-they dichotomy, which he calls "ethnic boundary," is the essential feature of this notion.[4]

Second, because ethnic groups do not exist in isolation, the salience of ethnicity varies according to the situation in which the particular ethnic group finds itself, alternating between relaxed interethnic relations and acute confrontations, depending on the expansion and contraction of opportunity structures.[5] The "choice of ethnic allegiance," as Patterson puts it, is contextual: ethnic salience varies with time and place depending on the needs of the groups concerned.[6] Moreover, it necessarily involves interaction between groups sharing a common social context: relations between different groups across national boundaries would not be considered ethnic, nor would being an Irishman be quite the same in Australia as, say, in Northern Ireland. In short, although peoples like the Cantonese, Hoklos, and Hakkas are cultural groups, they may be ethnic groups only some of the time. Moreover, "the fact that a segment of a cultural group becomes an ethnic group," says Patterson, "does not mean that all members of that cultural group thereby become an ethnic group." Nor is the group ethnic, even if so perceived by others, unless members of the group choose to interact with others in ethnic terms.[7]

This concept of ethnicity therefore stresses both the importance of conscious group identity in the formation of an ethnic, as against a cultural, group and the contextuality of the choice of ethnic allegiance. Given such a definition, it is reasonable to ascribe the term "ethnic" to the differences between groups speaking the Hakka, Yue (Cantonese), Min (Hokkien), or other "dialects" of Chinese. Elsewhere, such groups have been variously called "ethnolinguistic," "subcultural," or "a speech group," but while caution is undoubtedly called for, the more common anthropological usage of "ethnic" is preferable for our purposes.[8]

In China, as in many though not all other places, migration was the particular context in which ethnic consciousness and conflict emerged, in terms of a contradiction between "natives" and "newcomers," even though the "newcomers" may have been present for a long time. However, internal population movements in late imperial China have not received the attention they deserve, despite their direct bearing on demographic history, regional economic development, and law and order as well as ethnicity. This is understandable for, unlike overseas emigration, with its clear points of exit and entry that facilitated record keeping, internal migration tended to be invisible in the records.[9]

Like all premodern agrarian states, imperial China developed over the centuries policies and mechanisms to limit the freedom of movement of its subjects. An earthbound populace facilitated record keeping, the extraction of resources and manpower, and the maintenance of social order and imperial security. A (male) Chinese was identified by his native place, institutionally expressed by household registration, which endowed him and his family with rights and obligations. Territorial identity was powerfully reinforced by the ideology of kinship and localism. Anyone outside his native place with no legitimate business, such as officeholding or trade, remained an outsider in the eyes of the host community, sometimes for generations. In the eyes of the state, he was no different from a criminal evading taxes or plotting revolt. State policies accordingly favored natives over newcomers in the event of conflict.

Nevertheless, population movement was common in Chinese history, varying only in the forms it took. On the largest scale, a major theme of Chinese history is the peopling of South China by the Han people from the north. But, as this study will show, smaller-scale migrations constantly responded to and reflected the rhythm of regional economies as well as official encouragement or coercion and natural disasters.

Apart from ideas on ethnicity and migration, the third plank of the analysis in this study is Skinner's regional methodology, which divides late imperial China spatially into nine macroregions according to physiographical features. Map 1.1 delineates the macroregions within central and southern China to which Hakkas migrated. Regional boundaries do not necessarily coincide with administrative ones: for instance, the Lingnan region comprised the drainage

MAP 1.1. The macroregions of South-Central China in relation to river systems and provinces, showing major cities and the approximate areas of regional cores, ca. 1820. The boundaries shown are those of physiographic regions, since there is no empirical basis for delineating the precise limits of macroregional economies as of 1820. The Gan Yangzi is depicted as a separate regional system (rather than as a subsystem of the Middle Yangzi) since, during the first half of the nineteenth century, it was, if anything, more closely linked to the Lower Yangzi than to the Middle Yangzi. The depiction of regional cores supersedes that shown in previously published maps.

basins of the West River (including most of Guangxi) as well of the North River and the East River in Guangdong. The basin of the Hanjiang, including the Mei and Ting tributaries, which fell mainly within the province of Guangdong, belonged physiographically to the Southeast Coast.

Each region is characterized by internal differentiation, which Skinner analyses as a core-periphery structure. (See Map 1.1.) The river valleys and plains of core areas were distinguished by greater size and density of population, greater concentration of resources, better communications networks, and a higher degree of commercialization than the peripheral highlands. In addition to its unique spatial structure, each region had it own distinctive temporal cycles, and until modern times the various regions were only imperfectly integrated and their historical rhythms were often unsynchronized.[10]

It was above all in the context of those *regional* economic cycles that Hakka and Pengmin migration took place, and that those contextual factors that led to the formation of an ethnic consciousness emerged. Thus, we should view Hakka and Pengmin migration not in the context of administrative boundaries, but in relation to the physiographic, economic macroregions as conceived by Skinner.

Maps 1.2 and 1.3 show the Hakka heartland around 1550 and the extension of contiguous Hakka settlements up to 1850, in relation to topography and the macroregions (Map 1.2) and to administrative units (Map 1.3). Map 1.2 makes clear two key features of Hakka spatial concentrations: settlements were overwhelmingly concentrated in the highlands, and (in a related point) on the periphery of the macroregions. The counties of the Hakka homeland are in the mainly highland areas along the conjunction of the peripheries of the Gan Yangzi, Southeast Coast, and Lingnan macroregions. In the Gan Yangzi region, they lie in the upper Gan basin, in the Southeast Coast, on the Mei and Ting tributaries of the Hanjiang, and in Lingnan, on the upper reaches of the East (Dongjiang) and North (Beijiang) rivers. Later expansion took place in particular along the mountain ranges forming the border between the Gan and Middle Yangzi regions, and also in the southern Gan and along the frontier between Lingnan and the Middle Yangzi.

NOTE TO MAPS 1.2 AND 1.3 (overleaf). The Hakka heartland, ca. 1550, and areas of Hakka settlement, ca. 1850. The area of contiguous Hakka settlement as of 1850 includes small pockets of non-Hakkas not shown on these maps.

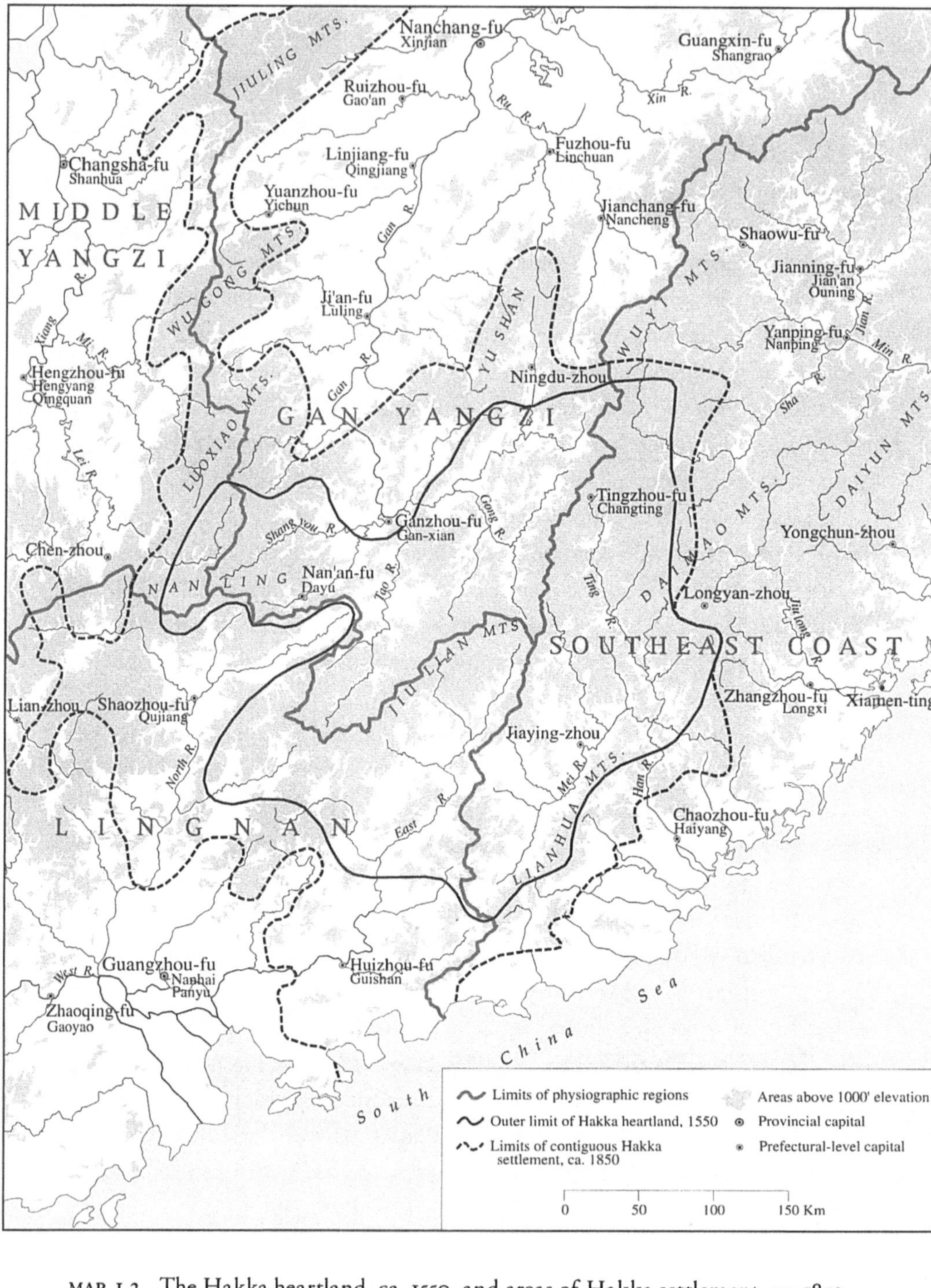

MAP 1.2. The Hakka heartland, ca. 1550, and areas of Hakka settlement, ca. 1850, in relation to topography and macroregions.

MAP 1.3. The Hakka heartland, ca. 1550, and areas of Hakka settlement, ca. 1850, in relation to Qing administrative units, 1820.

Bringing together the three elements of ethnicity, migration, and macroregional systems, a model can be developed suggesting four key hypotheses about Hakka and Pengmin migration and ethnicity during the great regional cycles of late imperial China up to the nineteenth century.

1. In general, migration is a demographic process reflecting the systemic interaction between the core and periphery within each region. An upturn in the temporal cycle creates economic opportunities, mainly in the core, which attract migrants from the periphery. Allowance must of course be made for some interregional migration, given the contiguity of the peripheries and the easy passage of people and goods through mountain passes.
   The comparative advantage of the Hakkas in mining and highland agriculture induced them to move mainly along higher ground toward upland areas close to major commercial centers, and to avoid the already heavily occupied plains.
2. A period of contraction may cause a reverse flow of migration away from the core; the movement may be back to the original periphery, to the periphery of another region, or overseas.
3. In a period of contraction, competition for resources brings into salience ethnic identity, group formation, and mobilization.
4. Since the Hakka cultural group migrated to different regions that were relatively unintegrated, each constituting a separate local social system, differences in ethnic expressions may be expected despite a shared culture.

Part One of this book applies this model to the history of the Hakkas mainly in the Lingnan and Southeast Coast macroregions. Chapter 2 traces the emergence of ethnically conscious groups of Hakkas in the course of migration in response to the regional cycles of that area: two major phases of migration are identified, one in response to the sixteenth century upturn in both macroregions and the other from the late seventeenth century, mainly limited to Lingnan, inasmuch as the Southeast Coast did not experience an upturn at that time. Ethnic consciousness and conflict emerged in the context of the economic downturns in both phases, and it was in Lingnan in the later phase that the Hakka ethos received its clearest expression, and indeed where historically the term "Hakka" was mainly used.

Chapters 3 and 4 examine changing Hakka identity in the nineteenth and twentieth centuries. From the mid-nineteenth century onward, the progressive breakdown of China's imperial order and the remaking of the nation's sociopolitical system opened up a competition for power among different groups in varying contexts. Formerly disadvantaged groups thrust themselves forward to seize opportunities for socioeconomic advancement. The Hakkas were one such group that, at various times in this period, played many prominent roles, only a few of which can be discussed in this book.

Generally, it is possible to examine these more recent Hakka activities in the context of two broad phases, one in the nineteenth century (Chapter 3) when Hakkas sought to minimize the risks to their survival as a group by means of ethnic mobilization, and the other in the twentieth century (Chapter 4) when they responded to the opportunities presented by a new political environment. Common to both phases was a readiness to accept new ideas with a revolutionary potential, and an emphasis on ethnic assertiveness—two strategies for surviving or enhancing socioeconomic status. Thus, the Taiping Rebellion with its Hakka leadership core reflected both strategies: a ready acceptance of a foreign religion, Christianity, and mobilization by means of the God Worshippers Society in the upper West River basin (Guangxi), where Hakkas were in conflict with neighboring groups.[11] The Hakka-Punti War during the same period (1854–67) saw the Hakkas in the Lingnan core similarly mobilized.[12] Receptiveness to new ideas as a means of social advancement later predisposed many Hakkas to join Sun Yat-sen's revolutionary movement.[13]

In the early twentieth century, ethnic self-awareness and a predisposition to social change attuned the Hakkas to the opportunities presented by the military profession, the introduction of modern education and associated new professions, and the rise of new political structures that opened up careers to the talented. Hakkas also followed avenues to commercial wealth that were closed to them in Lingnan but open in Southeast Asia and elsewhere. In this period, the Hakkas succeeded in achieving a degree of political and military influence out of all proportion to their numbers. In the Fujian-Jiangxi and Hunan-Jiangxi border regions, where the Hakkas were predominant, the location of the Communist rural soviets in the 1930s offered them new political opportunities. Both the Guomindang and the Chinese Communist Party politico-military establishments were to end up with a substantial Hakka representation.

Part Two broadens the analysis to take into account migrations of Hakka peoples in other macroregions. Both ethnic labels and ethnic identity were less clear than in Lingnan and the Southeast Coast and indeed the Hakkas are identified in the sources primarily as the predominant component of a larger category: the Pengmin.[14] As will be shown, there were three main concentrations of Pengmin, each of which produced specific problems belying the unity suggested by the single label: along the border between the Middle Yangzi and Gan Yangzi macroregions and in adjacent western parts of the Gan Yangzi (as well as a lesser concentration in the eastern Gan Yangzi); in the southern periphery of the Lower Yangzi macroregion; and in the uplands of the Hanshui basin, in the border area between the Middle Yangzi, Upper Yangzi, and Northwest macroregions.[15]

While the common themes of the regional and temporal nature of migration and ethnicity and the role of the state informs the analysis of all these areas, each presented somewhat different problems. In the Gan Yangzi (Chapters 6 and 7), the key issue was the handling of ethnic tensions between Pengmin immigrants and natives, tensions that particularly centered on local residence and examination quotas. In the Lower Yangzi (Chapter 8), the main problem was the environmental degradation caused by the type of upland agriculture practiced by the Pengmin, and the conflict between upland and downstream agriculturalists. Finally, in the Hanshui uplands (Chapter 9), the state faced problems of control over a wild frontier area, much less settled and wealthy than the Lower Yangzi.

Historiography of the Hakkas

In examining the literature that bears on the subject of the Hakkas, one inevitably begins with Luo Xianglin's *Kejia yanjiu daolun* (Introduction to the study of the Hakkas). The first and last scholarly investigation of the subject in the Chinese language, it appeared in 1933, and is cited as the authority by everyone whose research touches on the Hakkas. At the same time it has become a veritable Bible for the Hakkas themselves. Luo begins with a review of Chinese and Western writings on the Hakkas since the early nineteenth century. He then discusses Hakka origins and migrations, the geographical distribution and the ecology of Hakka communities, the Hakka dialect, Hakka cultural forms and values, Hakka ethnic characteristics, eminent Hakkas in modern times, and current developments among the Hakkas. The early chapters have appeared and reappeared in countless commemorative publications of Hakka organizations all over the world. Innumerable derivative accounts have also been written.

The popularity of Luo's work among the Hakkas stems from its unambiguous statement of a number of Hakka cardinal beliefs. Hakkas were originally migrants from the Central Plain in the north, true Han Chinese from the cradle of Chinese civilization, not hill aborigines, as their neighbors, out of ignorance or malice, frequently identified them. They were historically prominent as spokespersons of Han Chinese patriotism: they were patriotic loyalists of the Jin in the fourth century, Song loyalists against Mongol invaders in the late thirteenth and fourteenth centuries, and anti-Manchu patriots of modern times, as exemplified by the Taiping leader Hong Xiuquan and the anti-Qing revolutionary Sun Yat-sen. The Hakka dialect is unmistakably rooted in the prestigious speech of the northern Central Plain in the Sui-Tang period. Hakkas justifiably take pride in their womenfolk, renowned for their hard work and never known to bind their feet, in the academic achievements of their scholars, and in the possession by the group of all the orthodox Chinese cultural values.

The book is thus part scholarship and part ethnic rhetoric. It is well known in addition for positing a schema of five successive migratory waves: (1) A.D. 311–873, beginning with the fall of the Western Jin due to barbarian invasions; (2) 874–1276, indicating the critical impact of the Huang Chao Rebellion; (3) 1276–1682, particularly during the Song-Yuan transition; (4) 1682–1867, starting with the lifting of the ban against coastal habitation, originally imposed by the Qing against Taiwan-based opponents; and (5) 1867 to the present, a final diaspora since the end of the Hakka-Punti War in the Lingnan core. These phases are clearly too long and indeterminate to be of much value, beyond indicating the undoubted significance of their starting points. Moreover, Luo's sources are primarily Hakka genealogies, which pose serious problems of elite bias and reliability. In any case, his sample is disappointingly small.[16]

As to the critical question of when Hakka ethnic self-consciousness emerged, Luo dates it to the Five Dynasties and early Song. He believes the crucial factor at that time was the isolation of the Hakka forebears in a rugged terrain as a result of the political fragmentation and separatism of the time.[17] However, Luo is evidently speaking of the formation of the Hakkas as a cultural group, not as an ethnic group, since the latter, as we have argued, is predicated on interaction with others. It is even doubtful whether one can speak of the formation of a Hakka cultural group at this early stage, since the new migrants associated with the third wave were probably more numerous than the earlier settlers, and would have diluted any cultural consensus that might have existed and initiated a prolonged process of acculturation.

Luo came at the end of a long line of ethnically awakened Hakka scholars stretching back to the turn of the nineteenth century. Prominent Hakkas included the poet Song Xiang; the president of the Fenghu Academy in Huizhou, Xu Xuzeng; Wen Zhonghe, Hanlin academician and compiler of the 1898 edition of the Jiaying zhou gazetteer; the poet-reformer Huang Zunxian; Qiu Fengjia of Taiwan independence fame; Zou Lu, onetime Tongmenghui revolutionary and president of Zhongshan University in Guangzhou; and Lai Jixi, a *jinshi*, compiler of the 1911 edition of the Zengcheng and the 1920 edition of the Chixi gazetteers, and the first professor of Chinese at the University of Hong Kong. These men and others identified and codified Hakka cultural values and forms, and propagated a Hakka cultural past with a view to enhancing the depressed social status of a despised people.

Luo thus synthesizes the ethnocentric outpourings of these three or four generations of Hakka leaders. His work belongs to that phase of Hakka ethnicity that started early in the nineteenth century in Lingnan; it peaked about the time of the Hakka-Punti War in mid-century, and rose again from the 1890s, when the Hakkas joined the Republican Revolution to compete with their Cantonese and Teochiu coprovincials for a place in the emerging new order. In addition, however, he finds moral support for his views in the late-nineteenth-century writings of Westerners in China. The latter, missionaries and semischolarly officials, wrote enthusiastically of their discovery of the Hakka highlanders and unwittingly reflected the growing self-awareness of the group.

Myron Cohen deserves credit as the first modern anthropologist to interpret the Hakka material. He argues convincingly, contrary to Maurice Freedman, that ethnicity should be added to kinship and class as an organizational principle of Guangdong society.[18] More recently, in a sophisticated essay, Andrew Char elucidates more explicitly the basis of ethnic division between Hakkas and Cantonese and attaches fundamental importance to the localism of the

Cantonese, already potent when the Hakkas intruded into their midst in the seventeenth and eighteenth centuries.[19] Cohen implies that Hakka ethnicity was a nineteenth-century phenomenon while Char sees it as emerging from the moment of contact. Both limit their investigation to Guangdong, and neither examines the phenomenon in regional terms, thereby missing its spatial and temporal variations.[20]

Origins and Incubation of the Hakkas

When did the Hakkas develop as a cultural group with its own distinctive markers? This chapter only briefly explores this complex question, which should ideally be seen in relation to the histories of the contiguous groups, studies of which are unfortunately still lacking. Three questions need to be considered at the outset: the original nature of the population in the area that was to become the Hakka homeland; the history of the southern migration of the Han Chinese people; and the timing of the emergence of a distinct Hakka dialect.

The conjuncture of the Gan Yangzi, Lingnan, and Southeast Coast regions, where successive waves of migrants found refuge and came to be known as Hakkas, was originally populated sparsely by the She people, commonly identified as a subgroup of the Yao, who were spread across much of Lingnan. The She (first separately identified in Southern Song times),[21] like their Yao cousins, appear to have been mountains-and-hills people, living by hunting and slash-and-burn agriculture. This is in contrast to the Zhuang who, it is said, were valleys-and-plains people before they were assimilated or driven to the hills by Han Cantonese and others. These are crude generalizations drawn from the little research that exists.[22]

Most information on the second topic, the broad sequence of settlement of the south by Han Chinese, has been provided by Tan Qixiang, the historical geographer.[23] The first period of Han migration and settlement from the north occurred between the Jin (in the third century) and the end of the Tang.[24] It covered an area collectively known as Yangzhou, comprising the latter-day macroregions of the Lower and the Gan Yangzi, as well as the Southeast Coast. In the Southeast Coast, according to Hans Bielenstein, migrants originated from two main directions: those from the Lower Yangzi took to the coast, while those who crossed the Wuyi Mountains from the Gan Yangzi stayed inland. These two isolated strings of settlements were not bridged until mid-Tang.[25] The development of Zhangzhou and Quanzhou began some time in the Tang when uprisings of the She in that area led to Han conquest, colonization, and expansion as far south as the Hanjiang basin by the late Tang.[26]

The second period, lasting from the Five Dynasties to the Ming, saw the settlement of the Middle Yangzi region, and a large influx into Lingnan that joined earlier migrants slightly after the start of the period, giving the development of Lingnan a decisive push. The third, post-Ming, period saw the development of the Yungui region and the upper West River basin of Lingnan. Thus, of the areas that concern us, the Gan Yangzi and the Southeast Coast had been settled by the end of the Tang, and Lingnan had a sizeable population by Song times.[27]

The third indispensable piece of information concerns the development and crystallization of distinctive dialects, a critically important cultural marker that divides Han Chinese into subethnic groups.[28] Not only does the Hakka dialect play a crucial role as a subethnic marker, it is also important in Hakka mythology, supposedly backing up a claim to northern Chinese origins. Thus Hakka writers have argued that their dialect reflects the speech of the north, and was brought south by the Hakka people in the various migrations from the fourth and fifth centuries. Such a view once had some scholarly support, and one can back it up with early references, such as a pre-Ming visitor to Ting zhou, cited in the *Yongle dadian* (Yongle encyclopedia), who noted, "The speech of Ting is northern, unlike Min."[29] Another common conception about Hakka is that it has a close link to the Gan dialect, which again allows a view that the ancestors of the Hakkas settled first in the Gan Yangzi and subsequently moved to the Southeast Coast, and that migrants to the uplands of the Hanjiang, East, and North rivers originated from both the Gan Yangzi and the Southeast Coast. Here again, there is some evidence for this view in the sources: the 1518 edition of the Xingning gazetteer recorded that the speech of the county resembled Gan.[30]

Nevertheless, recent scholarship paints a very different picture, namely that Hakka is a development of Old Southern Chinese, a language spoken by Chinese migrants to the south in the Han dynasty and before, which split off from the northern dialects sometime long before the seventh century A.D.[31] Thus Hakka has no particular connections with northern Chinese or even with Gan.[32] The Min, Hakka, and Yue groups of dialects all originated in Old Southern Chinese and developed in somewhat different directions according to exposure to new groups of migrants from the north. In Hakka, this differentiation can presumably be dated at least from the Song, as a Song gazetteer of the Hanjiang basin noted that the speech of that area was an extension of the Zhangzhou and Quanzhou dialects, but that people in the highlands farther up the Hanjiang had a distinct speech of their own.[33]

Thus, while the ancestors of the Hakkas may indeed have come from the north, it is unlikely that they brought their language with them.[34] Rather, migrants from the north adopted (but also influenced) the language of their area of settlement, which predated their migration. Those going to Min areas became Min speakers, those going to Hakka areas became Hakka speakers. In general, Yue became the dialect most influenced by northern speakers, especially by Middle Chinese, the literary language of the Tang period.[35] Hakka was influenced to a lesser extent, while Min retained the greatest similarity to Old Southern Chinese.

This picture, which differs from the earlier Hakka orthodoxy, is corroborated by Chen Zhiping's research, though Chen does not frame his findings in the same terms. He cites many lineages who came south at the same time, and then "became" Hakkas, Yue speakers, or Min speakers, depending on the language of the area in which they settled.[36] Thus, many Yue as well as many Hakka lineages trace their origins in the Song to Nanxiong in northern Lingnan; they adopted a dialect depending on their destination.

With this background we can now turn to the migration of those who became Hakkas into the area at the conjunction of the peripheries of the Gan Yangzi, Lingnan, and Southeast Coast macroregions—in other words, the area that was to become the Hakka homeland. Most evidence suggests that the basic stage of Hakka settlement came in the late Song and the immediate post-Song periods. Nakagawa believes that the immigrants first settled Ting zhou in Fujian and in the fourteenth century moved on to displace the She in Jiaying zhou (Mei xian) in Guangdong.[37] By early Ming times the majority of inhabitants in the heartland would seem to have been descendants of immigrants of the late and post-Song periods, the start of Luo Xianglin's third wave. This conjecture is based partly on the impressive number of genealogies tracing ancestry to the late Song, and partly on Hakka scholarly opinion.[38]

Skinner's analysis of the regional cycles indicates that the period from the thirteenth to the fifteenth centuries, encompassing the Mongol invasion and Ming policies circumscribing foreign contact and trade, experienced an exceptional synchrony of depression in all three macroregions.[39] Skinner has also argued that the resulting community closure prevented the "Hakkas" from migrating down-valley, making contact with other Chinese, and eventually being assimilated.

These migrants thus experienced a prolonged period of enforced economic isolation and adaptation to a peripheral ecology.[40] It may be assumed that during their incubation they went through an early phase of borrowing from the preexisting practice of slash-and-burn agriculture of the She people before mastering irrigation using mountain streams and terracing. They must have learned from the She an inventory of crops suitable for the marginal agriculture of an upland and mountainous environment. As part of their adaptive strategy, they also developed such specialties as metals mining and stone cutting. It is also possible that the Hakkas took from the She the practice of women doing a large amount of fieldwork, and therefore in late imperial China retaining natural feet.[41]

How far the two groups intermarried and became assimilated is unclear. Jiang Bingzhao argues that many of the She became assimilated and called themselves Hakka: he visited three villages in Shanghang where the inhabitants had always regarded themselves as Hakka, but recently discovered a She identity.[42] Li Mo also stresses the extent to which She as well as other aboriginal groups in the area became assimilated as Hakkas.[43] Segawa goes so far as to argue that the She became so assimilated in Hakka areas that they virtually disappeared, while their maintenance of ethnic identity in other areas was at least partly based on cultural characteristics they shared with the Hakkas.[44] Others, however, stress that there is no evidence for Hakka-She intermarriage, and that such marriages were unlikely to have taken place.[45]

Late in the fifteenth century antagonism between early and recent settlers still kept a large part of this Hakka homeland in turmoil. The situation was serious enough for the court to dispatch a secretary of the Board of Punishment in 1485 to investigate and restore order. In his report, Hong Zhong, *jinshi* of 1475, identified the source of difficulties:

> The Fujian counties of Wuping, Shanghang, Qingliu, and Yongding, the Jiangxi counties of Anyuan and Longnan, and the Guangdong county of Chengxiang [later Jiaying zhou, now Mei xian] all have a confused mixture of vagrants, who are habituated to fighting and quick to resort to arms. They easily quarrel and brawl like packs of beasts. It is difficult not to expect them to grasp and bite. After they have settled down, local officials should be instructed, as a basic approach, to establish charitable schools to teach their young, deprive them of their weapons, and use the classics to inculcate civil virtues, so that their wickedness will be imperceptibly removed.[46]

It is not clear what role the She people played in the violence and banditry. However, in this area the Han Chinese, long-standing residents and vagrants alike, were "sojourners" (*ke*) in the eyes of the She, who viewed themselves as the original "masters" (*zhu*).[47] Superior Han numbers and competition with the She for resources led to spasmodic interethnic confrontation. From the 1480s to the 1650s the She revolted again and again, and were suppressed only by extensively coordinated imperial campaigns. The first campaign, mounted under the leadership of Wang Yangming in 1517–18, restored some interethnic peace for a few decades and hastened the assimilation of the She.[48] Thereafter, four more campaigns in different parts of the regional peripheries were waged—in 1553, 1566–67, 1572–73, and 1653—before the She were finally subjugated, never to rise again on any scale. Out of this crucible of prolonged interethnic conflict in an area that ultimately became purely Hakka, these Han Chinese immigrants must have emerged with a heightened sense of Han ethnic feeling and cultural affirmation (a subsequent Hakka ethnic characteristic), just as the She remnants, occupying the far periphery and greatly reduced by assimilation, slaughter, or expulsion, were determined to retain their own ethnic identity by barring interethnic marriages and persisting in their distinctive cultural forms and values.

Such a mountainous area afforded an environment that was atypical for Han Chinese—an ecological niche requiring special adaptations.[49] The "Hakkas" had had to make compromises, principally in developing an unorthodox sexual division of labor, which accorded with the higher value Hakkas placed on the labor of women than did their lowland neighbors. This practice was justified by appeal to ancient writings that extolled wife and husband working hand in hand to promote the family's well-being. This sexual division of labor may explain why Hakkas did not practice footbinding. An alternative explanation is, however, given by an early nineteenth-century Hakka scholar, who wrote that footbinding was practiced until the beginning of the Qing when, probably in response to imperial injunctions that the lowland Chinese ignored, the Hakka elite agreed that it should be banned among rich and poor alike.[50]

In the late imperial period the Hakkas expanded into new areas of both the core and the periphery of various macroregions. The rest of this book examines the way these migrations led to the formation of an ethnic consciousness.

PART ONE Migration, Ethnicity, and Nationalism Among the Lingnan Hakkas

2. Hakka Migrations in Lingnan and the Southeast Coast

It is impossible to say when the Hakka incubation period ended. Adaptive strategies continued to be refined. The development of cultural forms and the socialization of cultural values were ongoing. It is safe, however, to assume that sometime during the sixteenth century these Han Chinese had evolved distinctive cultural markers, including a separate dialect, and had emerged from their non-Han ethnic environment with a heightened sense of Han Chineseness. These people became Hakkas when some of them came into contact and conflict with other Han Chinese after migrating to other areas.

This chapter analyzes how they migrated in search of economic opportunities created by upturns in the regional cycles of the Lingnan and Southeast Coast macroregions in the sixteenth, late seventeenth, and eighteenth centuries. It shows that while prosperity continued conflict could be contained, but when the cyclical downturns came, in the seventeenth and again in the nineteenth century, ethnic conflict erupted and promoted the formation of an ethnic consciousness.

The Ethnic and Cultural Landscape of Lingnan

The population of the Lingnan macroregion, where the Hakka group and ethnic identification emerged most clearly, is, as observers, both scholars and laymen, have long been aware, highly diverse. Lingnan is populated by groups known as "Cantonese" and "Hakkas," as well as sprinklings of diverse non-Han aborigines; there are also isolated pockets of "Hoklos."[1] Each group entered the region at a different time and occupied a separate ecological niche. The earliest of the Cantonese ancestors arrived before Han times, although in significant numbers only in the Tang and later. Intermixing with the numerous preexisting aboriginal peoples, collectively known as the Baiyue, and linguistically influenced by them, they occupied the Guangzhou (Canton) delta lowlands before fanning out.[2]

As this chapter will show, the Hakkas penetrated the Lingnan macroregion from late in the sixteenth century, but in large numbers mainly from the seventeenth and eighteenth centuries. A final wave arrived in the second half of the nineteenth century following the Hakka-Punti War, when the authorities relocated displaced Hakkas in the poorer parts of the Leizhou Peninsula and on Hainan Island.

Two millennia of Han Chinese colonization and assimilation of the natives had produced a complex cultural landscape in Lingnan. The adoption of Han names by the non-Han and intermarriage between Han and non-Han contributed significantly to this complexity. Despite their ethnic rhetoric, none of the Han Chinese groups can claim a purely Han ancestry. But nothing had shaped interethnic relations as much as the forced migration of lesser groups. The Cantonese had, for example, disinherited the Zhuang people of the lowlands and the Yao of the higher ground; in the northeast, the Hakkas, and to some extent the Hoklos, had all but displaced the She aborigines. This environment engendered a sense of racial defensiveness; this may have been stronger in some ethnic groups than in others, but all the Han Chinese in the area at times felt the need to assert their racial purity with categorical certainty. One and all they were *Tangren* (people of Tang culture), descendants of migrants from the Central Plain (*zhongyuan*), that is, the cradle of ancient Chinese civilization in the north, and their ancestors were upper-class gentry families (*yiguan zhi zu*). Both the Cantonese and Hakkas had an implausible lore about how their ancestors entered Guangdong.[3] The history of settlement in the area makes intelligible the singular preoccupation of these groups with racial and cultural purity, which in turn accentuated the racial aspect of nationalism when that phenomenon emerged at the turn of the twentieth century.

Differences among the Han were almost equally sharp, though a recent study stresses the degree to which historically the boundaries between the major subethnic groups were fuzzy, with non-Hakka lineages becoming Hakka and vice versa.[4] The formation of the Hakka ethnic group and consciousness will form the major theme of this chapter. Among the other groups, the label "Cantonese" derives from the old Western name for Guangdong province. In the existing literature, the term serves two functions: it refers broadly to the preponderant group, but at the same time narrowly to the speech of the Guangzhou metropolis. Cantonese as spoken in Guangzhou happens to be only one of several different dialects, some varying to the point of mutual incomprehension. Cantonese people, however, would identify themselves to others of the province as Punti (*bendi*), meaning "native," or as *Guangfuren* (persons of Guangzhou prefecture), and to outsiders as *Guangdongren* (persons of Guangdong province).

"Hoklo," a term of confused origin and uncertain rendering in Chinese, and capable of connoting respect or contempt depending on the context, is a designation by others for the natives of the prefecture of Chaozhou (excluding the Hakkas), an area that lies within the eastern part of the province of Guangdong but from a physiographical perspective belongs to the Southeast Coast macroregion.[5] In fact, the label often includes the inhabitants of southern Fujian. The Hoklos of Chaozhou refer to themselves as "Teochiu," the local pronunciation for the name of the prefecture.

Development Cycles in the Southeast Coast and Lingnan

Figure 2.1 sums up G. William Skinner's delineation of the development cycles over the period 1000–1995 in the three main macroregions relevant to this study: the Southeast Coast, Lingnan, and the Gan Yangzi.[6] Elsewhere, he has outlined the specific development cycles in the Southeast Coast.[7] Essentially, one long cycle lasted from the seventh to the early sixteenth century. Within that cycle there was a middle phase (1000–1300) of great commercial development, especially related to the growth of foreign trade centered in Quanzhou.

Commercial expansion was subsequently halted by the Mongol invasion and the isolationist policies of the Ming court. As Mark Elvin explains, the period 1300–1500 witnessed an economic decline in China as a whole for several reasons: the disappearance of the frontier effect after the south had become increasingly populated; the Yuan policy of dealing with piracy through a ban on Chinese merchants going overseas and trading with foreigners; and the Ming

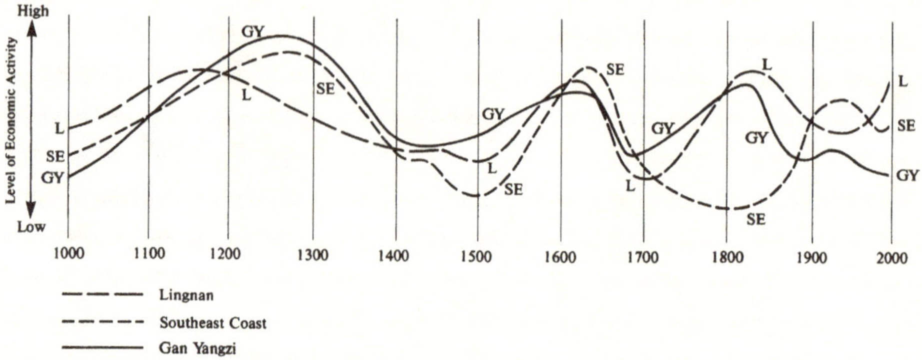

FIG. 2.1. Regional cycles of development: Lingnan (L), Southeast Coast (SE), and Gan Yangzi (GY), 1000–1995.

policies directed toward self-sufficiency and stamping out piracy. China also faced a liquidity crisis, the result of a flight of silver in response to inflation under the Yuan; the Ming attempt to deal with this by issuing their own inconvertible paper currency also failed. In addition, Elvin argues, the shift in Ming philosophical outlook from an investigation of nature to introspection and intuition halted the advances of the earlier period in Chinese science and productive technology.[8] Skinner adds to these factors the climatic downturn known as the Spörer minimum.[9]

A new cyclical upturn did not begin until the 1530s, with the arrival of the Portuguese around Macao, and obtained further impetus from the 1560s when the Spanish arrived in the Philippines. The Manila trade, dominated by the Hokkien (Fujianese) merchants, produced a great influx of silver.[10] Trade with Japan and Southeast Asia further contributed to stimulating a commercial boom in the economic core of the Southeast Coast.[11] Depression set in once again in the last decades of the Ming, deepened further by the Qing scorched-earth policy along the coast, aimed at Ming loyalists based in Taiwan. Granting Guangzhou the monopoly on trade with Westerners prolonged the stagnation, although Xiamen continued to trade with Southeast Asia. A new upturn had to await the expansion of trade following the creation of the treaty ports in the 1840s.

As Figure 2.1 shows, the Lingnan development cycles largely paralleled those of the Southeast Coast, because the economies of the two regions were connected by coastal trade and shared the same sea lanes of overseas commerce. There were significant differences, however. The initial upturn had come earlier in Lingnan, during the Tang, stimulated by the trade with the Arabs centered on Guangzhou; it was halted abruptly by the devastation of Guangzhou and its environs in 879 during the Huang Chao Rebellion. The Lingnan cycle then paralleled that of the Southeast Coast. There was an upsurge in the Song when Guangzhou had a thriving interregional trade in rice and salt and shared in the Quanzhou overseas trade.[12] Commercialization was further reflected in the Lingnan core increasingly becoming a rice-importing area, as agricultural land was turned over to fruit orchards, sericulture, and other cash crops.[13] If anything, the seventeenth-century downturn affected Lingnan even more severely than the Southeast Coast. The brutal evacuation of the population to 50 *li* (one *li* is about one-third of a mile) from the coast, a policy that lasted in Lingnan from 1662 to 1682, caused great loss of life and production.[14]

However, whereas the economy of the Southeast Coast did not really recover for one and a half centuries after the lifting of the scorched-earth policy, the granting of the foreign trade monopoly to Guangzhou enabled a much more rapid recovery in Lingnan, and thus the eighteenth century saw a sustained upturn in that region. Early in the nineteenth century, however, another downturn resulted from the severe silver shortage, opium consumption, piracy, and the loss of Guangzhou's preeminence to Shanghai.[15] Economic insecurity gave rise to massive emigration overseas, widespread local dissidence, and interlineage and interethnic feuding.

Hakka Migrations: The First Phase

The first phase of Hakka expansion into the foothills surrounding the major commercial centers of the Southeast Coast and Lingnan sprang from the new economic opportunities afforded by the sixteenth-century regional upturns. Tensions with the native population began to emerge at the time of the seventeenth-century downturns. Map 2.1 provides a somewhat impressionistic summary of Hakka migrations during the late Ming, showing how Hakkas converged on uplands close to major sea or river ports in at least four macroregions.[16]

The first recorded outward push of the Hakkas occurred in 1554, when

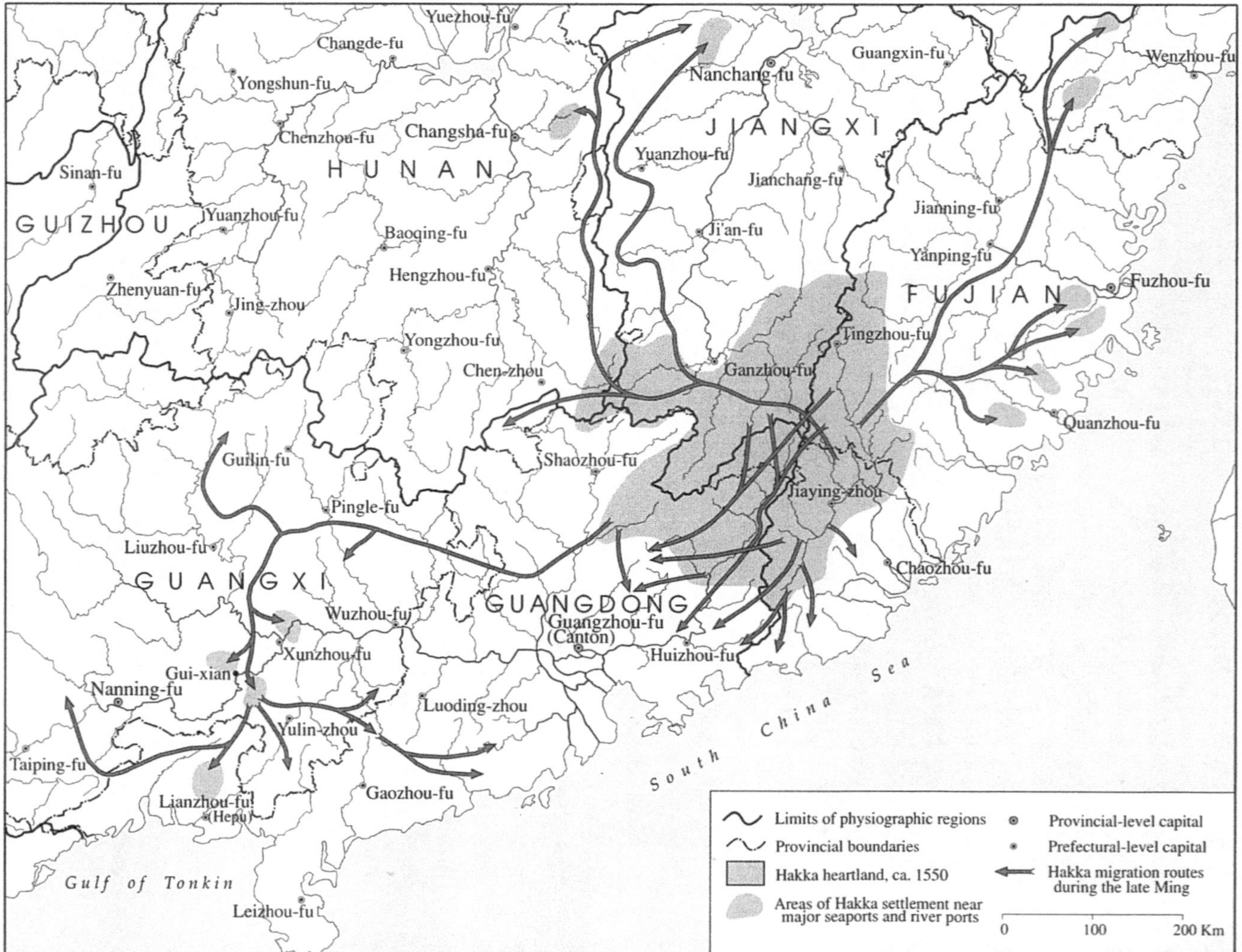

Yuezhou-fu
Changde-fu
Yongshun-fu
Chenzhou-fu
Changsha-fu
HUNAN
Sinan-fu
GUIZHOU
Yuanzhou-fu
Baoqing-fu
Hengzhou-fu
Zhenyuan-fu
Jing-zhou
Yongzhou-fu
Chen-zhou
Nanchang-fu
Guangxin-fu
Wenzhou-fu
JIANGXI
Yuanzhou-fu
Jianchang-fu
Jianning-fu
Ji'an-fu
Yanping-fu
FUJIAN
Fuzhou-fu
Tingzhou-fu
Ganzhou-fu
Quanzhou-fu
Shaozhou-fu
Jiaying-zhou
Guilin-fu
Pingle-fu
Liuzhou-fu
Chaozhou-fu
GUANGXI
GUANGDONG
Wuzhou-fu
Guangzhou-fu
(Canton)
Huizhou-fu
Xunzhou-fu
Gui-xian
Nanning-fu
Luoding-zhou
Yulin-zhou
Taiping-fu
Lianzhou-fu
(Hepu)
Gaozhou-fu
South China Sea
Gulf of Tonkin
Leizhou-fu
Limits of physiographic regions
Provincial boundaries
Hakka heartland, ca. 1550
Areas of Hakka settlement near major seaports and river ports
Provincial-level capital
Prefectural-level capital
Hakka migration routes during the late Ming
0
100
200 Km

migrants from the Mei basin headed south along the macroregional frontier to the coast, settling in the contiguous counties of Haifeng and Guishan (later Huiyang). They were drawn by the opportunity to mine zinc and lead, a highland specialty. Tens of thousands were engaged in illegal (i.e., unapproved, unsupervised, and untaxed) mining. As happened time and again, the immigrant miners roused local ire by interfering with *fengshui* (geomancy). Equally disruptive, in a terrain favored as a bandit hideout, local bandits also gravitated to the new source of wealth offered by mining. The resulting disorder brought official proscription. Ming and Qing official policies, which viewed any mining as administratively troublesome, were directed repeatedly toward closing off this logical avenue of Hakka advance. It is unlikely that so large a migrant population could have been repatriated, however; some must have been allowed to stay.

Around the same time, migrants from the eastern portion of the Hakka heartland also joined others in moving east and northeast and heading for upland areas near the major Southeast Coast ports of Quanzhou, Fuzhou, and Wenzhou. These movements are shown on Map 2.1 and summarized in Table 2.1. Near Quanzhou, Hakka migrants from Shanghang moved to Anxi, though it appears that many of them were assimilated to the local Hoklo population.[17]

Similarly, the increased demand for such marketable goods as indigo, cane sugar, and timber brought migrants from the Ting basin, along with some (Hokkien) natives of the prefectures of Zhangzhou, Quanzhou, and Yanping, to the hills of Yongfu (now Yongtai), Putian, Xianyou, and Fuqing, close to the regional metropolis of Fuzhou. In Yongfu, as the 1612 county gazetteer records, the migrants were willing to become tenants on land inaccessible to irrigation, and managed to derive more income by raising cash crops than the lowlanders did from their rice crop, exciting much native envy.[18] The precariousness of their existence, however, made these immigrants liable to become predatory. In 1561, led by a failed indigo farmer, they took to pillaging the surrounding villages.[19] In 1589 a temporary shortage of rice and resulting high

MAP 2.1 (opposite). Routes of Hakka migrations during the late Ming. Although we have attempted to draw on all available information, many of the routes shown here and in Map 2.2 (p. 58) are educated guesses. Both maps are highly stylized. In this map, the limits of Hakka settlement near ports are not precisely delineated.

TABLE 2.1

Hakka Migrations to the Environs of Southeast Coast Ports, Late Ming

Destination	*Macro-region*	*Time of Migration*	*Provenance*	*Economic Activities*	*Source*
			ENVIRONS OF FUZHOU AND QUANZHOU		
Yongfu, FJ	SEC	by 1612	Ting basin	cash crops	XZ (1612) 1: 42b–43a, (1748) 1: 19a–b
Putian, FJ	SEC		Ting basin	cash crops	
Xianyou, FJ	SEC		Ting basin	cash crops	
Fuqing, FJ	SEC		Ting basin	cash crops	Chen Zhiping, p. 75
Anxi, FJ	SEC	Ming	Ting basin, Shanghang		Chen Zhiping, pp. 87–88
			ENVIRONS OF WENZHOU		
Yunhe, ZJ	SEC	Ming?	Ting basin		XZ (1864) 15: 12b
Taishun, ZJ	SEC	Ming?, KX, YZ	Ting basin		XZ (1879) 2: 20a–b
Lishui, ZJ	SEC	late Ming	Jiangxi, Fujian, She	ramie, indigo	Chuzhou FZ (1635) 1: 16b–17a; XZ (1874) 13: 18a, 15: 14a, (1906) 12: 16b

NOTE: For conventions and abbreviations used in the tables, see p. xvii.

prices drove them into banditry again.[20] The natives complained with some exaggeration that "the *kemin* [guest people; the character *ke* is the first character of the term "Hakka," though the term was not restricted to the Hakkas] form gangs and oppress the natives, and yearly they resort to arms."[21] The 1748 edition of the Yongfu gazetteer repeated the charge, suggesting that 150 years later these immigrants were still not regarded as natives.[22] In 1873 an American missionary reported that nearly one-third of the Yongfu women had normal (in the Chinese parlance of the time, "large") feet, a sign that the Hakkas had remained unassimilated.[23]

As Map 2.1 shows, the third group of Hakka settlements was created when migrants from the Ting basin, including both Hakkas and She, came into the upper part of the Ou basin in the northernmost subregion of the Southeast Coast. This area was the boundary of the Southeast Coast, Lower Yangzi, and Gan Yangzi macroregions. Proximity to the Wenzhou-fu trading system was a major incentive for indigo and hemp growers to congregate there. Called *qingmin* or *qingke* (indigo farmers), they turned to banditry in 1638–42 when the dyed-cloth market in the Lower Yangzi Region collapsed. The revolt of the "indigo army" spread over twelve counties across the three southwestern prefectures of Zhejiang, spilling over the provincial border into Fujian and spreading even as far as Guangdong.[24]

The writings of Xiong Renlin, the official commissioned to suppress them, shed light on these immigrants. Hakkas from the Ting basin, it appears, had been working in the hills and mountains for some time. With accumulated capital they were leasing tracts of mountain land from native landlords, called *shanzhu* (mountain landlords). Called *liaozhu* (hut owners) themselves, because they provided makeshift huts for their farm laborers, the Hakkas invited the poor from among the She people in Shanghang to clear the forests by the slash-and-burn technique.[25] "The She come in the hundreds each year," wrote Xiong, "empty-handed and dependent on the *liaozhu* for a living as laborers. Some come in spring and depart in winter; others stay as long-term laborers."[26] Unassimilated as elsewhere, these Hakka and She immigrants left pockets of their distinctive speech down to modern times in such counties as Songyang, Taishun, and Yunhe: the *Language Atlas of China* reports isolated pockets of Hakka speakers south of Taishun and on the Fujian-Zhejiang border between Pucheng and Longquan. Pockets of She speech are spread more widely along the border of the Lower Yangzi and Southeast Coast macroregions.[27] In any case, the natives later came to apply the label "Hakka" indiscriminately to Hakka and She people alike.[28]

Substantial numbers of Hakkas also migrated within the Lingnan macroregion, as shown in Map 2.1; Table 2.2 outlines Hakka migrations in Lingnan during both the Ming and the Qing. Within Lingnan, one major push of Hakka migration was from the heartland to contiguous areas of the region to the west and southwest. Thus Hakka migrants moved in 1589 to fill an area that had been partially devastated by civil war with the She in 1572–73. Great loss of life was reported, especially in the counties of Guishan (Huiyang) and Yong'an (Zijin). These two counties were filled by Hakka immigrants from Xingning and Changle (Wuhua) in the Mei basin, from Wuping in the Ting basin, and from Anyuan in the upper Gan.[29] Some of this expansion also went in the direction of the border area of the Southeast Coast, namely to Haifeng,

TABLE 2.2

Hakka Migrations Within Lingnan and Adjacent Areas, 1550–1850

Destination	*Macro-region*	*Time of Migration*	*Provenance*	*Economic Activities*	*Source*
EASTERN LINGNAN AND ITS FRONTIER WITH THE SOUTHEAST COAST					
Longmen, GD	LN	ca. 1500	Mei basin	mining, iron ore	XZ (1936) 17: 210
Conghua, GD	LN	early sixteenth century	Heyuan, Yingde	mining	XZ (1730) 2: 104a
			Yingde, Changning	indigo, charcoal	XZ (1730) 2: 104b–5a
Hua xian, GD	LN	by 1687			XZ (1687) 1: 36a–b
Zengcheng, GD	LN	by 1686	Yingde, Changning, Yong'an, Longchuan		XZ (1686) 1: 21a, (1754) 3: 10a–b
Dongguan, GD	LN	by 1689	Fujian, Chaozhou	indigo	XZ (1689) 2.4
Xin'an (Baoan), GD	LN	late seventeenth century			XZ (1688) 3: 15b
Guishan (Huiyang), GD	LN	1554	Mei basin	mining	Haifeng XZ (1750): 40b
Boluo, GD	LN	1608–9	Xingning, Changle	indigo	XZ (1631) 1: 45b ff; Huizhou FZ (1595) 2: 51a, (1881) 17: 45a
Yong'an (Zijin), GD	LN/SEC	1589	Xingning, Changle, Wuping, Anyuan		Huizhou FZ (1595) 2: 55a–b
Haifeng, GD	SEC/LN	1554	Mei basin	mining, zinc, lead	XZ (1750): 40b
Lufeng, GD	SEC	Ming	Jiaying zhou, Chengxiang		Chen Yundong, pp. 177, 196
Jieyang, GD	SEC	seventeenth century			XZ (1779) 7: 7a–b
SOUTHERN LINGNAN					
Yongkang zhou (Tongzheng), GX	LN	late Ming		sugarcane	Tongzheng XZ (1933) 7:1b–2a

TABLE 2.2 (*cont.*)

Destination	Macro-region	Time of Migration	Provenance	Economic Activities	Source
Bobai, GX	LN	late Ming	Wengyuan, Yingde		
Rong xian, GX	LN	late Ming, KX	Huizhou, Chaozhou, Jiaying zhou, Fujian	paper	Wuzhou FZ (1770) 3: 27b; XZ (1897) 4: 26a
Cenxi, GX	LN	late Ming	Wengyuan, Yingde		Luoding ZZ (1687) 1: 22b–23b, 36a–b, 37b–38a, 9: 9b
Yangchun, GD	LN	late Ming			Zhaoqing FZ (1673) 4: 7a–b, 32b–33a, 5: 8b, 21: 4b–5a
Yangjiang, GD	LN	late Ming			Zhaoqing FZ (1673) 4: 7a–b, 32b–33a, 5: 8b, 21: 4b–5a
Enping, GD	LN	late Ming			Zhaoqing FZ (1673) 4: 7a–b, 32b–33a, 5: 8b, 21: 4b–5a
Xinning (Taishan), GD	LN	from 1732			XZ (1738/1804) 2: 38a–44b
(Chixi ting), GD	LN	mid-nineteenth century			Lo Wan
Kaiping, GD	LN				XZ (1823) 6: 23b–24a
Heshan, GD	LN	by end of seventeenth century			XZ (1754) 12: unpag.
Xinhui, GD	LN				XZ (1870) 10: 7
Gaoming, GD	LN				*Guangdong tong zhi* (1822) *juan* 171
Gaoyao, GD	LN	by nineteenth century			XZ (1863) 2: 29b–30b
		NORTHERN LINGNAN AND ITS FRONTIER WITH THE MIDDLE YANGZI			
Guiyang zhou, HN	MY	pre-1728			ZZ (1818) 4: 5a
Linwu, HN	LN/MY	late Ming		indigo	*Ming-Qing shiliao*, 8: 784
Lanshan, HN	MY	pre-1638		indigo	*Ming-Qing shiliao*, 8: 704
Jianghua, HN	MY	ca. 1717	Guangdong, Jiangxi		XZ (1870) 12: 9b

(*cont.*)

TABLE 2.2 (*cont.*)

Destination	*Macro-region*	*Time of Migration*	*Provenance*	*Economic Activities*	*Source*
He xian, GX	LN	late Ming, KX	Huizhou, Chaozhou, Jiaying zhou	mining	XZ (1890) 7: 13a, (1934) 2: 4b
Zhaoping, GX	LN	late Ming	Wengyuan, Yingde		XZ (1934) 7: 2a, 5b
Xiang zhou, GX	LN		Fujian, Guangdong		ZZ (1870) pt. 2: 21a–b
Huaiyuan (Sanjiang), GX	LN				XZ (1946) 2: 1a–9a

NOTE: For conventions and abbreviations used in the tables, see p. xvii. The destinations can be identified on Maps 2.1 and 2.2: basically, in the east, they go counterclockwise from Longmen in the northeast; in the west the list is from west to east, and in the north from east to west.

which had also suffered devastation; most of Haifeng and a small part of Yong'an were in the Southeast Coast region. Haifeng, where Fujianese expansion had occurred as far back as Song times,[30] also received Fujianese immigrants from Zhangzhou and Quanzhou.

Within five years of the arrival of the Hakkas in the Lingnan counties such as Yong'an and Guishan, tensions with the locals were running high. The 1595 edition of the Huizhou fu gazetteer describes the Hakkas as "violent" and "belligerent"; initially they "buttered up" their prospective landlords but later became so overbearing and unruly that the landlords feared taking them to court.[31] As might be expected, the fixed quotas of taxes and corvée restrained landlords and local officials alike from taking drastic action to curb the Hakkas.

Further down the East River from Guishan, a wave of Hakka immigrants, similarly originating from Xingning and Changle, arrived at Boluo in 1608–9. There the locals were ready to drive out the intruders but were restrained by the authorities, who were fearful of antagonizing so large a group of vagrants and more concerned with meeting the tax quotas than with appeasing the natives. In the 1632 edition of the Boluo gazetteer, the ruling magistrate permitted himself a long lecture to the natives concerning the unresolved problem of the immigrants. He called attention to the vast tracts of arable land in the county that remained idle, causing much poverty. The immigrants, after all, were Han Chinese who had been crowded out of their native places, and should be allowed to stay. As in Guishan and Yong'an, the policy of the local government was that, rather than expel the immigrants, they should be brought under control by means of the institution of a *xiangyue* (village league).[32]

The Ming *xiangyue* system had been introduced to the Hakka area in the upper Gan by Wang Yangming during his campaign against the She.[33] As a rural district pledge system, the *xiangyue* involved mutual surveillance and responsibility among villagers, and the nomination of a responsible person who kept records of each household and reported suspects to the authorities. The village head was charged with the responsibility of overseeing the social conduct of the villagers and had in his possession registration slips for each male immigrant, indicating precisely his place of origin, his new place of residence, the name of his landlord, and the names of family members accompanying him. These slips were issued by the county office, the official attitude being that knowledge about the immigrants was the first step toward controlling them. The system was introduced to the whole of Huizhou prefecture in 1623.[34]

Rather than restraining the Hakkas, however, the *xiangyue* system actually encouraged ethnic solidarity and mobilization. When the immigrants arrived, they already fell into groups according to the locality where they originated. Those of the same provenance tended to reside in the same villages, giving rise to Xingning and Changle villages. In the face of the hostility of the natives, it was but a short step for this territorial bond to merge into an ethnic one. The villages had the capacity to affiliate and expand into a hierarchy of units, with leadership provided by the village heads. Leadership, organization, and shared cultural markers constituted the resources for mobilization in interethnic feuding.

It was the downturn of the economic cycle that brought confrontations between immigrants and natives to a head in Boluo. A major conflict erupted in the winter of 1630 and spring of 1631 when Hakka indigo farmers originating from Fujian raided and held for ransom numerous native subsections of the county.[35] Equally troublesome were the miners. In 1640, in response to the suggestion of the Board of Revenue that silver and tin mining be allowed in the hills, the native gentry and commoners expressed alarm and opposition.

The miners had come, their petition argued, in their hundreds and thousands and organized themselves into a *Xing-Chang yue* (Xingning-Changle League, referring to two counties in the Hakka homeland from whence the immigrants had come).

> They occupy all the good land but disown any tax obligations. They have seized others' land to make pathways to the mines, and have dug up fields and graves. They feed themselves by plundering the villages, rendering the natives incapable of paying tax and rent. Setting fire to anything in order to repel the forces of the law, and brandishing the sword whenever provoked, they detain landlords and government functionaries, and kill or repulse government troops and runners.

The petition goes on to detail some of the atrocities committed by the immigrants. A landlord was killed in a ritual to their flag; another was flogged in public and had his leg broken; a third was forced to kneel and was shot with an arrow, and his land and house were confiscated. An assistant magistrate had his quarters burned while conducting an inquest. "The lands of the natives are all ruined, the taxes unpaid, and the minerals exhausted. How extreme is the poison spread by these bandits!"[36]

Close by at Longmen and Conghua, other Hakkas arrived as part of the migration from the heartland. As early as the Hongzhi reign (1488–1506), Longmen had attracted Hakkas from the Mei basin, who came as illicit miners of iron ore.[37] The Hakkas from Heyuan (up the East River) and Yingde (up the North River) also came to mine iron ore in Conghua where, in 1560–64, gathering a force of 30,000, they rose in a major revolt that spread to the prefectures of Shaozhou and Huizhou.[38] Others subsequently arrived as indigo farmers and charcoal burners from Yingde, Changning (later Xinfeng), and from as far as the Ting basin. There were also some people from Zhangzhou. Along with the miners, they were reported to have pillaged in 1616 and again in 1623.[39]

As Map 2.1 shows, Hakka migration in the late Ming also extended far beyond areas contiguous to the Hakka homeland, with migrants skirting the Lingnan core to settle in the West River basin. Migrants tracking to the north of the region settled in Linwu, in Hunan province but on the Lingnan side of the macroregional border.[40] Hakka miners also appeared in He xian.[41] Substantial numbers of Hakka migrants also ended up in Zhaoping, to the north of the Wuzhou subregion, while others pressed on still farther west to Huaiyuan (Sanjiang) in the Liuzhou subregion.[42]

Other migrants turned to the southwest to settle in many areas of southern Lingnan. Thus Hakka papermakers in Rong xian originated in the upper East, Hanjiang, and Mei river basins and were described in the gazetteers as "Hui-Chao-Jia," that is, from the prefectures of Huizhou and Chaozhou and from the department of Jiaying.[43] At the southern end of the Wuzhou subregion, Cenxi received a substantial number of Hakka immigrants from Wengyuan and Yingde in the upper North River basin, some of whom also settled in Bobai in the Maoming subregion. In the 1640s both Cenxi and Bobai were to experience bloody interethnic feuding, which the gazetteers reported as "the massacre of Weng-Ying."[44] This concentration of Hakka migrants also probably extended both to the west, where Hakkas of unspecified provenance moved to Yongkang zhou (Tongzheng), in the Nanning subregion, as sugarcane farmers,[45] and to the east in the direction of Guangzhou, with Hakka settlements in the counties of Yangjiang, Yangchun, and Enping by 1673: given the early Qing ban on coastal settlement, such migrants would have had to have arrived in the late Ming.[46]

A final route of advance of the Hakkas in the late Ming was northward along the macroregional frontier between the Gan and Middle Yangzi macroregions. Although covered in Map 2.1, this migration will be dealt with separately in the text, when discussing the Pengmin in Chapters 6 and 7.

Thus this first phase of Hakka migration already shows a clear pattern. In times of economic upturn, migrants moved to upland areas mostly around the regional core in order to take advantage of burgeoning economic opportunities. Although there was some tension with local populations, these were kept in check so long as there were sufficient opportunities for everyone. When the downturn began to restrict opportunities, however, open ethnic conflict began to emerge.

The Second Phase of Hakka Migration

The second phase of Hakka expansion in Lingnan began immediately upon the lifting of the ban on coastal settlement in 1682–83. The developmental cycles of the Southeast Coast and Lingnan regions diverged at this point: as indicated earlier, the Southeast Coast entered a prolonged phase of stagnation, while Lingnan enjoyed an economic upturn. Thus the Lingnan economy offered opportunities for migrants to earn a living, whereas such opportunities were scarce in most of the Southeast Coast. Consequently, the second Hakka push was mainly confined to Lingnan.

THE SOUTHEAST COAST AND TAIWAN

No evidence, therefore, can be found of Hakka advance toward the core area of the Southeast Coast.[47] The exceptions, movements to some peripheral parts of the region, in fact prove the rule. Migration did take place to the upper Ou basin where the economic depression was partly mitigated by proximity to the Lower Yangzi. Taishun, for example, received immigrants from the Ting basin during the Kangxi and Yongzheng reigns.[48]

Taiwan, which may be regarded as peripheral to the Southeast Coast, is a more important case. By the 1920s some 16 percent of Taiwan's population, or more than half a million people, were Hakka speakers. The origins of this community are not as clear as they might be. Some useful recent publications in Taiwan unfortunately do not always cite sources, and thus it is difficult to judge between different versions. Nevertheless, it is possible to say on the basis of what we know that Hakka migration to this area generally shared common features with other Hakka migrations.[49]

What is clear is that Hakka migrants went to Taiwan over a long period between the late seventeenth and early nineteenth centuries. What is less clear is the more detailed temporal pattern of migration. Chen Yundong says that as soon as the Qing government opened up the coastal areas following the reconquest of Taiwan, Hakka migrants went to Taiwan, mainly from Jiaying zhou. However, Hakkas from the prefectures of Chaozhou and Huizhou had to cross the boundary between the provinces of Guangdong and Fujian. As migrants from another province, they were subject to official discrimination. The restrictions were somewhat relaxed after the death of Shi Lang in 1696, but it was only after the prominent role Hakkas played in suppressing the Zhu Yigui Rebellion in 1721 that local officials moved to increase Guangdong residents' access to the island. Thus it would appear that the majority of the Hakka migrants came to Taiwan in the last three quarters of the eighteenth century. Migration continued in the nineteenth century, but at a lower level.[50]

Although, as usual, most Chinese sources, contemporary and otherwise, stress push factors in the motives for migrating, in fact Taiwan offered considerable economic opportunities in the seventeenth and eighteenth centuries, and thus its attraction for Hakka migrants fits largely into the pattern identified in other chapters of this work. Despite the generally depressed state of the Southeast Coast for more or less the whole period, growth in Taiwan was strong following the suppression of the Ming loyalists: exports of rice and other commodities boomed.[51] By the mid-eighteenth century, Taiwan exported as much as one million *shi* (a *shi* or picul is about 133 pounds) of rice a year, mostly to make up the deficit in the Zhangzhou-Quanzhou area; also of considerable importance were sugar exports, which went first to the regional city of Xiamen and thence into the Lower Yangzi macroregional system through the metropolis of Suzhou.[52] How far Hakkas in particular concentrated on the production of these export commodities is, however, not clear from the sources.

Nearly all the Hakkas migrating to Taiwan came from Hakka areas in the Southeast Coast macroregion, as part of the great exodus from that region due to the overexpansion of its population during the sixteenth-century boom.[53] Thus, about half came from Jiaying zhou, the center of the Hakka homeland. A further 20 percent or so came from Chaozhou and a much smaller number from Ting zhou, both of which areas were also in the Southeast Coast.[54] These migrants tended to come down the Hanjiang River to the vicinity of Shantou and then either embarked directly on small boats to make an illegal crossing to Taiwan, or proceeded along the coast to Xiamen where an official permit for a legal crossing could be obtained.

Finally, about 20 percent or so of the Hakkas came from the prefecture of Huizhou in Guangdong. Although the largest part of Huizhou belonged to the Lingnan macroregion, there is nevertheless reason to believe that many, and probably most, of those from Huizhou came from the Haifeng-Lufeng area, which was precisely the part of Huizhou that belonged to the Southeast Coast. Thus Chen Yundong's study cites the Jiangs of Beibu and the Fans of Guanxi as both originating in Lufeng.[55]

Once the Hakkas reached Taiwan, they settled in pockets stretching the length of western Taiwan, but generally they came to be concentrated in the more inland and upland portions of the coastal strip.[56] The major concentrations of Hakka people are found at Pingdong in the south (which was settled by Hakkas as early as the 1690s), and a larger area encompassing Miaoli, Xinzhu, and Taoyuan in the north.[57]

The major question has, however, been their physiographical distribution, which was generally in hilly areas. For a long time this was interpreted as indicating that they arrived later than the Hokkien (Quanzhou and Zhangzhou) people who occupied most of the plain;[58] such a phenomenon was similar to the situation in much of Lingnan, where Cantonese (Punti) occupied the lowlands, renting higher land to the Hakkas. Similarly, in the areas of Pengmin migration to the Gan Yangzi, it was almost universal for Pengmin Hakkas to exploit the poorer hill land, leaving the valleys to the natives.

More recently, however, it has become clear that this explanation cannot hold in many cases, because the Hakkas entered many areas at the same time as or even before the Hokkien people. Thus attention has shifted to two other explanations for the pattern that emerged. First, some scholars argue that this distribution of populations essentially reflects the nature of the areas from which each group came. The Hakkas came from marginal upland areas and had developed skills that were best used in that context. We can discern a similar phenomenon both in Lingnan and in the Gan Yangzi, where, as outlined in the model in Chapter 1 and as shown in this and subsequent chapters, Hakka migrants moved toward upland areas close to higher-level trading systems in search of economic opportunities; in many cases the opportunities they seized were those for which they were particularly suited. Thus, it was Hakka skills in the cultivation and processing of key commodities such as indigo that provided them with a role in the development of the production of those commodities in the southern and western Gan Yangzi uplands.

Second, others have postulated that Hakka occupation of the hilly areas was the result of their losing out in communal strife and essentially being driven out of the plains areas by the more numerous Hokkien.[59] Thus it was substantially after the Hakkas first migrated to Taiwan that they moved into the hilly areas that they currently occupy.

Such a phenomenon can also be addressed through the model outlined in Chapter 1. While the Taiwan economy was in an upturn, and while there remained new land for settlement, intercommunal tensions were kept in check and the various Han Chinese communities adopted attitudes mainly of collaboration. When, however, economic opportunities began to decline, whether because of an overall downturn in the regional economy or because of the using up of available land, then tensions rose and ethnic conflicts became accentuated. Therefore, although the earlier period was by no means pacific, the most severe period of subethnic tension in Taiwan lasted from the 1780s to the 1860s.[60]

Thus Yin Zhangyi argues that development of the Taibei basin and specifically the Xinzhuang region began in the early and mid-eighteenth century as a cooperative enterprise between different subethnic groups, who lived in largely unsegregated communities. The construction of the Temple of San Shan Guo Wang (King of the Three Mountains) in the mid-eighteenth century signified growing subethnic consciousness, in this case acting as a focus of loyalty for Chaozhou Hakkas.[61] Tensions sharply increased at the beginning of the nineteenth century and continued until the Hakkas were forced out of the area by around 1840 and moved to the areas of Taoyuan, Xinzhu, and Miaoli.[62]

LINGNAN

The Hakka thrust into Lingnan drew migrants from the Hakka heartland into counties still closer to the regional core than had been the case with their predecessors in the Ming. At the same time, further expansion took place in the west and north of the Lingnan region, with several counties on the frontier with the Middle Yangzi receiving immigrants. Map 2.2 takes the history of Hakka migrations within the Lingnan macroregion beyond the Ming period covered in Map 2.1 and up to the mid-nineteenth century (see also Table 2.2). Map 2.3 shows for comparative purposes areas of Hakka speech relative to Cantonese and other forms of speech around 1980 from the *Language Atlas of China*. Broadly, this comparison emphasizes that the historical evidence of Hakka migrations in the Ming and Qing provides a basis for understanding the current distribution of Hakka speakers.

Thus, soon after the beginning of the Lingnan upswing, Hakka migrants moved into Zengcheng, farther down the East River basin from their earlier destinations at Guishan and Boluo; in 1686 they had a dozen villages, by 1754

NOTE TO MAP 2.2 (overleaf). Routes of Hakka migrations within Lingnan and adjacent areas, 1550–1850, in relation to river systems and upland areas. Like Map 2.1 (p. 44), this map is stylized, depicting routes of migration that remain conjectural. This map omits entirely the diversion of Sichuan-bound migrants to counties southwest of the Pearl River.

MAP 2.2.
Routes of Hakka migrations within Lingnan and adjacent areas, 1550–1850, in relation to river systems and upland areas.

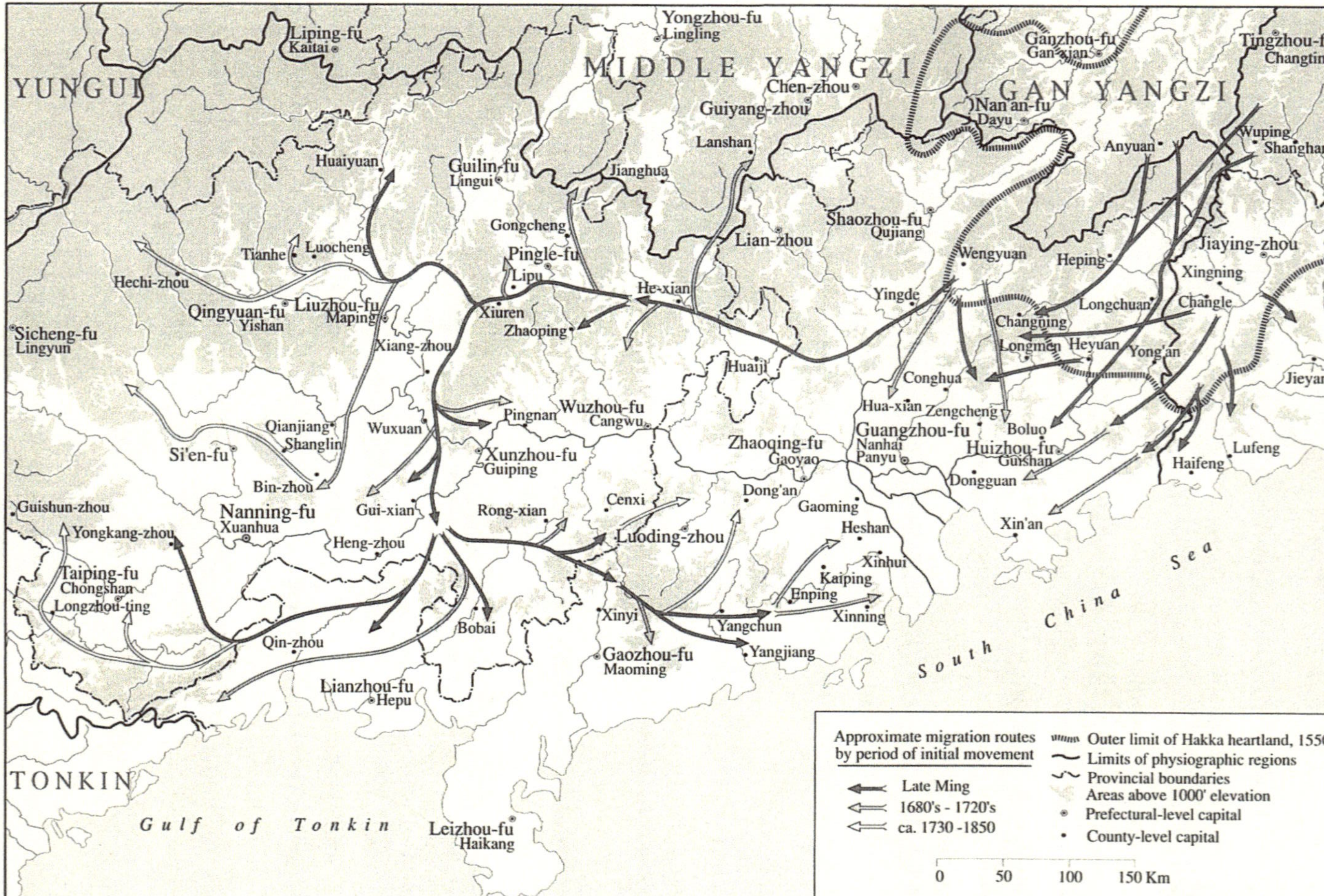

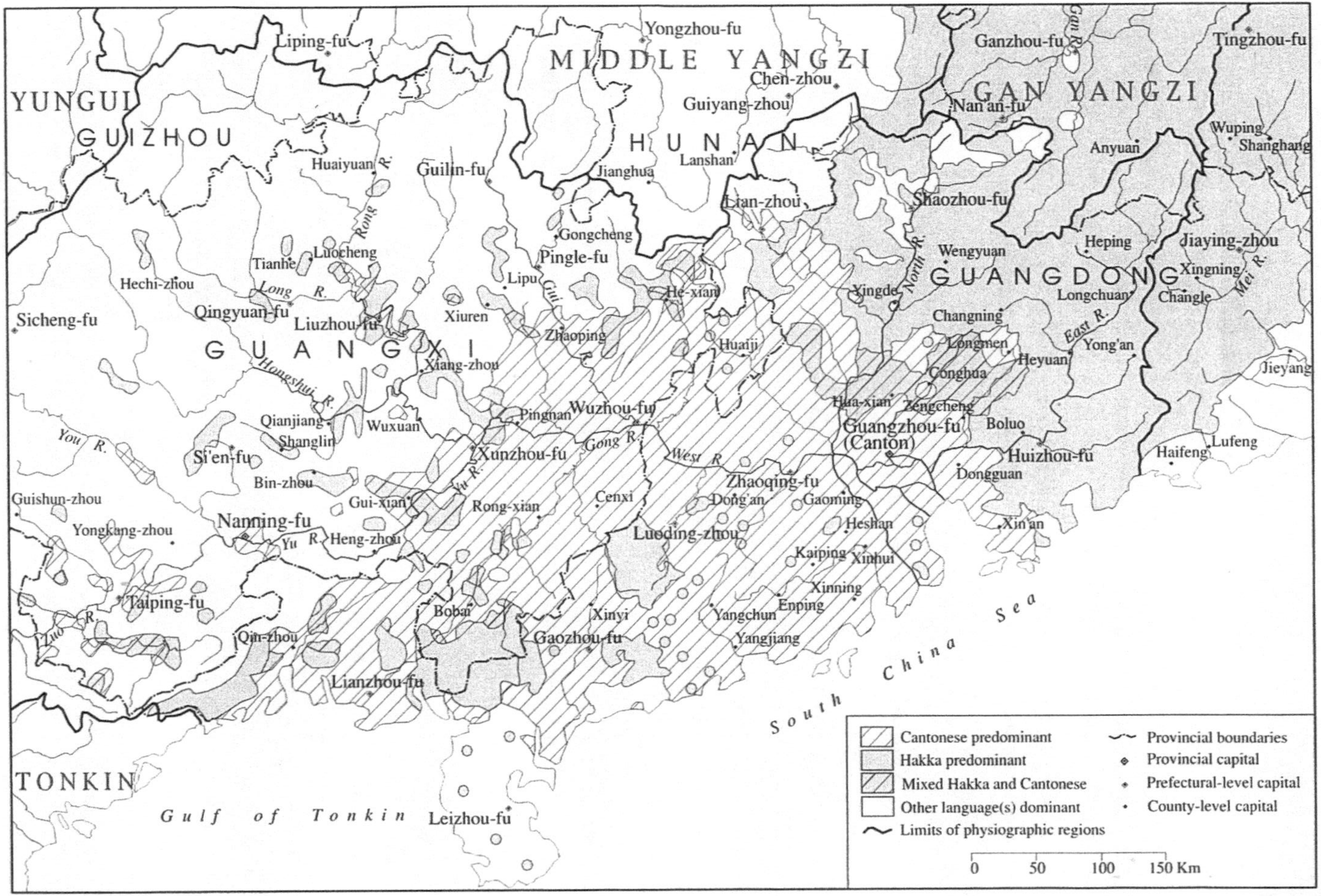

MAP 2.3.
Areas of Hakka speech in relation to areas of Cantonese speech within Lingnan, ca. 1980, showing administrative capitals as of 1820.

a hundred.[63] Still in the East River basin, they were present in the core county of Dongguan by 1689.[64] By the same time, they had reached Xin'an (Baoan), again in the core, farther to the south.[65] Along the north of the outer core, they entered Hua xian in about 1687.[66] Also by the end of the seventeenth century they could be found in the central delta county of Heshan;[67] as Map 2.2 suggests, however, it may be that the Hakkas arrived in Heshan from the west, from the settlements established during the Ming in counties such as Enping and Yangchun.

However, the real influx into the immediate vicinity of Guangzhou occurred late in the Kangxi period and especially during the Yongzheng reign, because the Yongzheng court accepted the advice of its local officials and diverted into this area what had by then become a huge stream of Hakka migrants heading toward Sichuan.[68] Starting in 1732, a call from Grain Intendant Tao Zhengzhong for settlers to open wasteland initiated an influx of Hakkas into Xinning (Taishan) and other counties to such an extent that, by the middle of the nineteenth century, they constituted as much as a third of the population.[69]

To take Xinning as an example, the 1738 gazetteer describes the kinds of economic opportunities—again at least partly in the exploitation of the uplands—available to the immigrants who had followed the economic upturn to Lingnan:

> Tens of thousands of people from other counties have come, some having been invited by the natives, some coming without being asked, and others following relatives who arrived earlier. Working the hillsides, they cultivate indigo, *chongxiangfen*, and mushrooms, or engage in timber and charcoal production. Others work in salt production, peddle rice and wine, or occupy themselves as collecting merchants of seafood or as boatmen.[70]

However, most of the Hakka immigrants, identified as having originated from Huizhou and Chaozhou prefectures, worked as tenant farmers. Under the government policy of bringing wasteland under cultivation, wealthy individuals, both natives of the county and outsiders, received parcels of land by the thousand *qing* (one *qing* equals approximately 6.5 hectares), invited tenants, and acquired formal title to the land, which would become subject to tax only six to ten years later. On low-lying land, a substantial outlay of some thousands of taels of silver went into the building of dikes to keep out the tidal water, and the tenants were provided with animals, seed, food, and village quarters, so that the capital spent per *qing* amounted to over one hundred taels. The normal tenant-landlord arrangement was sharecropping, with the tenant retaining 90 percent of the rice crop in the first year, 80 percent in the second when the landlord no longer provided animals, seed, and tools, 70 percent in the third, and 60 percent in the fourth and thereafter.

By contrast, far less capital was needed to open hill land, the investment being limited to building water-storage ponds where water was available, at the cost of a hundred or more taels per pond. The tenants in this case received no assistance from the landlord in the form of food, implements, seed, or shelter, and their obligation was that of a fixed rent; the rent was normally four times the amount of seed sown, payable variously from the sixth to the tenth year of cultivation.[71]

The large influx of immigrants inevitably engendered a steady buildup of interethnic tensions in the Lingnan core. In the eyes of the natives, the Hakka immigrants were clearly intruders, alien in speech and outlandish in social and cultural practices. The sight of Hakka women laboring alongside their menfolk in the fields, or unashamedly "showing their faces" in the marketplaces, unrestrained by footbinding and mixing freely with the menfolk, was considered by a community that observed a strict separation of the sexes to be corrupting the moral tenor of native society. Moreover, where the tenants worked for absentee non-native landlords, their labor was considered to be of no benefit to the local community.

The immigrants, on their part, felt ostracized by the community of natives who were bound together by powerful ties of kinship, territory, and community. On the interpersonal level, pejorative ethnic labeling, the taunting of Hakka women by native men, lack of permanent tenancy rights, competition for water and other resources, and countless other sources of conflict kept the ethnic boundary alive.[72] In Zengcheng, as the gazetteer of 1754 reveals, the *kemin*, originating from Yingde and Changning and subsequently joined by those from Yong'an and Longchuan, were viewed ambivalently. Although appreciative of the industriousness of the Hakka tenants, the natives nevertheless detested their litigiousness and easy recourse to violence. The natives were particularly alarmed by Hakka occupation of old deserted villages, often in uncomfortable proximity to their own settlements, even though Hakka villages were mostly segregated from native ones. Most threatening of all, local officials were allowing the Hakkas to develop a hierarchy of intervillage leagues, the small ones numbering tens of households, the largest more than a hundred villages.[73] The gazetteer lists all the villages in the county, carefully differentiating those populated by *kehu* ("sojourner households," or "guest" households; again the *ke* is the same character as the first character of the term "Hakka") that had been taken over entirely by them, and the small number that were mixed.[74]

But the essential point is that so long as the Lingnan economy flourished, these tensions were kept in check. A degree of peace could be based on the symbiotic relationship whereby one group depended on the other for land or labor. When the economic downturn set in from the start of the nineteenth century, however, interethnic feuds erupted, at first on a small scale as in Dongguan and Boluo in 1808.[75] Likewise, in Xinning and the surrounding counties, Hakka tenants were reported to be absconding or resisting rent payment.[76] It was here that, as the decades of depression wore on, the latent tensions exploded into a large-scale war at mid-century, with the battle lines drawn along those of dialect.[77]

Economic competition between the Hakkas and the natives had gone hand in hand with political competition. As the Hakkas prospered economically, some of them turned their ambitions to academic success. As early as 1760, Hakka students in Kaiping petitioned the authorities to be allowed formally to establish permanent residence so that they could sit for the examinations; the petition was refused. Later, as interethnic tensions mounted, the Qing government established separate examination subquotas for Hakka candidates of Xinning in 1788, Kaiping and Dongguan in 1811, and Xin'an and Gaoming in 1812.[78] Hakka aggressiveness on the economic front, and dogged competitiveness in the civil service examinations, during a period of shrinking economic opportunities and intensified academic competition, eventually brought on a crisis insoluble, in the view of the natives, short of exterminating the competitor.

"Hakka": Origin of an Ethnic Label

While people speaking the Hakka dialect were, as shown in Maps 1.2 (p. 24), 1.3 (p. 25), and 2.3, widely spread throughout the peripheries of the southern macroregions, the label "Hakka" itself emerged in the areas of Lingnan where Hakka migrants found themselves in contact and conflict with lowlanders; it was subsequently transmitted to the Hakka homeland in the Mei and Ting basins. The "Hakkas" of the upper Gan basin never identified themselves as such; instead, they called themselves *bendi* ("natives") in relation to immigrants, a large proportion of whom had in fact come from the Mei and Ting basins. The label was carried by these immigrants to various parts of the Gan basin, but was subsequently eclipsed by the label *keji*. Even more significant, the "Hakkas" in the North River uplands, though within the Lingnan macroregion and Guangdong province, dissociated themselves from the label when Hakka ethnic self-awareness reached one of its peaks. This may be explained by the fact that the North River "Hakkas" had migrated to the Lingnan core in far fewer numbers, and that the Shaozhou subregion enjoyed a relatively advantageous economic position on the north-south artery of trade. In sum, Hakka ethnic assertiveness in Lingnan in the nineteenth and early twentieth centuries should not be construed as an all-Hakka phenomenon. The "Hakkas" were segmented by regional contexts of time and place, and some had more reason than others to assert their ethnicity.[79]

Peripherality holds the key to explaining many of the cultural peculiarities of the Hakkas. In contrast to other ethnic groups such as the Cantonese or the Hokkien, the Hakkas, "alone of all Han Chinese groups," writes Skinner, "had no drainage basin to call their own."[80] The consequences were far-reaching. The Hakkas developed traditions of mobility and sojourning, and of unorthodox male and female roles. Their speech was characterized by a degree of homogeneity unknown to any other Chinese dialect because they lacked a prestigious center based upon a metropolis in the core area.

The effects of peripherality extended to the primacy of ethnic over territorial bonds and to the ethnic label ("Hakka," or in Modern Standard Chinese *kejia* or "guest family") itself. Unlike the Cantonese and the Teochius, each of whom had a major urban center to identify with, namely, Guangzhou-fu and Chaozhou-fu respectively, the Hakkas could find no comparable locus to express their identity. This has given rise to forced and tortuous mythmaking by Hakka writers endeavoring to endow the label with respectability. Writers like Gu Zhi and Luo Xianglin traced the term to the Eastern Jin, with inevitable injury to historical fact.[81] Wen Zhonghe speculated that the term derived from Song census categories, which distinguished between native (*zhuhu*) and immigrant (*kehu*) households, forgetting that the distinction was applied throughout the empire.[82] Others asserted without evidence that the name was already prevalent in vernacular usage in Song times.[83] Lai Jixi, on the other hand, maintained that the label was given to the Hakkas by the Cantonese, a belief shared by many.[84]

The origin of the label, as with so many of its kind, remains buried in history, unrecorded as it came into currency among beleaguered and illiterate immigrants. In printed sources, the earliest recorded appearance of the word *ke* to refer to the people now known as the Hakkas was in the context of interethnic conflict in Jieyang county in the lower Hanjiang basin (a Hoklo area). The thrust of the Hakkas into this county (the western half eventually ending up in their hands) and elsewhere in the lower Hanjiang is not recorded in any of the local gazetteers. Nevertheless, it is clear that some Hakkas penetrated most of Chaozhou prefecture. Huang Zanfa reports a saying, backed up in pre-1949 statistics, that in Chaozhou prefecture and Jiaying zhou, "only in Dabu are there no Hoklo, only in Chenghai are there no Hakkas."[85] The Jieyang gazetteer of 1779 cryptically reported that in 1644 and 1646 "*ke* bandits" (*kezei*) sporadically slaughtered and committed other crimes against the natives, "being hateful of their different speech."[86]

The term "Hakka" seemed, however, more prevalent on the Cantonese-Hakka boundary, appearing in the gazetteers of Yong'an, Changning, and Dongguan, all in the East River basin of Lingnan. Yong'an, which was created in 1569 from sections of (Hakka-dominant) Changle and (Cantonese-dominant) Guishan, received an influx of Hakka migrants after a prolonged conflict with She and local bandits. The label was not found in the 1586 edition of the county gazetteer, but appeared in the 1687 edition: "The county has many fine people whose ancestors arrived four generations ago from the provinces of Jiangxi and Fujian and the prefectures of Chaozhou and Huizhou [in Guangdong], and they are called *kejia*."[87] Recitation of the classics could be heard from house to house, rich and poor alike seeking academic success as opportunities for social advancement opened up with the upswing of the Lingnan regional cycle.[88]

Changning, a county on another tributary of the East River, was founded also in 1569 after local turmoil similar to that in Yong'an. It was constituted from sections of Heyuan, Wengyuan, and Yingde counties. As Map 2.3 shows, Changning, like Yong'an, would become predominantly Hakka in population after the Hakka immigrants gained the upper hand over the Yao and the She, as well as over the other Han Chinese inhabitants. Here the term *kejia* seems to have arisen originally to distinguish two variants of the Hakka speech. According to the earliest extant edition of the Changning gazetteer (1756), "Tradition has it that when the county was founded, those of Fujian ancestry spoke *kejia* while those of Jiangxi ancestry spoke *shuiyuan*."[89] Thus, the label appears to have served, in the first instance, to differentiate two immigrant groups of generally the same speech. Whether it expressed a significant ethnic difference at one time is unclear; the two groups were reported to be in harmonious coexistence between 1756 and 1839.[90] In Yong'an, on the other hand, the label acquired a broader usage than that of simple reference to people of Fujian origin.

In Dongguan, where the first handful of Hakkas arrived in the 1680s and grew to over a thousand in sixteen villages in 1720, the immigrants were classed in the gazetteer with the aborigines, loosely called Yao, among whom the Hakkas had settled in the hills. These "Fujian and Chaozhou vagrants" (*Min-Chao liuren*) were engaged in indigo cultivation. In the 1689 edition of the gazetteer, the natives referred to them as *ngai-lou* (*ailiao*), and in the 1720 edition, as *liu-ngai* (meaning "Ngai vagrants"). The word *ngai* was newly coined to convey a double insult. It was written with the "dog" radical to give emphasis to the native view of the Hakkas as subhuman, and it was a slur on their peculiar speech, *ngai* being how the Hakkas pronounced the first-person pronoun. The 1689 edition noted that the Hakkas spoke a dialect called *he*, and the 1720 edition reported that they called themselves by the name *kejia*.[91] This contradicts the common belief that the label was an ascription by others. Indeed, the natives of Dongguan and other Cantonese would continue to call them "Ngai" well into the nineteenth century before yielding to Hakka ethnic sensitivity. Those who knew better, like the great Cantonese scholar Qu Dajun, would use a less offensive character, without, however, avoiding the dialectal pun.[92]

Just how the term "Hakka" was derived remains, of course, a mystery. It seems probable that, rather than originating in some distant past, "Hakka" was simply the Hakka way of saying *kemin* or, more accurately, *kehu*, in which category they were enrolled in the local population registers. This was required by the machinery of local social control known as the *baojia*, introduced in the late Ming especially vis-à-vis immigrant households, and subsequently adopted and expanded by the Qing.[93] This hunch receives some confirmation from the appearance of the label in the gazetteers of Xinchang (later Yifeng) and Xingguo, counties in the Gan Yangzi region. As will be discussed in Chapters 6 and 7, these counties began receiving Hakka immigrants in the late Ming, and in both instances the name appeared in connection with the *baojia* system.[94]

Alternatively, a recent article by Jiang Bingzhao has argued that the term emerged in the context of Han migration into the minority nationalities areas of Southeast China: it does not come from the term *kehu*, which mainly refers to landholding or the lack thereof, but arose to distinguish between the Han immigrants and the non-Han original inhabitants of the area.[95] On the other hand, Li Mo has argued that the term originates in part in the assimilation of the She with the migrating Han, and that the She used to call themselves *shanke*.[96]

In the West River basin of Lingnan, the ethnic situation was greatly complicated by the coexistence not only of Zhuang, Yao, and other aborigines, but also of old Cantonese and Hakka settlers as well as new ones, not to mention immigrants from other provinces. The terms *kejia* or *keren* (referring to the speakers) and *kehua* or *kejiahua* (the speech) tend to be common primarily in twentieth-century local gazetteers, whereas native-place identification is more common in earlier compilations, which probably reflected the immigrants' own self-perception.

On the other hand, the label *ngai* seems to have been carried far and wide by the Cantonese emigrants from the Lingnan inner core to these parts, appearing in many variations. Another common label, again intended as a slur on the peculiarity of the immigrants' speech, was *ma-gai*, one rendering of which is the interrogative "what" in Hakka speech.

The label *lai* was far less common than some scholars have assumed; it probably means "comer," unless it turns out to originate in the Zhuang language. It was given to the Hakka immigrants by the Zhuang people, particularly of the Gui-xian subregion. In this subregion, the concentration and numerical strength of the immigrants made a real difference. Hakkas of different native provinces, Guangdong, Fujian, and Jiangxi, showed themselves capable of acting in solidarity against hostile neighbors, although it is unclear under what ethnic banner they rallied. Here they found themselves simultaneously in conflict with Cantonese landlords and competing with Zhuang and other aboriginal tenants during the second downturn of the Lingnan cycle. By the mid-nineteenth century, the ethnic lines were clearly drawn, frequent feuding having erupted since 1842. In the eyes of the Cantonese, the Hakkas were not Han Chinese at all, but to be classified along with the Lang, Zhuang, Yao, and Tan, and referred to as Ngai or Lai. The temptation for the Cantonese landlords to exact more than the normal rent would have been strong, given the industriousness of the Hakkas and their greater productivity from combined male and female fieldwork. The 1874 edition of the Xunzhou fu gazetteer puts the situation succinctly:

> The Lai people (*lairen*) are found in all four counties of Xunzhou prefecture, being especially numerous in Gui xian. They migrated here from Guangdong, Fujian, and Jiangxi, for which reason they are called lai. Because they habitually utter the sound *ngai*, they are also called Ngai. Their customs are no different from those of other residents. However, the men and women all engage in farming, not shrinking from hardship, and are consequently able to double the yield from the land, compared to others. All the wealthy landowners prefer them as tenants. Although they dwell in solitary huts within the fields, without neighbors, their sentiment of ethnic solidarity (*zudang zhi yi*) is very strong. In an emergency, a hundred will respond to a call, arriving with spears and spades on their shoulders, fearless of death. Altercations between them and the aborigines often lead to armed feuds.[97]

Faced with enemies on two fronts, it is hardly surprising that so many of the Hakkas should join the God Worshippers Society and that the Gui-xian subregion should become the staging area for the Hakka-led Taiping Rebellion.[98]

To conclude, the hypothesis outlined in Chapter 1 fits, to a large degree, the evidence presented for Lingnan and the Southeast Coast. The demographic interaction of the core and the periphery is shown, in both macroregions, by the power of the economic upturn of the sixteenth century to attract highland Hakkas as miners and cash croppers to upland areas closer to the core. Similarly, when the Southeast Coast stagnated while the Lingnan core experienced an upturn from the late seventeenth century, Hakka migrants avoided the Southeast Coast and instead, as shown in Map 2.2, headed south for upland areas adjacent to the Lingnan core and even into the core itself. I have found no evidence of a reverse flow back to the periphery in times of economic difficulties, but the migration of Hakkas along with others from the Southeast Coast to Taiwan and Southeast Asia in the late seventeenth and eighteenth centuries, and the overseas migration out of Lingnan in the nineteenth century, may be viewed as movement to a more extreme periphery.

Moreover, it was during economic contractions in the relevant macroregions that Hakka ethnicity manifested itself in contradistinction to the interests of the locals. Thus, ethnic tensions emerged during the seventeenth-century downturns in both the Lingnan and the Southeast Coast macroregions, and again during the nineteenth century when Lingnan entered a severe contraction.

3. The Formation of the Hakka Ethos in the Nineteenth Century

The previous chapters of this study have concentrated on the history of the Hakkas up to the early nineteenth century.[1] The environment within which the Hakkas lived changed substantially during that century, with the emergence of Chinese nationalism, as well as the disintegration of the imperial state. Thus new themes begin to emerge in Hakka history, with the sharpening of ethnic consciousness and the forging of a link between Hakka ethnicity and Chinese nationalism in the twentieth century. This chapter and the next examine these later pages in the history of the Hakka people.

Hakkas in Lingnan in the Early Nineteenth Century

As a result of the processes discussed in Chapter 2, by the early nineteenth century the Hakkas around the Lingnan core and up and down the West River basin had begun to form an ethnic group and to interact with their neighbors in ethnic terms. However, at no time did all the Hakkas unite in ethnic solidarity, partly because the Hakkas straddled three different macroregions, each with a distinctive developmental cycle. Hakkas and Hoklos, for instance, interacted without a single incident along the isogloss all through the second half of the nineteenth century.[2] One reason for this was that the Southeast Coast regional cycle, unlike that of Lingnan, began an upturn following the Opium War and the creation of treaty ports along the coast.

An important feature of the Hakkas in Lingnan was that their disabilities were primarily economic. This was true of Hakkas everywhere: the home base was invariably described by the stock phrase *shan duo tian shao*, that is, more mountains than arable land. Close to the Lingnan core the Hakkas were typically tenants of Punti landlords, a dependency relationship that lay at the root of Hakka-Punti conflict. The Hakkas everywhere were not specially disadvantaged by any deliberate government policy. Indeed, institutional arrangements and imperial policies tended to promote equality of opportunity and were sensitive to interethnic rivalry. Hakkas in the home base were, of course, able to acquire gentry status by means of the prefectural examinations and, in such predominantly Hakka areas as Jiaying, Huizhou, Nanxiong, and Shaozhou in Guangdong, Tingzhou in Fujian, and Ganzhou and Nan'an in Jiangxi, they competed among themselves. In mixed prefectures where Hakkas formed a substantial minority, special quotas were set aside for them, usually after interethnic altercations, in order to defuse tensions. This policy had been first adopted for the "Hakkas" in Yuanzhou prefecture (Jiangxi) in 1730.[3] Later the precedent was extended to the prefectures of Guangzhou and Zhaoqing in Guangdong. Thus, civil and military examination quotas were set aside for Hakkas of the counties Xinning (1788), Dongguan (1801), Xin'an (1802), Kaiping (1807), and Gaoming (year unknown).[4]

By the nineteenth century, the Hakkas of Lingnan were differentiated by spatial and temporal variations in migration and settlement (as shown in Chapter 2). The isogloss of Hakka and Cantonese can be fairly accurately delineated immediately beyond the purely Hakka areas, i.e., along the line of the Guangzhou regional core, cutting through the East and North River basins. (The exception was the western basin of the North River above Yingde, which had a large Yao population.) Moving inward from the first line of intergroup contact, there are significant variations in the comparative numerical strength of Hakkas vis-à-vis Cantonese. Reliable demographic data are unavailable; the impression given by the sources is that, by the mid-nineteenth century, only Boluo county had a Hakka majority and, according to one source, Hakkas there were paying ground rent to Punti owners residing in the towns. In Zengcheng, Conghua, and Hua xian Hakkas and Punti were approximately equal in number. Hakkas were slightly outnumbered in Dongguan and Xin'an, while in Xinning, Kaiping, and surrounding counties they still amounted to up to one-third of the population.[5]

The relative size of the Hakka community was obviously of critical importance in its effect on the resources available, the scope and duration of ethnic mobilization, and the decision between confrontation or accommodation. Hakka settlement patterns, too, enhanced the potential for interethnic conflict, as Myron Cohen has shown.[6] Since Hakkas were immigrants from a culturally different population, their settlements tended initially to be small and widely interspersed among the Cantonese who were already organized in localized agnatic groupings. This did not mean, however, that Hakkas and Cantonese generally lived in the same villages. On the contrary, Hakka settlements tended to be segregated from Cantonese villages. Indeed, in some counties for which gazetteer information is available, the Hakka community occupied an entire section of the county, generally cleaving to the hillier and poorer lands.[7] This pattern of settlement suggests that the purely Hakka villages facilitated the endurance of distinctive cultural traits, which formed the basis for ethnic identification and mobilization.

This settlement pattern stemmed from the type of land available to Hakka immigrants: generally marginal land, already claimed by the Cantonese but not yet in use. Initially, the relationship was symbiotic: Hakkas worked the land in permanent tenure and the Cantonese collected ground rent. A great many of the settlers had arrived under government sponsorship in the eighteenth century; these were given the right of landownership conditional upon the land being brought under cultivation and the taxes being paid. But, as so often happened, no sooner was the "waste" land made productive than previously unknown claimants appeared, which, according to a local official in the eighteenth century, was the reason for settlers' hesitation in responding to the official call.[8]

These initially small and dispersed Hakka communities would grow, drawing a constant stream of immigrants who congregated, in the stock imagery used by Cantonese, "like ants and bees." The tendency of the Hakkas to develop sizable village settlements and to increase their landholdings became a pressure increasingly difficult to resist, while the rapacity of Cantonese landlords grew with economic contraction. In 1867, E. J. Eitel of the London Missionary Society wrote that "the Hakkas are everywhere to be found, either dispersed in small villages between the hills and paying ground-rent to the Puntis, or congregated in large villages, and then continually fighting with the Puntis for the ownership of the hills and fields occupied by them."[9] A government official, endeavoring to reason with the Puntis and mediate in the Hakka-Punti War, remarked: "Concerning these feuds, are the Hakkas entirely to blame? For decades, the natives (*tu*) have been treating the Hakkas like slaves. Native humiliation and oppression of the Hakkas are no different from the present Hakka treatment of the natives."[10]

As we have seen, the *xiangyue* institution, a form of social control promoted by the government in the countryside, had facilitated extralocal organization for interethnic conflict ever since the sixteenth century; it continued to be a basis for ethnic mobilization right up to the nineteenth century.[11] Residents of different villages came together periodically for moral lectures by elders. These intervillage "compacts" had the capacity to federate, to use Philip Kuhn's term, into "multiplex" organizations, providing a ready forum for ethnic issues and the emergence of ethnic leadership.[12]

The most famous example of Hakka subethnic mobilization in the nineteenth century was, of course, the Taiping Rebellion. Map 3.1 shows the areas in Guangxi province where Taiping mobilization started: mainly Hakka areas.[13] Given the amount of material on the Taiping Rebellion and the fact that it soon outgrew its Hakka origins, it is only touched on in this work. Nevertheless, all sources make clear the importance of the Hakka origins of the rebellion in Guangdong and Guangxi.

The background to the rebellion was just the sort of increase in interethnic tensions in the context of a major downturn in the Lingnan regional economy that is suggested by the hypothesis outlined in Chapter 1. The increased conflict between Hakkas and Punti and also between Hakkas and Zhuang was particularly acute in Gui xian and Guiping, the centers of the development of the God Worshippers Society. The conflict led to the dispossession of many Hakkas and left them little alternative but to embark on rebellion; Taiping leader Shi Dakai from Gui xian was precisely such a Hakka who entered on the road to rebellion when his fellow Hakkas were driven from their homes by local Puntis.[14] Early in the rebellion, leaders like Shi were joined at Bobai by an additional group of Hakkas who had been driven from their homes.[15]

Many other leaders also had Hakka origins: Hong Xiuquan was himself a

MAP 3.1 (opposite). Areas of Taiping (Godworshippers Society) mobilization, 1848–50, and the area most severely affected by the Hakka-Punti wars, 1854–67.

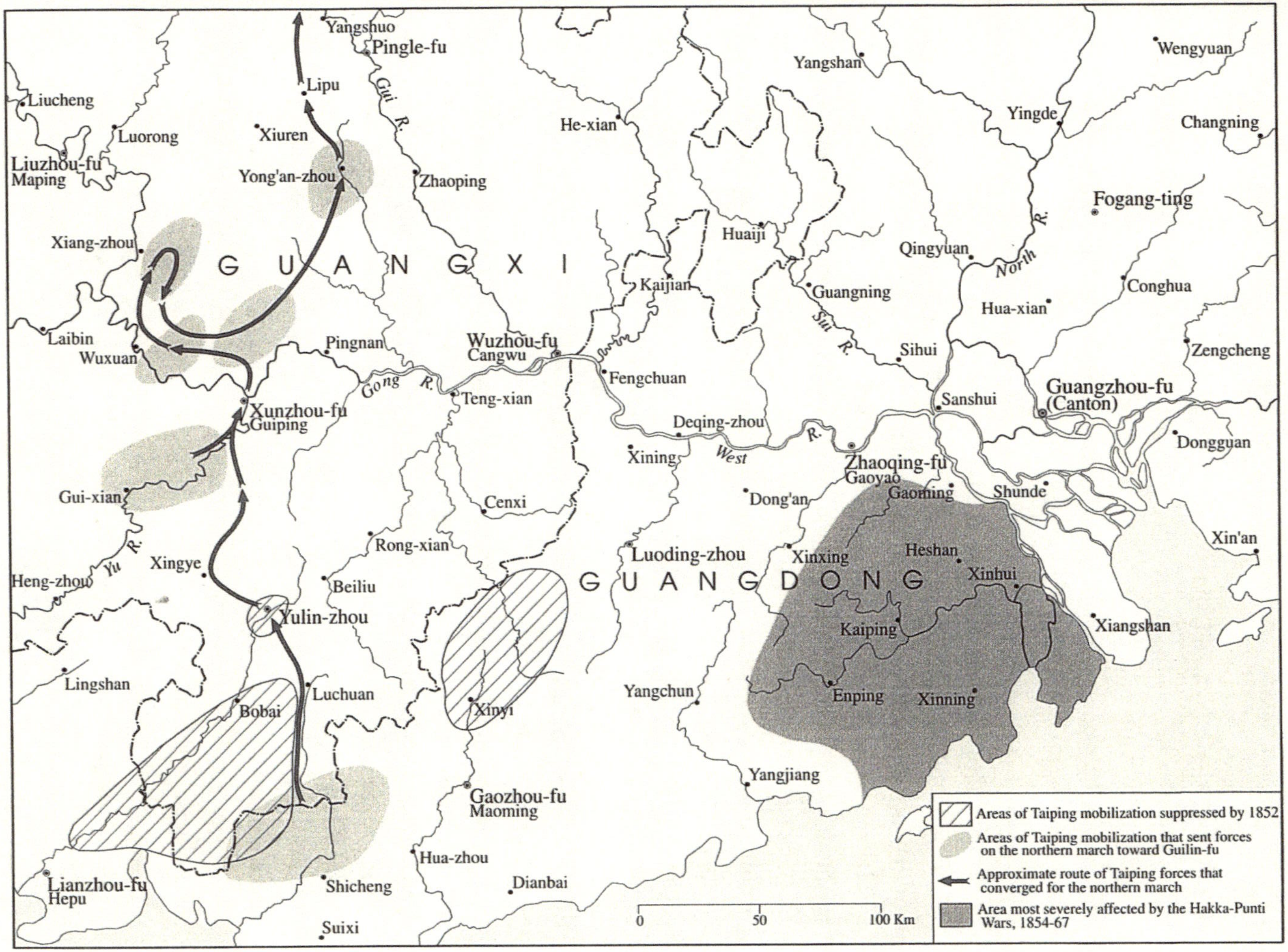

GUANGXI
GUANGDONG
Yangshuo
Pingle-fu
Lipu
Gui R.
Liucheng
Luorong
Xiuren
Liuzhou-fu
Maping
Yong'an-zhou
Zhaoping
He-xian
Yangshan
Wengyuan
Yingde
Changning
Fogang-ting
North R.
Qingyuan
Conghua
Hua-xian
Huaiji
Kaijian
Guangning
Sui R.
Sihui
Zengcheng
Xiang-zhou
Laibin
Wuxuan
Pingnan
Wuzhou-fu
Cangwu
Fengchuan
Sanshui
Guangzhou-fu
(Canton)
Gong R.
Teng-xian
Xunzhou-fu
Guiping
Deqing-zhou
West R.
Xining
Zhaoqing-fu
Gaoyao
Gaoming
Shunde
Dongguan
Gui-xian
Cenxi
Dong'an
Rong-xian
Luoding-zhou
Xinxing
Heshan
Xin'an
Yu R.
Xingye
Heng-zhou
Beiliu
Xinhui
Yulin-zhou
Kaiping
Xiangshan
Lingshan
Luchuan
Yangchun
Enping
Xinning
Bobai
Xinyi
Yangjiang
Gaozhou-fu
Maoming
Hua-zhou
Lianzhou-fu
Hepu
Shicheng
Dianbai
Suixi
0
50
100 Km
Areas of Taiping mobilization suppressed by 1852
Areas of Taiping mobilization that sent forces on the northern march toward Guilin-fu
Approximate route of Taiping forces that converged for the northern march
Area most severely affected by the Hakka-Punti Wars, 1854-67

Hakka from Hua xian, and Yang Xiuqing a Guangxi Hakka from Guiping.[16] Hong's version of Christianity became a medium through which Hakka ethnic mobilization could take place in the still-frontier society of Guangxi.[17] Although the Hakka character of the rebellion became less important as it advanced toward Central China, large numbers of Hakkas did participate. This can be seen as an exceptional instance of Hakka migration. Right at the end of the rebellion, after the defeat of the main Taiping army, remnant forces led by Wang Haiyang retreated to the Hakka heartland of Tingzhou prefecture and Jiaying zhou before their final destruction by government forces.[18]

Hakka-Punti tensions also set the scene for the widespread and uncontrolled conflict along ethnic lines that erupted in the Lingnan macroregion and lasted from 1854 to 1867, engulfing like "a prairie fire" as many as eight counties: Xinning, Gaoming, Heshan, Yangchun, Yangjiang, Enping, Kaiping, and Xinxing.[19] Map 3.1 shows the main area affected by that war: a continuous area of Hakka settlement—but generally an area where the Hakka were a minority—to the west of Guangzhou. The ethnic consciousness of the Hakkas more than made up for their inferior numbers. At the height of the conflict, speaking to an official sent to mediate, a Cantonese leader observed: "Peace is possible where the two groups are equally strong or equally weak, or where one is stronger than the other. Where the natives are stronger than the Hakkas, the former offer to discuss peace if the latter so wish. But here the natives are weaker and the Hakkas reject peace proposals from the natives."[20] These may have been self-serving remarks of a member of the group bent on extirpating the enemy, but Hakka strength could scarcely be exaggerated.

Ethnic antagonism between the two groups was absolute. As observed by Eitel, Punti animosity was as extreme as their well-known xenophobia toward Westerners: "If you were to ask a thorough-bred Punti about the character of the Hakkas, he would certainly, in the case of his condescending to acknowledge that he ever heard of such people, turn up his nose and tell you that the Hakkas are quite beneath your notice, that they are a kind of semi-barbarians, living in poverty and filth."[21]

The Hakkas, on their part, reciprocated with an image of the Puntis as "a clever but malicious and sneaking set of people," calling them "those snakes."[22] As the Puntis "refused to be sheltered by the same heaven with them,"[23] the solution had to match the depth of ethnic division. After 200,000 died on each side, a new dependent subprefecture, called Chixi ting, was carved out of a section of Xinning county at the edge of the sea.[24] Hakkas were urged to exchange acre for acre and move to Chixi. Others were resettled in the Leizhou Peninsula and on Hainan Island. Many no doubt remained behind in fortified villages but at a safe distance from the Cantonese for, as W. F. Mayer noted, "wherever their clans have been intermingled with a Punti population, they have been ousted and overwhelmed."[25]

Articulation of the Hakka Ethos

The most disastrous aspect of the conflict in the western districts of the Lingnan core was that the gentry on both sides engaged directly in mutual belligerence. This signified extreme community closure of the "coercive" kind, culminating in the militarization and fortification of one group against another.[26] In times of community openness, the gentry might be expected to use their extralocal contacts to perform the role of mediators. Now, as heads of warring groups along a cultural divide, and with imperial authority at the local level at its most impotent, they provided the leadership and resources for large-scale, organized, and uncontrolled warfare. Thereafter, the most visible aspect of Hakka ethnicity lay in the articulation by the Hakka elite of a particularistic ethos that would bolster Hakka pride and cohesiveness. Successive generations of Hakka elites would seek to foster a uniformity of self-perception for Hakkas everywhere. In discussing Hakka "cultural orientation" as perceived by Hakka ethnic writers, it is well to recall Patterson's distinction between an ethnic and a cultural group. The culture of an ethnic group tends to be mythmaking, while the traits of a cultural group are objectively verifiable.

Associated with the symbolic articulation of Hakka identity was the rise of Jiaying zhou (a county and also a prefectural-level unit; the county was later called Mei xian) as the spiritual center of the Hakkas. The emergence of what Frederik Barth calls an "ethnic boundary" occurs in the interaction between cultural groups.[27] As one would expect therefore, ethnicity as marked by the emergence of the label "Hakka" first developed in the zone of contact between Hakkas and Cantonese.

Ethnic sentiments, however, get transmitted to the home community; the humiliation of members of a group at the hands of another reflects upon the group as a whole. Thus, by the mid-nineteenth century, according to Eitel, "Hakka" was prevalent as an ethnic label "even in the Department of Kiaying-

TABLE 3.1

Comparison Between Examination Success in the Hakka Area of Jiaying with Two Metropolitan Counties

County	*Jinshi* graduates	*Juren* graduates	*Jieyuan* (first place in *juren* exams)
Jiaying	49	302	9
Panyu	37	300	1
Nanhai	47	402	9

SOURCE: Gu Zhi, 2: 13a.

chow [Jiaying zhou]."[28] Jiaying's prestige among the Lingnan Hakkas arose in part from its academic success and in part from the multitude of emigrants from the Mei basin. According to one computation, over a two-hundred-year period from the mid-seventeenth to the mid-nineteenth century, this economically deprived county outperformed Panyu and, to some extent, Nanhai, two of the metropolitan counties (see Table 3.1).

Late in the eighteenth century, in a series of examinations for the *juren* degree in Guangzhou, four Hakka candidates from Jiaying and one from Dabu, contiguous to it, performed the consciousness-raising feat of successively carrying off first prize, to the discomfort of their Cantonese rivals.[29] The beleaguered Hakkas at the Lingnan core and elsewhere would increasingly look to Jiaying, in American Baptist missionary George Campbell's words, "for vindication from calumny."[30]

The first spokesman for the Hakka ethnic group was not in fact a native of Jiaying. Although Hakkas had been roused before, the first ethnic statement did not appear until the early nineteenth century, following the interethnic feuds in Boluo and Dongguan in 1808. The spokesman was Xu Xuzeng, a native of Heping in the East River upland and *jinshi* of 1799. As director of the Fenghu Academy in Huizhou, he considered in a lecture why, despite centuries of settlement, the Hakkas were still known by a name that denoted "sojourning." In his lecture, which is preserved together with his genealogy, Xu introduced all the themes that would be repeated tirelessly in Hakka ethnocentric writings.[31] Like all such statements, these are neither all myth nor all truth. Xu's lecture was a statement of all the essential elements of Hakka self-identification, of the claim to a Chineseness that was equal, if not superior, to that of other Chinese.

Xu began with the origins, a search for greatness. First, the Hakkas were descendants of northerners, bearers of the ancient civilization of the Central Plain. Their migration to the south was motivated by the spirit of patriotic loyalism. Some of the Hakka ancestors in the south were Song loyalists, old upper-class families who had accompanied the Northern Song court in the move to Hangzhou in the early part of the twelfth century, in the wake of barbarian invasion. Most of them, however, had migrated during the Song-Yuan transition to avoid Mongol rule. To continue in Xu's own words:

> Then the Mongol armies came further south, the Song court moved hither and thither, finally to the southern mountain ranges. The old upper-class families along with commoners uprooted themselves and followed . . . battling the Mongol armies with bare hands on the way. . . . Accompanying the emperor to the south, only one in ten thousand survived, scattering everywhere. Though bereft of family and country, they did not emulate the five hundred on Tianheng Island, who committed suicide, but instead determined to live on and nurse their vengeance. Avoiding the unhealthy climate of the lowlands and unwilling to live among people of different customs and speech they selected an area [in the highlands of the Guangdong-Fujian-Jiangxi border] to be close to provinces of the interior. Moreover, as survivors of the same cause, they felt they should reside together [and] preserve their customs and speech . . . so that their patriotic spirit would not diminish.

The Hakka brand of loyalism was in fact xenophobia. It was not such as to be unique to them by any means, for their Punti neighbors also exhibited it in their "origin myth." Unlike the Hakkas, however, the Puntis never felt the need to assert repeatedly this aspect of their origin, or indeed any other, displaying the serenity and self-assurance of a dominant group.

Antiforeign patriotic sentiment among the Hakkas may be historically significant, although the extent to which the Taiping leaders were inspired by this tradition is unclear. What is certain is that the patriotic antiforeignism of the Hakkas predated the rise of anti-Manchu nationalism. Moreover, this view of the past has been carried forward to a historical view of the Taipings and of Sun Yat-sen and his Hakka followers that fits in with that tradition.

As to the timing of the departure from the center of Chinese civilization, most Hakka writers would agree that the majority of the Hakkas were descended from the migrants of the Song-Yuan transition. The claim was already made in Xu's time, however, that some Hakkas were descended from earlier immigrants. Xu stated that his Hakka contemporaries, Song Xiang, a renowned scholar-poet of Jiaying, and Zhou Shenxuan of Qujiang (Shaozhou-fu), were of the belief that some of the *keren* of Jiaying zhou, and of Tingzhou and Shaozhou prefectures, could trace their origins to the fall of the Western Jin dynasty early in the fourth century A.D., a significant indication that Xu was not alone in his concern with the group's origin.[32] Circumstances in the fourth century, when the earlier immigrants arrived, resembled those of the later migration in essential detail. During both the fourth and the twelfth centuries, the reigning Chinese dynasties had been forced out of the Yellow River valley by barbarian invasions, one to be restored in present-day Nanjing, the other in present-day Hangzhou. In each instance, the expelled court was accompanied by loyal officials and their families, to whom Hakkas traced their ancestry.

The assertion of an origin in the north by all Han subethnic groups in the south was in part a function of their forced coexistence with non-Han aborigines. The claim was made by Hakkas, Cantonese, and Hoklos alike.[33] Moreover, each group had a story of their entry into Guangdong province that was simplicity itself. Major Hoklo lineages traced their descent from the state-sponsored colonists of the late Tang, who emigrated from Henan to the Zhangzhou-Quanzhou and Chaozhou areas in the Southeast Coast.[34] Similarly, leading Cantonese lineages propagated the lore of descent from the 97 families, made up of 33 surnames, who forgathered, after the long trek from the north following the Mongol invasion, at an obscure place on the Guangdong border, Zhujixiang (Pearl Ward) in Nanxiong zhou, before arriving in the Lingnan lowlands.[35] The Hakkas on their part propagated the lore of Shibicun (Stonewall Village) in Ninghua county, Fujian, where their ancestors had found shelter from the Huang Chao Rebellion in the late ninth century. Later, at the time of the Mongol invasion, they crossed the provincial border to the counties of Jiaying and beyond.[36] The claims of all these groups were carefully recorded in the genealogies of their families and lineages.

To return to Xu's elaboration on the origins of the Hakkas, Hakka society, physically isolated in the peculiar highland ecology of their new homeland, evolved distinctive values and customs. No Hakka ever served the Mongol regime: Hakka refusal to do so was celebrated as a mark of patriotic loyalism. No matter how destitute, Hakkas combined the high culture of scholarship with farming and the martial arts. Hakka women, rich or poor, did not practice footbinding, in response, Xu implied, to early Qing decrees.[37] Consequently Hakka women, unlike others, excelled in fieldwork, in addition to household management, handicrafts, and child rearing. Frugal by habit, they never had to resort to prostitution. Finally, the speech of the ancient north was preserved in the Hakka language. "In essence," exulted Xu, "the Hakkas are diligent by habit, thrifty and unostentatious in customs, courteous, modest, elegant, and polished by disposition"—all the prized virtues believed to inhere in the uncorrupted people of the Golden Age of great antiquity.[38]

This elaborate articulation of an ethos for the Hakka group by a *jinshi* of the realm marked a new level of ethnic consciousness that was to fragment the Lingnan elite along ethnic lines. The feuds in Boluo and Dongguan, which had prompted Xu Xuzeng's ethnic statement, had quickly been brought under control, thanks to both the presence of imperial military units close at hand and the mediation of the elite on both sides.[39] The feuds that erupted in the western districts in mid-century, however, were to prove unmanageable. The imperial forces were then preoccupied with the Taiping rebels. Other local dissidents could be put down only by ad hoc recruitment of local mercenaries. Incredible as it may seem, Hakka and Punti braves were among the recruits used to suppress the Red Turban (Hongtou) rebels, who were ethnically Punti.[40] It was in the nature of the Chinese local elite that, in times of extreme local instability, loyalty to lineage and community tended to overshadow that toward the regime, impelling some to cultivate dissidents in the interest of self-preservation. In these circumstances, Hakka braves could not suppress the rebels without at the same time attacking their Punti elite supporters. In a situation of simmering interethnic tensions, this spelled disaster. The Puntis, alarmed by the "excessive zeal" of the Hakka mercenaries in going after the rebels and their supporters, real or imaginary, responded by declaring war on all Hakkas. The battle line was drawn on the sound of speech alone. This thirteen-year-long war was to leave a legacy of mutual hatred that affected high and low on both sides beyond the immediate battle zone.

In the mid-1860s, when a less beleaguered government was able finally to intervene to bring about a settlement, two Hakka officials who were not native to the war-torn region spoke up to ensure fair treatment for the Hakka group. Ding Richang, a native of Fengshun and governor of Jiangsu province, wrote to his opposite number in Guangdong, advising an evenhanded approach and enlightening him on Hakka origins and culture in order to obviate disadvantageous treatment of the Hakkas as if they were non-Han aborigines.[41] Lin Daquan, a native of Dabu and *juren* of 1861, who was in Ding's employ, circulated a treatise on the Hakkas and strongly criticized the official handling of the feuds. In particular, he attacked the local authorities for referring to the Hakkas involved in the feuds as "Hakka bandits" (*fei*) and for aiding the Puntis in driving them out. Like Xu's lecture, Lin's treatise was a spirited glorification of the Hakkas: true sons of the Golden Age, descendants of the upper class of the Central Plain, with a speech that showed a clear affinity with the ancient speech of the north.[42]

The Punti gentry on their part were decided in their characterization of the Hakkas as bandits and thieves, and beyond the Chinese racial and cultural pale. This stereotype was fostered in the county gazetteers, which served as an important repository of local particularism. Thus, in the section recording the feuds, Hakkas were labeled as *fei* in the gazetteers of Gaoyao (Zhaoqing-fu) (1863), Xinhui (1870), Xinning (1893), and Gaoming (1894).[43] The Gaoyao gentry, in the Xuantong edition of the gazetteer, improved on that of 1863 by describing the Hakkas as Yao aborigines.[44] As late as 1925, the Yangjiang gazetteer still referred to the Hakkas as bandits (*kefei*).[45] But the Enping gazetteer of 1934 topped them all: the name "Hakka" was written as "Chilao," a subbranch of the Lao aborigines; a dozen verses written by a Punti talent at the time of the feuds cursed the Hakkas for the calamity they had caused, and were included in the section on literary works of the county.[46]

The publication in 1898 of the gazetteer of Jiaying zhou, by then the undisputed spiritual heartland of the Lingnan Hakkas, was something of a milestone in the articulation of the Hakka ethos. Its chief compiler, Wen Zhonghe, was a Hanlin academician. The gazetteer included an extensive treatise on Hakka customs and manners and a detailed exposition of all the main rituals, to dispel any doubt of Hakka Chineseness. The Hakka language had received its first scholarly treatment at the hands of the Hakka poet-classicist Huang Zhao in his Zhenping (Jiaoling) county gazetteer of 1880.[47] Wen's chapter on the Hakka dialect carried this a step further. The tonal affinities of Hakka with Sui-Tang speech were set out to show the unmistakably northern origin of the dialect.[48] Finally, and most significant of all, there was a handy brief history of the Hakkas, which was more self-assured and less grandiloquent than those purveyed by Xu Xuzeng and Lin Daquan. Wen was uncertain of the precise origin of the label "Hakka," but he surmised that it might have originated with the census category *kehu* ("immigrant households") used in Song times.[49]

The significance of such gazetteers as a means of mobilization for ethnic interaction can scarcely be overstated. Compiled by respected members of the community, they fostered group cohesiveness and maintained the ethnic boundary, even though these were not their only purposes.

4. Ethnicity and Nationalism in the Twentieth Century

The turn of the twentieth century witnessed an upsurge of nationalism among China's elite. That nationalism contained multiple strands that impinged on ethnic separateness in various ways. On the one hand, the primary strands of anti-imperialism and national integration required the subordination of ethnic differences. On the other, a lesser strand, which seemed particularly strong in Lingnan, stressed the racial aspect of Chinese nationalism. Since Lingnan was one of the most ethnically complex areas of China, the tantalizing question arises: what connection was there between the position of the Hakkas in Lingnan and their strong representation in the anti-Manchu revolutionary movement? At any rate, the involvement of the Hakkas in the revolution unfolded side by side with their assertion of a Han racial origin, against the background of Punti animosity.

Thus, even as nationalism rapidly took hold among the Hakka elite, the ethnic rhetoric was kept up. In 1901 there appeared an anthology of poetry based on the work of poets who hailed from the Mei River valley between Song and Qing times. It was called *Meishui shizhuan* (An anthology of poetry from the Mei valley), there being no higher cultural credential in Chinese society than excellence in poetry. The noted poet-reformer Huang Zunxian lent his prestige to this enterprise by furnishing a preface, in which he wrote, "I have often said that the *keren* are an ancient race of the Central Plain, a fact borne out by their spoken and written language."[1]

The year 1905 was another landmark in the development of Hakka self-consciousness. That year, the Cantonese scholar Huang Jie wrote a school history of Guangdong, called *Guangdong xiangtu lishi* (A local history of Guangdong). The volume was issued with the approval of the provincial educational authorities for use in the new schools being set up under the imperial reforms. An offending lesson in the text dealt with the racial composition and origins of different groups. It stated, "Among the races of Guangdong are Hakkas and Hoklos; they are not Cantonese and are not of the Han racial stock."[2] The text provoked a storm of protest among Hakka scholars, while the Hoklos showed their sense of security by ignoring it altogether. As Campbell relates:

> A circular was sent out by some Mei-chau [i.e., Jiaying] scholars, containing an answer to the calumnious statement in the school history and also a call to all interested to attend a meeting in the Yamen to concert measures to secure its excision. . . . In the spring of 1906 . . . the called meeting was held. Mr. Yong, editor of a Swatow daily, was Chairman. After due discussion, a "Society for Investigation of the Origin of the Hakka People" was formed. A printed prospectus was issued, providing for the cooperation of every surname in the roster of Mei-chau clans. Each of the thirty-six townships into which the county is divided was to have a special committee to secure material for the memorial to be prepared. The provincial authorities did not await the collection of these facts before taking action. The offending statement was cut out.[3]

During this episode, the Hakka elite (numbering among them Huang Zunxian, Qiu Fengjia, and Zou Lu) threw their full weight behind the newspaper and pamphlet campaign for the affirmation of Hakka racial purity.[4] In the early years of nationalism, these men, many of whom, like Qiu and Zou, were active members of the Tongmenghui led by Sun Yat-sen, saw no contradiction between their ethnic assertiveness and the broad political goals of the revolutionary movement. They were working simultaneously toward the acceptance of Hakkas as a rightful section of Guangdong society and toward the establishment of a new political order in which they intended to have a place. For Hakkas these were not antithetical but interdependent goals. In this light their ethnicity may be viewed as mobilization in a competition for power.

The strategy was transparent in the ethnic rhetoric itself. Although quick to react to insults and to correct misconceptions of Hakka racial origins, Hakka leaders were careful to project themselves as Chinese nationalists above all else. Thus, Zou Lu and Zhang Xuan, both Hakkas, coauthored the pamphlet *Hanzu ke fu shi* (A history of Hakkas and Hoklos of the Han race) in response to the Guangdong school history, with the view of promoting national unity. In a foreword, Qiu Fengjia expressed the fear that ethnic separateness, if unchecked, would destroy the Hakka people as well as the Chinese nation, at a time when China was engaged in a struggle for survival.[5] Another Hakka writer, Zhong Yonghe, made the startling assertion that all three groups in Guangdong—Cantonese, Hoklos, and Hakkas—were descended from a mixture of Yue natives and Han immigrants. Common racial origin was more significant for the three groups than variations in speech.[6]

Ethnicity and Nationalism

By all accounts, Hakka involvement in the Republican Revolution was impressive. Leaving aside Sun Yat-sen—whose Hakka ancestry is still a matter of dispute—of the 112 Guangdong members of the Tongmenghui in Tokyo in 1905–6, 50 were Hakkas from the Mei River valley.[7] The desire for modern education had drawn many young Hakkas to Japan as private students.[8] Hakka participation in the revolutionary cause was all the more prominent since many of the early martyrs came from this cultural group: all four who perished in the uprising at Ungkung (Huanggang) near Chaozhou in 1907 were Hakkas, as were as many as one-third of the 72 martyrs of Huanghuagang in Guangzhou in March 1911.[9] In the years leading up to the 1911 Revolution, Hakkas were visible in various proto-revolutionary spheres: in journalism, in the new schools, and in the provincial assembly. In Shantou, the *Zhonghua xinbao* (New China journal) was started by Hakka businessmen in 1908 and edited by the Tongmenghui member Ye Chucang. Its policy was to attack the old regime and to act as a voice for the Hakkas in eastern Guangdong. Qiu Fengjia was vice-president of the Guangdong provincial assembly, Chen Jiongming a prominent assemblyman, and Zou Lu an assistant secretary.[10]

After the revolutionaries seized Guangzhou, the Hakkas quickly achieved a strong representation in the new regime. Chen Jiongming was lieutenant military governor, second only to the Cantonese Hu Hanmin; Liao Zhongkai headed the ministry of finance, and Deng Geng the army ministry. Qiu Fengjia was education minister and concurrently Guangdong's representative at the Shanghai conference for the establishment of a central government. Yao Yuping was marshal of the Guangzhou troops, and Liu Yongfu commander in chief of the volunteer corps.[11]

In the Shantou-Chaozhou area, where the revolutionaries resisted the distant control from Guangzhou, the Hakkas had a harder time; they nevertheless played a highly visible role. There the revolutionaries were divided into three ethnic groupings: Cantonese, Hoklo, and Hakka. As witnessed by the U.S. consul B. G. Tours, a "Cantonese revolutionary party" led by the American-born L. K. Goe (Liang Jin'ao) and following Guangzhou's example, took over Chaozhou "as representative of the Republic of China" on 10 November 1911. "There is no actual government of any kind in Swatow at the present time," Tours reported. "There is considerable friction between the Cantonese party who engineered the revolution in Swatow, and the Swatow revolutionary party who were at first content to follow the Cantonese lead but who now expect the lion's share of the spoils. Some open quarrelling between the two factions will be hard to avoid."[12]

In fact the spoils seemed to be going to a Hakka party that had occupied the police headquarters in Chaozhou and seized control of the army. On 11 November, "swollen greatly by new recruits and armed adherents with police rifles," the Hakka party elected Zhang Licun "Commander of Chaozhou Prefecture," to the great resentment of the Cantonese and Hoklo parties.[13] But when Zhang subsequently left to fight for the revolutionary cause in Central China, military command was seized by Chen Honge, a Hoklo who was a nonrevolutionary New Army officer but who had the support of the Hoklo merchants. In the 1912 elections for the new government, Hakkas and Hoklos backed different political parties.[14]

To bring the Shantou-Chaozhou area under Guangzhou's control, acting military governor Chen Jiongming sought to replace Chen Honge with one of his own trusted lieutenants, the Hakka Lin Jizhen; the latter forcibly landed at Shantou and ousted Chen Honge. "Lin's venture," Edward Friedman writes, "was opposed and denounced as criminal and capricious" by the army of Colonel Chen Honge, the Shantou Chamber of Commerce, the Chaozhou newspaper *Tuhua bao* (Illustrated news), and by Chaozhou military men.[15] The Hoklos called Lin "the aboriginal chieftain from Taiwan," denying him any Chinese racial credential. Lin, like so many Hakkas including Qiu Fengjia, had returned from Taiwan to participate in the anti-Manchu revolution.[16] In the end, Guangzhou backed down and replaced Lin with a complete outsider, Wu Xiangda, a native of Zhejiang, in order to alleviate interethnic tensions.[17]

Although the revolutionary regime in Guangdong ended abruptly in the summer of 1913 with Yuan Shikai's counterrevolution directed from Beijing, and although Guangdong was occupied by the alien army of Long Jiguang of Guangxi, the Hakkas had demonstrated their capacity for a spectacular push upward. Individual Hakkas would continue to exploit the opportunities, military, educational, and professional, inherent in a society undergoing modernization. And as an ethnic group, Hakkas would be quick to respond to ethnic insults, as shown in the Wolcott incident described below. At the same time, the realization that the new environment permitted socioeconomic improvement combined with the demands of idealistic nationalism to temper Hakka ethnicity itself.

In 1920 the Commercial Press in Shanghai published an English textbook called *Geography of the World*. The author was not a Cantonese, but a foreign schoolteacher at the Taowu Middle School in Suzhou, R. D. Wolcott. An entry under Guangdong reads, "In the mountains are many wild tribes and backward people, such as the Hakkas and Ikias [She]." The offending passage had been taken from a nineteenth-century work by the Welsh missionary Timothy Richard, *Comprehensive Geography of the Chinese Empire*. For a foreigner to slur the Hakkas through the nation's most prestigious publishing house was not a matter the Hakkas would take lightly. Hakka sojourners in Shanghai, students as well as leading personalities, bestirred themselves at the insult and organized the United Hakka Association (*Kexi datonghui*), with a branch in Guangzhou. In January 1921 the association held a conference in Shanghai to discuss how to deal with the Commercial Press. Subsequently, the Press issued a public apology, notified the schools that had purchased the book of the error, and agreed to destroy unsold stock. That year, in Shantou, Zhou Huifu launched a newspaper, *Datong ribao* (Unity daily), to promote public understanding of Hakka culture and to foster ethnic solidarity.[18] At the same time the Hakkas in Hong Kong organized the Chongzheng (Revere the Orthodox) Association. This aspired to be the headquarters for all overseas Hakka organizations, which were to be known by the same name.

Significantly, there was strong opposition from some Hakkas to the formation of an ethnic organization. The Hakka student association in Japan, for example, declared such a step "retrogressive," "unduly parochial," and "out of step with the times." It urged that the United Hakka Association be disbanded and the funds raised be spent on charity: "At a time when the nation is faced with great difficulties and threatened by powerful neighbors, the problems of internal administration and external diplomacy, not to mention reconstruction and reform, require urgent attention. It is doubtful that these problems can be overcome even with complete unity of purpose and effort. How is it possible for us to engage in divisiveness and weaken ourselves?"[19] It was probably these considerations that caused the organization and the newspaper to go quickly out of existence.

The Hakkas in Lingnan in the 1930s

By the early 1930s, the Hakkas had achieved a position in Guangdong's political and military life that was, to say the least, anomalous. The view of a foreign observer of Guangdong in 1932 highlights this extraordinary situation. Late that year, the Japanese consulate general in Guangzhou forwarded to Tokyo a report entitled "The Hakka Ethnic Group, Past and Present," in which the (unknown) author spoke of "Great Hakkaism" (*daikyakka shugi*). He saw as real "the prospect of a great Hakka leader emerging on the basis of Hakka spiritual solidarity to take national power."[20] With hindsight this may seem chiliastic; the author underestimated the integrative power of Chinese nationalism, which was then gathering momentum against Japanese aggression, and he was probably unduly influenced by Hakka ethnic rhetoric or by Cantonese perception of a threat. In any case, the report captures the anomalous prominence of the Hakkas in Guangdong and the dynamic push of individual Hakkas in the military and political spheres.

To begin with, the anomaly was that, since the Republican Revolution, the political and military power of Guangdong was time and again in Hakka hands. The report spoke of the following as Hakka eras: Chen Jiongming, 1912 to August 1913, and November 1920 to January 1923; Zhang Fakui, October 1927 to March 1928; Chen Mingshu, February 1929 to April 1931; and the current era of Chen Jitang since April 1931, which was not to end until 1936.[21]

At the time of the report, Chen Jitang controlled Guangdong in virtual autonomy from the Nanjing government of Chiang Kai-shek (Jiang Jieshi). Along with Chen Mingshu and Zhang Fakui, he had climbed a wide-open military ladder. All three men had their initial military training at the Whampoa (Huangpu) Military Preparatory School during the early years of the republic. The school was then headed by the Hakka Deng Geng, ex–army minister of the Guangzhou revolutionary regime, and in 1918 Chen Jiongming's chief of staff. In 1921 Deng rose to become a divisional commander of the Guangdong army organized by Sun Yat-sen.

For reasons of geography as well as political preference, the fortunes of all these men were bound up with Sun and the Guomindang. Chen Jitang, for example, enjoyed a rapid rise in the Guangdong army: he was a brigade commander in 1923 while Li Jishen, a native of Jiangsu, had overall command; in 1925 Chen was a divisional commander, in 1928 a commander of one of the field armies, and in 1929—replacing Li Jishen—chief commander of Guangdong province. With the secession from Nanjing in May 1931, he assumed both political and military power over the province until he was outmaneuvered by Chiang Kai-shek in 1936.[22]

Chen Mingshu had joined the army of another Guangdong Hakka, Yao Yuping, and participated in the siege of Nanjing in November 1911. After military training, Chen rose in the Guangdong army: he became a regimental commander in 1920, and a divisional commander in 1925; in 1927, after a meritorious role in the Northern Expedition, he was promoted to field-army command. In 1928 he succeeded Li Jishen as chairman of the Guangdong provincial government, a post he held until his eclipse by Chen Jitang. Dissociating himself from the latter's secessionist move, Chen Mingshu was rewarded by Nanjing with garrison duty in Shanghai. There, in January 1932, he and his Nineteenth Route Army won national acclaim by stubbornly fighting the Japanese. Jealousy in Nanjing, however, caused Chen's army to be transferred to Fujian where, in November 1933, Chen launched his famous challenge to Nanjing in a bid for greater power, only to plummet into oblivion after its failure.[23]

Zhang Fakui's career was much the same as those of his two fellow Hakkas. He was involved early on with the Guomindang and rose rapidly through the military ranks. During the Northern Expedition he led a division that earned the name "Ironsides" for defeating Wu Peifu's army. His command subsequently expanded over several armies, some of which became infiltrated by Communists, such as Guo Moruo (a Sichuan Hakka), who served as chief of the political department of one of the armies, and Ye Jianying (a Mei xian Hakka), who was chief of staff of another. In October 1927 Zhang returned to Guangzhou and ousted Li Jishen, only to find a Communist coup on his hands, which he suppressed with difficulty. Subsequently, he was pushed out of Guangdong by the combined forces of Li and the two Chens. He placed his army under the temporary command of Miao Peinan (a Wuhua Hakka), and in 1928 it rejoined the Northern Expedition. Zhang resumed command in 1929 when in combination with Guangxi generals he tried unsuccessfully to retake Guangdong from Chen Jitang. He was later to rejoin Chiang Kai-shek and take on a succession of military posts during the Sino-Japanese War.[24]

As of 1932, when the Japanese report was compiled, the combined armies of Chen Jitang, Chen Mingshu (whose troops were mostly Hakka), and Zhang Fakui would have amounted to a powerful force of 150,000 to 160,000 men. This strength, as well as the national fame of the Nineteenth Route Army, induced the Japanese observer to anticipate the emergence of a Hakka national leader, despite the admitted rivalry among these men.[25]

Examining the current regime of Chen Jitang more closely, the Japanese observer painted a picture of Hakka military, political, and financial strength that probably alarmed the Cantonese and Hoklos. In the army headquarters it was "whispered" that, except for the deputy chief of staff, all the leaders from the chief of staff down to the chief medical officer were Hakka: "To give a concrete example of the Second Army, beginning with army commander Xiang Hanping, there are seven Hakkas out of ten division commanders, and all four brigade commanders of the Independent Regiment are Hakka." In the Third Army, beginning with commander Li Yangjing, Hakkas numbered 20% of regimental and superior officers.[26]

In the political sphere, the most respected leader was Zou Lu, a Dabu Hakka and president of Zhongshan University. Those who exercized real power in the provincial administration were provincial chairman Lin Yungai (probably a Hakka from Xinyi county) and the departmental head of civil administration

Lin Yizhong, also a Hakka. The Guangdong branch of the Guomindang was headed by the Hakka Huang Linshu. In finance, the head of the Bank of Guangdong was a Luoding Hakka by the name of Shen Daihe; the Liang-Guang salt commissioner was Chen Jitang's brother Chen Weizhou; and the chief of Guangzhou maritime customs was yet another Hakka, Zhou Baoheng.[27]

Thus by accident or design, the gathering of power in the hands of individuals of the Hakka ethnic group was a reality in the early 1930s. The Japanese report then took up the question of why the Cantonese continued to treat their Hakka neighbors with contempt even though the Hakkas had lived among them for centuries.

> The basic reason is said to be that the Hakkas are excessive in preserving their original customs and manners and boastful of their Central Plain origins, not conducting themselves as refugees or vagrants who had lost their homes. . . . There is something in the Hakka character that arouses Cantonese animosity. For example, while the Hakkas pride themselves in their habits of thrift and economy, the natives see this as greed and stinginess. And while the Hakkas take pride in their good custom of ancestral reverence and the strength of communal and group feeling, the Cantonese see superstition and obstinate parochialism. The Cantonese also hold them in contempt for their treacherous cunning.[28]

The prominence of the Hakkas in Guangdong affairs in the immediate prewar years seems to have produced a surface calm, masking Hakka vigilance and troubled interethnic tensions. Only in view of those tensions can one explain the vehemence of the Hakka response to yet another Cantonese slight. In 1930 a Cantonese by the name of Li Zhenfang published a piece called "Hakka Customs and Manners" (*Kejia fengsu*) in the weekly organ of the Department of Reconstruction of the Guangdong government. Li, an employee of that department, wrote: "The Hakkas are made up of two kinds, the main stock (*dazhong*) and a branch (*xiaozhong*). The former speak a bird-like chatter and are not quite civilized; the latter in recent years, after much contact with Puntis, are quite unlike their former barbarous state [*zhenbei*, literally, barbarous tribes of the wilderness]." Predictably, Hakkas responded with an uproar. Departmental head Deng Yanhua offered a public apology for such a lack of discrimination, the author of the article was summarily cashiered, and the editor of the weekly offered an apology, all of which failed to mollify the Hakkas. As the Japanese report recounted:

> The incident led to a kind of social equality movement by the Hakkas who, after years of contempt at Cantonese hands, erupted in a fury. Hakka residents in Guangzhou huddled together in discussions and nominated Rao Qingzhong as their representative to ask the provincial government chairman Chen Mingshu for a thorough investigation. At the same time, on 3 August, a united conference of all Hakka organizations in Guangzhou was held . . . and it elected eighteen representatives to deliver a long statement of protest to the head of the Department of Reconstruction. The statement read: "Hakkas absolutely cannot overlook the article, which incites ill will among local people on the basis of communalism and sows the seeds of division among the people." Three demands were then stated: (1) a formal apology by the head of the Department of Reconstruction; (2) the dismissal of the responsible author; (3) the apology to be widely publicized.[29]

The matter was closed only after the demands were met and after provincial chairman Chen Mingshu intervened personally by demoting and transferring the weekly's editor.[30]

Conclusion

In their study of the Hakkas in modern times, Chapters 3 and 4 have been more suggestive than definitive in some areas. What emerges clearly is the manner in which during the nineteenth century the Hakkas at the Lingnan regional core coped with the problem of survival, in the face of Cantonese animosity, by means of ethnic mobilization. In the new political environment of the twentieth century, as an ethnically aroused group, they sought to achieve socioeconomic progress. During the latter phase, they were helped by the fact that their social disabilities were scarcely comparable to disadvantages of color or creed. Cultural difference, mainly linguistic, was easily overcome by a shared written language, by Hakkas acquiring another speech, and by the elevation of the "national language" (*guoyu*), which placed the Cantonese and the Hakkas on an equal footing.

This chapter has touched only on the significant roles played by the Hakkas in the nationalist movement. As a disadvantaged group who saw their future in a new, integrated national order and who directed their energies toward that larger goal, they may have served as a check on the naturally localist tendencies of the more secure dominant groups, the Cantonese and Hoklos. But this is only speculation. Similarly suggestive is the exceptional upward social mobility among members of this ethnic group, and their predisposition to social change; yet within their own community they were often socially conservative and worked to preserve their traditional social customs and organizations.

PART TWO The Pengmin: Migration, Ethnicity, and the State

5. The Pengmin and Government Policies Toward Migration

Outside the Lingnan macroregion, the Hakka ethos and consciousness was much less well developed, and the ethnic designation "Hakka" was hardly ever used before the twentieth century. Any study of the Hakkas in other regions therefore has to use different categories. In the macroregions lying within the Yangzi watershed, Hakka migrants became known as part of a broader category mostly called Pengmin, or shack (shed) people.[1] "Pengmin," used as a label both by the host community to denote a social category and by the state to designate an administrative category, was highly elastic, indicating a range of persons, modes of existence, and economic activities.

Nor were such migrants always known as Pengmin. In the Southeast Coast, as mentioned before, the immigrants into the Ou basin and those close to the Fuzhou metropolis were called *qingmin* or *qingke* (indigo people), while those in Yanping fu in the upper Min were known as "Pengmin."[2] In Lingnan, migrants to the East River basin were known by their provincial or county provenance, while others were called *liaomin* (shack people).[3] In the Gan Yangzi, immigrants were known in late Ming times as *mamin* or *mapeng* (hemp people). "Pengmin" seemed more common in Qing times.

Because of its derogatory connotation, "Pengmin" was not a label favored by the immigrants themselves. However, it gained local official usage in Jiangxi from 1649 when, following a revolt, immigrants were permitted to enroll in the local population registers and remain permanently. As the Yichun gazetteer of 1683 noted, this was the first time that the Pengmin household category appeared.[4] The more neutral form *keji* subsequently replaced "Pengmin" in official usage and came to be adopted by the immigrants.

The earliest phase of widespread Pengmin migration occurred in the latter part of the sixteenth century. The impetus seems to have derived from a conjuncture of several circumstances. First, there existed people, particularly in the Southeast Coast, with modest capital to invest; here an economic boom was taking place roughly from the third decade up to the end of the sixteenth century. Zhangzhou and Tingzhou capitalists figured prominently in upland cash-crop farming.

Second, there was a pool of manpower accustomed to opening up mountain land by the slash-and-burn technique. The first Pengmin came almost exclusively from the resource-poor upland of the Hanjiang in the Southeast Coast, the areas drained by the Ting and Mei tributaries. This was the home of the Hakkas, whose speech and lifestyle had been evolving for some centuries. During that time, the preexisting She aborigines had been progressively sinicized, dispossessed and displaced, and harnessed for Hakka Chinese purposes. The area's seclusion from the traumas of the coastal raids of the so-called Japanese Wako (*wokou*) probably resulted in increasing congestion, adding impetus to emigration. Identified in the sources as "Min-Yue" or "Fujian and Guangdong" people, these highlanders proved to be extremely mobile. Itinerant merchant peddling by the menfolk appears to have been one way of acquiring information about economic opportunities in distant places.

Finally, some of the areas receiving immigrants had been depopulated, making local officialdom and host communities receptive to outsiders who might share an invariable and burdensome tax quota. Depopulation was commonly caused by such local disruptions as the Wako raids as in the northern parts of the Southeast Coast, by excessive official exactions, or by the rapacity of the locally powerful. Thus, as the 1635 edition of the Chuzhou fu gazetteer observed, "the natives are greatly reduced in number, while the roving people (*liuxi*) enter stealthily to erect shacks and usurp the land, filling up the hills and ravines."[5] In Yunhe county, probably an extreme case, the immigrants numbered 60 percent of the total population.[6]

Generally, the contrasts between the Pengmin and the host community were those between dryland farming and irrigated agriculture; between varying degrees of transience and permanence; between scattered, solitary families, or small lineages and phratries on the one hand, and larger localized kinship groups on the other; between heterodox and orthodox social practices, for example in the position of women and in the sexual division of labor; between martial and civil values; and between bandit organizations and secret or open religious and nonreligious entities on the one hand, and various organized expressions of orthodoxy on the other. The highlanders were almost invariably linked to the lowlanders as the latter's tenants, for most land, however remote or barren, was already claimed by private persons or was in state hands.

The natives generally viewed these immigrants as intruders and would have expelled them except that some native landowners sought to benefit from their labor. Local administrators, given their natural bias against rootless vagrants, naturally favored the natives in the event of conflict. Thus, the Pengmin were culturally deviant, socially marginal, and politically weak, and consequently some scholars have mistaken them for one of the "mean" (*jianmin*) classes.

Mobility remained a distinguishing feature of the Pengmin: some moved from the lowlands to the hills and mountains of the same province, but the larger proportion traveled great distances from outside the province. The simple makeshift huts that gave the dwellers their name were a reflection of the impermanence of their stay. There were varying degrees of this impermanence.[7] The Pengmin were initially true sojourners, seasonal migrants who came in spring and returned home in winter. Moreover, in the early stages, the slash-and-burn technique of opening up the mountain land dictated that the cultivators move from hill to hill as the soil of each became exhausted. This may explain why the Hakka migrants were often accompanied by the She people, true practitioners of slash-and-burn. A two-way acculturation between Hakkas and She had long been taking place in their shared homeland, and now the She were again providing the knowledge for exploiting a raw wilderness.

At any time between the late sixteenth and the early nineteenth centuries, one might have found peasants, individually or in groups, arriving before the spring season and departing in winter to return the following year. Some, however, had been joined by their families and had settled down. The more successful ones had sent for more members of their home villages as farmhands or subtenants, and made only infrequent journeys back to their native place to fulfill ritual and other obligations. The most successful owned land, lived in closer proximity to the native community, and built up modest lineages. Their offspring sat for the civil service examinations. Success hinged always on perseverance, the luck of good harvests, and opportunities for commercial activities. But mostly there was an uphill struggle against an inhospitable environment, the sporadic hostility of the native population, unfair rents and prices, and the ever-present danger of crop failures.

Market dependency, as well as impermanence, was a distinguishing feature of the Pengmin.[8] Although always involved in subsistence agriculture, the Pengmin nevertheless were more deeply involved in the market than most other peasants. This explains why their migration was not random or directionless; the migrants generally gravitated to the hinterlands of high-order commercial cities, where economic opportunities were to be found, not just to areas with unused land and other resources. One has, therefore, to view the Pengmin in their regional context in order to appreciate their internal variation and diversity. Migration was not continuous from the late sixteenth century onward, but coincided each time with the expansionary economic cycles of the particular regions concerned; timing therefore varied from region to region.

Not all the Pengmin were destitute peasants. The term rather referred to all those people who were engaged in the opening up of unused land in the hills and mountains, producing goods that could be transported and fed into marketing networks. Farming, whether for subsistence or for cash crops, was only one facet of a varied highland economy. The highlands afforded many resources suitable for commercial exploitation: timber and minerals, and edible forest products such as mushrooms, tree fungi, bamboo shoots, and medicinal herbs. The processing industries that developed in conjunction with cash crops produced ramie cloth, indigo, paper, bamboo ware, tobacco, varnish, and sugar; labor was provided either by full-time workers or by agriculturalists during the slack season. The extent of commercialization in the specific local system concerned determined whether the Pengmin moved as individuals or in groups, whether they had a simple sharecropping relationship with the landlord or their farms were organized as capitalist enterprises by merchant-investors, and whether they grew a wide or narrow range of crops.

The Pengmin were widely distributed in the peripheries of the macroregions along the Yangzi watershed. Tables 6.1 (p. 112), 8.1 (p. 148), and 9.1 (p. 166), together with their accompanying maps, lay out the information culled from local gazetteers on the Pengmin: their time of migration, their provenance, and their economic activities. The information should not be taken as complete, because gazetteer compilers frequently chose to ignore the immigrants altogether. Nevertheless, the information makes clear that the major Pengmin concentrations were on the peripheries of the Gan Yangzi region, where wide areas in the south, west, and even northeast of the region were targets of Pengmin migration, and the mountains on the border between the Upper Yangzi, Middle Yangzi, and Northwest macroregions.

As shown in Chapter 2, some of the Hakka migrants around the periphery of and even toward the core of the Lingnan region were also described in the sources as Pengmin.[9]

Migration and the State

Since Pengmin migration involved large numbers of people and took various forms, the government had to develop different ways of dealing with it. The specific problems created by internal migration in each region came in the context of the limited capacity of the late imperial state to exert social control. As Skinner has pointed out, overall administrative effectiveness had been compromised by the need to balance the requirements for the extraction of resources (in the cores) and the maintenance of security (in the peripheries) against the dangers of an overblown, uncontrolled apparatus capable of threatening central power and impoverishing the people through overtaxation. The result over time was that the administrative machinery failed to keep pace with territorial and population growth and the intensity of administration steadily decreased. Much of the fascination of Chinese field administration lies precisely in the intricate arrangements developed to counteract this tendency.[10]

Given the administrative constraints, one might assume that, as in other agrarian states, the Chinese government would have adopted a rigid stance toward unauthorized population movement. In fact the trend in the Ming-Qing period was toward greater flexibility, and by the end of the eighteenth century the Qing state all but formally sanctioned migration. Each small shift in attitude was, however, forced upon the government, as a post facto recognition of the inevitable, and new regulations were always formulated with regard to those who had already moved rather than to those who intended to move.

According to Liu Min's careful study, until the latter half of the sixteenth century the Ming government rigidly applied the law requiring household registration in one's native place.[11] A (male) individual together with his family was tied to the place where the family was enrolled in the yellow register. The Ming penal code identified "fugitive households" (*taohu*) and "displaced people" (*liumin*) as lawbreakers; the policy with regard to these two categories was repatriation, varying only in the methods employed. It was the attempt to repatriate settlers in the upper Hanshui basin that provoked the Yunyang revolts, at the end of which, it is recorded, "in 1471, 1.4 million were ordered to be repatriated, of whom 70 percent perished en route."[12] A few decades later a survey revealed three-quarters of a million still remaining, and these were allowed to establish "sojourning status" (*fuji*); such people were referred to as "sojourning households" (*kehu*), and their offspring were barred from the civil service examinations, although in practice the immigrants were allowed to stay indefinitely.[13]

From the Wanli reign (1573–1620) onward, the government made ad hoc decisions that, although not sanctioning population movement as such, nevertheless amounted to a significant shift in policy. Some "displaced people" were permitted to establish permanent resident status (*ruji*), and to own or lease land, and were viewed as subjects on a par with the natives. Continuing this trend, the Qing rulers gradually tended toward making voluntary migration legal. In an effort to consolidate Manchu rule speedily, the first emperor permitted, on an ad hoc basis, residents of twenty years who were married and had ancestral tombs to establish permanent residence and to sit for the examinations.[14]

The freedom to migrate, though still permitted only tacitly, was included in the changes to the *baojia* registration in 1757, whereby local officials were instructed to keep a record of households moving in and out of a locality. The next year, individual Pengmin with relatives to sponsor them were allowed to apply for a permit to join those relations.[15]

This loosening of the household registration system is explained by the broader developments taking place in the political and fiscal systems, which enabled the state to be more relaxed about population movement. Other agrarian states often desired an earthbound population to facilitate military conscription, the collection of poll tax, and of course the maintenance of social control. In China, however, the Ming and Qing states maintained a relatively small armed force; moreover, soldiering was a hereditary profession.[16] Any fiscal reasons the government had to limit its subjects' freedom of movement were also less compelling in China than elsewhere, for taxation was levied in relation to the area and productivity of land. The aspect of population movement that did concern the Chinese state was labor service: each adult male was liable to render compulsory labor services, an essential way of minimizing government expenditure. When, during the late Ming, the labor services were gradually commuted to money payments, the fiscal imperative for holding the adult male to a fixed locale weakened further. It was all but gone when, in 1712, the labor service taxes were frozen at the 1711 level; they were then merged with the land taxes, and so became, in Ho Ping-ti's words, "completely divorced from the adult-male population."[17]

That the Qing government did not cease to control population movement altogether was clearly the result of concerns about internal security and the need for social stability. It is against this background that we must evaluate the policy deliberations concerning the Pengmin early in the Yongzheng reign. The existing instrument of social control, the *baojia* system, was designed more or less for an earthbound populace, with neighborhoods of fairly concentrated households within easy reach of supervision and control. The Pengmin, on the other hand, were not only mobile but scattered, sometimes deep in the peripheral highlands. They settled typically in the administrative no-man's-land of interprovincial boundaries, also the typical locus of antistate activities.

Policies Toward the Pengmin During the Yongzheng Reign

The Pengmin question forced itself upon the personal attention of the Yongzheng emperor when his accession to the throne was inauspiciously marked by an uprising of the Pengmin in the border area between the Gan and Middle Yangzi regions (this area, which had a large concentration of Pengmin, is mostly referred to in this study as the Xiang-Gan border). This was the first time any government had articulated an overall policy to deal with the masses of unregistered and uncontrolled highland settlers, whose numbers were soon to increase greatly under the stimulus of a rapidly expanding population. The monarch himself, well known for his security consciousness, returned frequently to the issue of the Pengmin during his reign.[18]

The decision-making process was set in motion when the emperor called upon Grand Secretary Bai Huang and President of the Board of Revenue Zhang Tingyu to memorialize their views. Next, governors-general and governors were instructed to conduct a thorough field investigation and to assess the memoranda in the light of concrete realities. The principal draft policy statement, as memorialized by Zhang Tingyu in 1724, perceived the Pengmin problem as one of "settling them in peace"; it recognized that forcible repatriation was impractical.[19] The dilemma was already familiar. Local officials had attempted to expel the Pengmin from the western Gan highlands after a revolt led by Zhu Yiwu in 1674–78, and from the southern Gan highlands following a similar uprising; but in the end expulsion had had to be limited to the ringleaders. The incensed natives, who had demanded wholesale expulsion, remained unpacified, the more so when new settlers arrived.[20] The state was caught on the horns of a dilemma: forcible repatriation of so numerous a mass of illegal migrants might drive them into revolt, and the practical difficulties associated with resettling them were considerable; on the other hand, allowing the immigrants to remain was likely to keep conflict between natives and immigrants in a perpetual boil. The situation was complicated by the 1649 decree of the first Qing monarch, anxious to speed the process of consolidation, that the Pengmin on the Xiang-Gan border be enrolled as residents even though some of them had revolted.[21]

Zhang Tingyu's solution was to rely on the personal authority of the county and departmental magistrates over the native gentry, an authority that tended to be somewhat stronger in the periphery than the core. This motivated his emphasis on the selection of experienced and competent persons to serve as magistrates. Magistrates with Pengmin under their jurisdiction, according to Zhang, should be selected under the "preferment" (*ti*) category, that is, selected and recommended by governors and governors-general; or else, Zhang suggested, they should be selected by the emperor in audience. Later, in the next reign, such posts were designated "important" (*yaoque*) and were not filled by anyone over 60 years of age.[22]

Zhang's statement further recognized the inevitability of internal migration. It drew the significant distinction between the lawless, who should be brought to justice, and the peaceable, who had been forced out of their native place after losing their means of livelihood and therefore deserved compassion. Not to make this distinction, said Zhang, would render any blanket edict of expulsion a dead letter. His recognition that there were good among the bad was echoed by governors and governors-general, who were apprehensive of possible consequences to their careers in carrying out an order of forcible expulsion that was sure to backfire.

Having once committed himself to the position that the Pengmin should be permitted to remain, Zhang put forward a number of practical measures to regain control over them, including offering them some possibility of acquiring native status. Those who had long resided in a locality and been law-abiding, he recommended, should be treated on a par with the natives. The more recent and still mobile settlers, on the other hand, should form units of five families each for self-policing, with their records updated and verified at the same time as the regular *baojia* registration. Taking the final step, Zhang proposed that those aspiring to participate in the civil and military examinations be "separately examined" so as to "share in the civilizing influence of the Sacred Dynasty." In suggesting a separate quota, Zhang evidently had in view the Xiang-Gan border area, a place fraught with interethnic conflict.

None of Zhang's ideas were new in themselves, only in their application to the Pengmin. In 1671 immigrants to Sichuan had been granted the right to establish permanent residence, and in 1690 to sit for the examinations, although in that case their migration had been encouraged by the state.[23] Separate examination quotas, always given stintingly, had existed since the early Qing, although only for the Yao and Miao aboriginal people and for the merchants of the salt monopoly.[24] This precedent of separate examination quotas for the Pengmin of the Xiang-Gan area was in the late eighteenth and early nineteenth centuries extended to the Hakka immigrants in the Lingnan regional core.[25]

Despite these precedents, Zhang's proposals were so novel that they have caused some scholars to misconstrue the Pengmin as one of the "mean" classes who were "emancipated" by the Yongzheng emperor along with others in that category. Thus the Japanese scholar Morita Akira asserts that the Pengmin were classified as "mean."[26] Indirectly this opinion was based on an early twentieth-century missionary source, which considers the Pengmin to be among the déclassé and adds the following comment: "The 'hut people' . . . were descendants of strangers who had come from barbarous border regions to establish themselves in Jiangxi, Zhejiang, and Fujian."[27] This misunderstanding partly reflected the original source, *Huangchao tongzhi*, which misleadingly lists the emperor Yongzheng's decree for Pengmin to be enrolled in *baojia* registers immediately after the decrees emancipating the various classes of the "mean" category.[28]

Another Japanese scholar, Terada Takanobu, is, however, surely right in believing that the Pengmin were not among the "mean" under Qing administrative law, though he is without grounds in asserting that toward the end of the dynasty, their vagrant status combined with native hostility to cause them to be treated as "mean" in the eyes of Qing law.[29] The difference between the Pengmin and the "mean people" was simply that until their emancipation the various classes of the "mean people" suffered legal disabilities and were barred from the civil service examinations, whereas the Pengmin would not be legally debarred from the examinations were they to return to their original native place. In short, so far as one can tell, the Pengmin did not suffer any special legal disabilities.

Morita recognizes that the Pengmin were different from other déclassé groups, but believes nevertheless that the Qing state treated them as "mean" because of native discrimination and the threat their mobility posed to state security. Thus Morita's belief that the Pengmin were emancipated by decree of the Yongzheng emperor is unsupported by the evidence.[30] In fact, rather than legally emancipating the "mean" people, the proposals show the sensitivity of Qing administration to interethnic tensions.

In any case, when the proposals were referred to the relevant governors and governors-general, these field administrators carried out for the first time a detailed investigation of Pengmin settlements. Governor Pei Shuaidu of Jiangxi reported the presence of Pengmin in nine out of thirteen prefectures, while Governor Li Wei of Zhejiang discovered them in 27 counties.[31] Each man underlined the mixture of the law-abiding and lawless, and the varied nature of these settlements, ranging from seasonal to permanent. Explicitly or implicitly, they were not in favor of a blanket policy of self-policing by means of the *baojia*.[32]

It was two years before an edict was issued specifically bringing the Pengmin under control by means of the *baojia* apparatus. Previously, the monarch had chided those officials who were "afraid that the *baojia* is difficult and troublesome to implement, regarding it as an old ineffective method," and had threatened with "severe" punishment all local officials from the magistrate up to the governor-general "who do not perform their duties with real earnestness."[33] The edict concerning the Pengmin reads:

> The Pengmin are to be enrolled in *baojia* registers for verification by county and department magistrates. Where they are scattered, they should form a *jia* [normally 100 households], no matter what the number. . . . Those who have established productive property and are willing to become permanent residents by assuming the tax quota of extinct households are to be enrolled together with the natives (*tuzhu*) and discharge fiscal obligations. Where the Pengmin households number four to five hundred, the responsible officials are to select *bao* and *jia* headmen, and investigate each unit during the slack farming season. Yamen functionaries [conducting the investigation] are not permitted to extort money or goods on any pretext. Those Pengmin wishing to return to their native places shall have their names removed from the registers and are not permitted to return. Landlords and *bao* headmen who do not report bandits concealed in the registers are equally liable for punishment. Officials who fail to detect the bandits during their rounds of investigation will also be punished.[34]

The thrust of the new policy lay in achieving control over the immigrant population and forestalling banditry by self-policing and joint responsibility, at no cost to the state coffers. What is more striking was the absence of any intention to stem the tide of further immigration, the regime now recognizing that such a measure would be either impractical or dangerous. It is also clear from this policy that only a small and fortunate minority would benefit from the right of equivalent native status; those who qualified would, in any case, have ceased being Pengmin in the strict sense. The official attitude toward this category was evenhanded. Indeed, after a visit to the Xiang-Gan area, the Liangjiang governor-general, Zhao Hongen, deplored the natives' oppressive treatment of the Pengmin permanent residents. The latter, he observed, were more prompt in their tax payments. He enjoined his subordinates to treat them on a par with the natives.[35]

The *baojia* affected the entire Pengmin population, but it depended for its effectiveness entirely on the energy and integrity of the local supervisory officials, and it was prone to atrophy as local officials became increasingly overtaxed by more urgent matters. For this reason, the Qianlong emperor found it necessary to reaffirm its application in 1757.[36] In 1763 detailed regulations were also issued to achieve control of the particularly troublesome solitary immigrants who were without dependants and harder to keep track of. They were required to produce identification papers issued by the local authorities of their native place, and to possess a guarantee given by immigrant kinsmen before being allowed to enter a new area. Those who had already arrived were required to produce similar sponsorship or face forcible repatriation.[37]

The Qing state implemented these policies in each of the three interregional border areas where the Pengmin were concentrated, namely, the Xiang-Gan, the periphery of the three macroregions—the Gan Yangzi, the Southeast Coast, and the Lower Yangzi—and the upper Hanshui basin. The unique problems and characteristics of each region shaped the way the policies were implemented.

6. Pengmin Migration to the Gan Yangzi Region

Chapters 2 to 4 examined Hakka migrations and ethnic self-consciousness in the Lingnan and Southeast Coast macroregions, and showed how the migrations of the Hakka cultural group reflected the regional developmental cycles of late imperial China. This chapter and the next will show that the model outlined in Chapter 1 also fits the data for the Gan Yangzi region, although there the label "Hakka" never became prominent and the Hakkas can mainly be identified as a majority of the larger category of Pengmin. As in Lingnan and the Southeast Coast, migrants from the Hakka homeland in the highlands at the junction of the peripheries of the Gan Yangzi, Southeast Coast, and Lingnan macroregions responded to economic opportunities and migrated mostly to upland areas close to higher-level trading systems in the Gan Yangzi, while ethnic self-consciousness emerged mainly in response to regional downturns. Below we first delineate the Gan Yangzi developmental cycles before proceeding to examine the population movements. Figure 2.1 (p. 42), which compares the regional cycles of these three macroregions, shows again the specificity of the cycles in different regions.

Regional Cycles in the Gan Yangzi

The arrival of settlers during the Tang dynasty initiated a long cycle in the Gan Yangzi, sustained in part by further increases in population as refugees fled the Huang Chao Rebellion in the ninth century. By Northern Song times, the area around Lake Poyang was heavily populated, with substantial concentrations up the Gan around Jizhou (Ji'an), Qianzhou, Ganzhou, and Yuanzhou.[1] Economic growth and agricultural revolution in the Gan basin paralleled and were stimulated by similar developments in the Lower Yangzi and the Southeast Coast between the tenth and the twelfth centuries. The economic importance of the basin derived in part from its location on the north–south route of migration, and in part from trade out of the Lower Yangzi to Lingnan.[2] A ten-mile mountain highway across the Lingnan pass was laid as early as the eighth century, and it was bricked in Song times.[3]

During the Song, the Gan basin, along with the Middle Yangzi, began to assume its historic role as the breadbasket of much of the empire. Rice from the Gan Yangzi found its way to Nanjing and Hangzhou.[4] The area around Longxing and Jizhou was especially productive. The region's economic prosperity was reflected in the prominence of its scholars and statesmen, such as Wang Anshi, Ouyang Xiu, and Li Gou. Indeed, the Gan basin paid more taxes than Liangzhe, one of the richest areas in the empire. Longxing contributed more revenue than any other prefecture in the country. Not far behind was Jizhou, where "the rivers disappear beneath the fleet of boats" carrying the tax grain.[5]

Other locally produced items figured prominently in long-distance trade: paper and silk from Raozhou, copper ware from Linchuan and Nanchang, porcelain from Jingdezhen and Jizhou, and fish from Jianchang.[6] In the south, Qianzhou grew in importance as a commercial node, dealing in a cattle trade to Lingnan, and an illicit trade in salt and tea.[7] In addition, the revolution in water transport in the eleventh century made Qianzhou a leading center for construction of grain transport boats, helped by its ready supplies of wood, tung oil, iron nails, hemp, and charcoal.[8] The Gan basin also exported timber as far as Nanjing.[9]

As on the Southeast Coast, in the Gan Yangzi region the first cycle came to an end with the Mongol conquest (see Figure 2.1, p. 42), during which both the Gan and Middle Yangzi were battlegrounds. The upswing of a second cycle began in the sixteenth century when, once more, the commercial expansion in the Lower Yangzi served as a powerful stimulus. Commercial rice farming in the Gan basin flourished. Other items also assumed great commercial importance. Four major collecting centers emerged at Jingdezhen, Zhangshuzhen, Wuchengzhen, and Hekouzhen for porcelain, herbal medicines, timber, and paper, respectively. The commercial boom in the Lower Yangzi, Southeast Coast, and Lingnan, particularly in the textile and handicraft industries, had a direct impact on the Gan region, stimulating the opening up of the highlands.

The second cycle ended, as elsewhere, as a consequence of the disruptions caused by the Ming-Qing transition. The Gan was racked in 1648–49 by the Jin Shenghuan Rebellion. But recovery began here earlier than in Lingnan, coming in the third rather than the last quarter of the seventeenth century, although it was halted briefly by the War of the Three Feudatories (1673–81). Although the most devastating effects of Wu Sangui's campaigns were confined to the Xiang basin, the Gan basin was affected to some degree by Wu's associate in revolt, Geng Jingzhong, whose men overran the eastern and southern parts of the Gan basin from Fujian in 1674–77.

From the last quarter of the seventeenth century onward, recovery and rehabilitation initiated a new cycle in the Gan Yangzi that was to last over a century, with a tremendous growth in population and economic development.[10] Once more, a boom in grain exports to the economically flourishing Lower Yangzi region and elsewhere occupied center stage.[11] This third cycle entered a downturn from the early nineteenth century owing to severe deflationary pressures, culminating in the Taiping Rebellion, the destructiveness of which was particularly felt in the Gan as well as the Middle Yangzi.

A new cycle began in the second half of the nineteenth century, stimulated again by the economic development of the Lower Yangzi, now centered in Shanghai, the opening of the Yangzi to foreign shipping after 1861, the introduction of steam ships, and the opening of treaty ports in Hankou, Changsha, and Jiujiang. But most important now was the urbanization and industrialization of North China and Shanghai. By the early twentieth century, the Gan Yangzi, notwithstanding severe population pressure of its own, had once more resumed the burden, along with the Middle Yangzi, of supplying food grain to other regions.[12]

Pengmin Migration to the Gan Yangzi

In the Gan Yangzi, the Pengmin were concentrated in three main areas: the border between the Middle Yangzi and Gan Yangzi macroregions (Xiang-Gan), the upper Gan basin, and the northeastern highlands drained by the Xinjiang, Le'anjiang, and Changjiang. This chapter and the next will analyze the situa-

TABLE 6.1

Pengmin In-migration Within the Gan Yangzi and Along the Xiang-Gan Frontier, 1550–1850

Destination	Macro-region	Time of Migration	Provenance	Economic Activities	Source
		DESTINATIONS ON THE XIANG-GAN BORDER			
Wuning, JX	GY	Qing	Hubei	charcoal, maize	XZ (1824) 7: 2a–b, (1870) 14: 23b; Cao (2), p. 25
Jing'an, JX	GY	pre-1755			XJZY 3: 31b
Fengxin, JX	GY	mid-Qing	Fujian, Guangdong, Jiangxi		XZ (1826) 1: 8b, 5: 2b
Xinchang (Yifeng), JX	GY	1620s and later	Fujian, Guangdong	indigo, tobacco	XZ (1683) 2: 107a–b, 123b–26a; ZPYZ, 15: 19b, 39: 24b; XXZ (1917) *juan* 2
(Tonggu), JX	GY	mid-Qing		paper, tree oil	ZPYZ, 29: 25a; Cao (2), pp. 24, 26
Yining zhou (Xiushui), JX	GY	pre-1674 and mid-Qing	Fujian, Guangdong, Jiangxi	indigo	ZZ (1824) 2: 3, 10a, (1873) 2: 13b, 17b
Pingjiang, HN	MY	pre-1674 and later	Fujian, Guangdong, Jiangxi	indigo	Yuezhou FZ (1746) 12: 1b–4b; XZ (1874) 7: 6a–b
Liuyang, HN	MY	late Ming, mid-Qing	Jiangxi, Guangdong	indigo, ramie	Changsha FZ (1685) 8: 25b, (1747) 37: 33a; XZ (1733) 1: 32b–33a, (1907) p. 89 ff
Wanzai, JX	GY	late Ming, early and mid-Qing	Fujian, Guangdong, Jiangxi	indigo, ramie, tobacco, paper	XZ (1683) 3: 7a, (1733) 12: 11b–12a, (1872) 7: 40a, (1940) *juan* 3; Cao (2), p. 24
Shanggao, JX	GY	pre-1755			XJZY, 3: 31b
Fenyi, JX	GY	pre-1681	Fujian, Guangdong	ramie, sugarcane, sweet potatoes	XZ (1683) 2: 42b, (1822) 12: 3a
Yichun, JX	GY	late Ming, early and mid-Qing	Fujian, Guangdong	ramie, lacquer, coal	XZ (1683) 6: 3a, 23a, (1871) 5: 17b–18a; Yuanzhou FZ (1803) 12: 2b
Pingxiang, JX	MY/GY	late Ming, early and mid-Qing	Jiangxi		XZ (1683) 1: 18b, (1784) 2: 56b, 5: 18a, (1872) 1: 6b–8a, (1935) *juan* 3–4

TABLE 6.1 (*cont.*)

Destination	Macro-region	Time of Migration	Provenance	Economic Activities	Source
Liling, HN	MY		Fujian, Guangdong	indigo, pottery, tea oil	XTZ (1926), pp. 18–19
Anfu, JX	GY	pre-1726			ZPYZ, 1: 16a
You xian, HN	MY	mid- and late Qing	Fujian, Guangdong	indigo, ramie, sweet potatoes, tobacco, tree oil	XZ (1789) 52: 1b, 6b–8a, 54: 7b, 9b, (1871) 7: 6a–b; Cao (2), p. 26
Lianhua ting, JX	MY/GY	pre-1726			ZPYZ, 1: 16a
Chaling zhou, HN	MY	early Qing			ZZ (1695) 7: 20a, (1871) 7: 19b
Yongxin, JX	GY	pre-1726			ZPYZ, 1: 16a
Yongning (Ninggang), JX	GY	1560s and later		indigo, paper	XZ (1750) 5: 32b
Ling xian, HN	MY	mid-Qing	Jiangxi, Guangdong, Fujian		XZ (1766) 7: 1a, (1873) 7: 1b
Longquan (Suichuan), JX	GY	1560s and later	Fujian, Guangdong	indigo	*Ming Muzong shilu*, 26: 3a; XZ (1873) 5: 18a, 6: 6a, 18: 6b
			Fujian, Guangdong	timber, tree oil	XZ (1824) 18: 13b, (1873) 18: 7a; Cao (1), p. 35
Shangyou, JX	GY	pre-1674	Guangdong		XZ (1881) 7: 8a; Nankang XZ (1823) 7: 6b
Guidong, HN	MY	mid-Qing	Jiangxi, Guangdong	mining, indigo, mushrooms	ZPYZ, 37: 2a–3b, 54: 46b
Xingning (Zixing), HN	MY	early Qing			XZ (1758) 10: 22b
Guiyang (Rucheng), HN	MY	early Qing	Guangdong		Rucheng XZ (1870) *juan* 28–31, (1932) *juan* 29
Chongyi, JX	GY	mid-Ming, pre-1710	Guangdong, Fujian	tin, timber	XZ (1710) 3: 22b–23a, (1867) 11: 1b, 15a–b; Cao (1), p. 24

(*cont.*)

TABLE 6.1 (*cont.*)

Destination	*Macro-region*	*Time of Migration*	*Provenance*	*Economic Activities*	*Source*
Dayu, JX	GY	late Ming, mid-Qing	Fujian, Guangdong	mushrooms	Nan'an FZ (1609) 15: 17a, (1768) 1: 30b
		OTHER DESTINATIONS IN THE SOUTHERN GAN			
Longnan, JX	GY	pre-1734	Fujian, Guangdong	iron ore, charcoal	ZPYZ, 57: 80a; XZ (1709) 4: 9a
Dingnan ting, JX	LN/GY	mid-Qing	Guangdong		TZ (1779) 7: 21a
Anyuan, JX	GY/LN	pre-1683	Fujian, Guangdong	indigo, ramie, tea, tobacco, tree oil	XZ (1751) 1: 9b, 28a, 35a
Huichang, JX	GY			tobacco, timber, tree oil	XZ (1872) 11: 3a–5b
Ruijin, JX	GY	mid- and late Ming, early and mid-Qing	Fujian, Guangdong	tobacco, grain, tree oil, forestry	XZ (1683) 2: 8b, 27b–28b, (1710) 2: 9a–10b, 4: 62a, (1753) *juan* 21; Cao (1), pp. 28, 35, 40
Shicheng, JX	GY	late Ming	Fujian	ramie, tree oil, sweet potatoes	XZ (1660) 8: 8b–9a, (1745) 24a–b; Cao (1), p. 36
Ningdu zhou, JX	GY	late Ming	Fujian	indigo, ramie, tree oil,	XZ (1592) 3: 11b; Wei Li, 8: 100b
Le'an, JX	GY	pre-1755	Fujian		XJZY, 3: 31b
Yongfeng, JX	GY	mid-Qing	Fujian, Guangdong	charcoal, iron ore	ZPYZ, 57: 80b
Jishui, JX	GY	pre-1755			XJZY, 3: 31b
Luling (Ji'an), JX	GY	late Ming	Fujian, Guangdong, She		XZ (1920) *juan* 8–11; Ji'an FZ (1776) 6: 1, (1875) 1: 28a–b
Taihe, JX	GY	mid-Ming, pre-1670, mid-Qing	Fujian	indigo, sugarcane	XZ (1826) 30: 32b, (1878) 2: 25a; Ji'an FZ (1876) 1: 28a; Cao (1), p. 25
Wan'an, JX	GY	mid-Ming, pre-1674	Fujian, Guangdong		XZ (1873) 3: 4b–5a, 4: 23b; Cao (1), p. 23
Xingguo, JX	GY	mid-Ming, early and mid-Qing	Fujian, Guangdong, She	indigo, ramie, tree oil	XZ (1683) 1: 19b, 2: 3b, (1711) 17: 1a, (1771) 13: 9a–10a, 14: 15a–21a, 17: 1a–2a, (1872) *juan* 46; Cao (1), pp. 35, 40

TABLE 6.1 (*cont.*)

Destination	*Macro-region*	*Time of Migration*	*Provenance*	*Economic Activities*	*Source*
Yudu, JX	GY	pre-1662	Fujian	sugarcane	XZ (1662) 1: 35b–36b, (1757) 1: 38b–39a
Gan xian, JX	GY	mid- and late Ming, mid-Qing	Fujian, Guangdong	indigo, tobacco	XZ (1756) 1: 35b, 3: 20b–21a; Ganzhou FZ (1621) 7: 35a, (1782) 2: 43a, (1873) 33: 1a; Cao (1), p. 40
Nankang, JX	GY	mid- and late Ming, mid-Qing	Fujian, Guangdong	sugarcane	XZ (1710) 3: 17a; Nan'an FZ (1609) 15: 17a; Cao (1), p. 40

NOTE: For conventions and abbreviations used in the tables, see p. xvii. The destinations can be identified on Map 6.1: basically, destinations listed on the Xiang-Gan border are found from north to south starting from Wuning; those in the southern Gan run counterclockwise from Longnan in the south. Areas on either side of the Gan–Lower Yangzi and in the northern section of the Gan–Southeast Coast borders are covered in Table 8.1.

tion in the first two areas, where most of the Hakkas were found, while Chapter 8 will examine the Pengmin in the Lower Yangzi and contiguous areas of the Gan Yangzi and Southeast Coast. Map 6.1 and its supporting Table 6.1 summarize the available data on the Pengmin in the Xiang-Gan border and upper Gan basin. The geographical distribution of the Pengmin will be broadly clear from Map 6.1 and Table 6.1: that is, Pengmin migration was concentrated across the highlands of the southern Gan, including the area of the original Hakka homeland, and along the mountains dividing the Gan and Middle Yangzi macroregions (see also Map 1.2, p. 24). The pattern of upland settlement was typical of the Hakkas in Lingnan and can also be seen here, though here again, as in Lingnan and the Southeast Coast, it was the upland areas close to river ports or economic centers such as Changsha, Ji'an, and Nanchang that were targeted.

NOTE TO MAP 6.1 (overleaf). Areas of Pengmin in-migration within the Gan Yangzi and along the Xiang-Gan frontier, 1550–1850. Areas of Pengmin in-migration are shown shaded only within the Gan Yangzi and Middle Yangzi regions. In fact, there was some spillover into Lingnan and the Southeast Coast. The county seats of Ninggang and Tonggu are plotted for reference, even though these counties had not yet been established as of 1820.

MAP 6.1. Areas of Pengmin in-migration within the Gan Yangzi and along the Xiang-Gan frontier, 1550–1850, showing administrative capitals as of 1820.

MAP 6.2. Areas of Hakka speech in relation to areas of Gan and Xiang speech within the Gan Yangzi and along the Xiang-Gan frontier, ca. 1980, showing administrative capitals as of 1820.

Maps 6.1 and 6.2 allow a comparison between the areas of Pengmin settlement in the Ming and Qing and those of Hakka speech in the 1980s.[13] It is clear that there were substantial similarities in the distribution, though current areas of Hakka speech along the Xiang-Gan frontier are no longer continuous or as widespread as the areas of Pengmín settlement. One point about this comparison, however, needs to be stressed: much of the area in the southeast of the Gan Yangzi was part of the Hakka homeland. Although Pengmin also settled there, the use of Hakka speech predated their arrival. So Map 6.2 should not be taken to indicate that all the indicated areas of Hakka speech date from the time of Pengmin settlement. Some of the Hakka speech along the Xiang-Gan frontier also originated in Hakka migration before the arrival of the main body of Pengmin in the late seventeenth and early eighteenth centuries.

The rest of this chapter will discuss the temporal aspects of Pengmin migrations, and the economic activities and provenance of the Pengmin, with particular reference to their Hakka origins. From various sources one can derive at least an approximation of the temporal aspects of these migrations in the Gan Yangzi. Some deductions can be made from references in general or local histories. Thus, revolts of the Pengmin in 1643–44 are taken to mean that the immigrants involved had recently arrived in these areas. Similarly, the revolts of 1674–77 suggest arrival either in the late Ming or the early Qing. Second, the dates of the earliest gazetteers or official documents in which the Pengmin appear provide a rough indication. Genealogical information, mostly contained in local gazetteers, can show when influential Hakka families arrived in a given area. Finally, recent information on village formation, if it is reliable, opens up the possibility of a more exact dating of the migrations.[14]

The broad picture that emerges from these sources suggests that the movements of the Pengmin from the periphery to the core coincided with upturns in the regional cycles of the Gan Yangzi. By the end of the eighteenth century, there had been not one continuous wave, nor two separate waves, but three: in the late Ming, the early Qing, and the mid-Qing. Thereafter, some migration followed in the wake of the Taiping devastation, but on the whole overseas emigration proved more attractive. Whether the Pengmin moved out during an economic depression is difficult to say, although movement back to their native place was common even among overseas migrants. There is also evidence that the introduction of sweet potatoes and corn enabled the Pengmin to alternate between cash cropping and subsistence farming (and thus avoid migration back to the periphery), depending on the market situation.[15]

The first wave of migration is recorded in the Veritable Records of the Longqing reign (1567–72): in the Wanyang Mountains "sojourning merchants" from various provinces gathered to produce indigo, a commodity that fed into the Ji'an-fu trading system, and for which demand was increasing with the growing use of cotton.[16] The Veritable Records give no hint of the exact provenance of these merchants, nor of those they hired to grow the crop; both were noticed only because they were engaging in predation. Those downriver at Taihe, however, came from the Hakka area of Tingzhou, via central Jiangxi.[17] Some of these migrations are suggested in Map 2.1 (p. 44).

Such migrants could be found also in other areas of the Gan Yangzi. To the north on the Xiang-Gan border, during the Tianqi reign (1621–27) Fujianese immigrants came to Xinchang as indigo farmers.[18] In Yichun, the gazetteer of 1683 records that Pengmin from Fujian first arrived at the end of the Wanli reign; but at that time they were merely isolated sojourners. By the Chongzhen reign (1628–44), however, much larger numbers were coming, densely populating the hills, where they produced hemp and lacquer for the market and grew yams for food.[19] To the southeast of the region in Ganzhou, the 1621 edition of the Ganzhou-fu gazetteer commented: "Today Ganzhou prefecture is no longer a peaceful place; displaced people from Fujian and Guangdong are gathering in the hills, perpetrating unlawful acts and becoming more and more restless."[20]

In some parts of the southern Gan, such as Ningdu and Shicheng, there had been immigrants since Ming times. They were not purely Hakka and should perhaps be treated apart from the Pengmin. For reasons unique to these areas, half of the land of Ningdu was farmed in the early Qing by immigrant tenants, whose families had been there, according to Wei Li, a great landowner, for three, four, or as many as ten generations. These tenants came originally from counties just across the border in Fujian, 70–80 percent of them from Jianning and Ninghua, the rest from Shanghang and Liancheng.[21] In Shicheng, the tenants came from Ningdu and Ruijin within the Gan basin, as well as from Ninghua. These along with the peasant tenants of Ningdu and elsewhere united under an organization, called *kegang*, to engage in rent-resistance revolts during the Ming-Qing transition.[22] Nevertheless, in the twentieth century both these countries are Hakka-speaking, though in a few remoter areas of Shicheng, the Ninghua subgroup of the Min dialect is spoken.[23]

The division between the first and the second waves was marked by warfare on the Xiang-Gan border, particularly in those areas where Pengmin were concentrated. The Yuanshui valley on one side and the Lushui valley, along which lay Pingxiang and Yichun, on the other, formed the route of easiest access between the basins (which are now linked by railways). The strategic and economic significance of this section of the border was thereby enhanced. Here, in 1642–44, Zhang Xianzhong's troops fought the Ming, only to be overwhelmed by the Qing. Here, too, in 1648–49, were battles between Qing troops and those of Jin Shenghuan who, after first declaring for the Qing in 1644, had then revolted against it.[24]

The War of the Three Feudatories, which began when Wu Sangui rebelled against the Qing in 1673, marked the division between the second and third waves. Again, the Lushui-Yuanshui basin was a key focus of contention, and was the route through which, after taking Changsha, Wu also mounted his invasion of the Gan basin. Wu's troops crossed the border at Pingxiang in the eighth month of 1674 and seized the prefectural city; they then turned south and captured Longquan, Wan'an, and Ji'an-fu, but failed to take Ganzhou-fu. Meanwhile, Wu's ally Geng Jingzhong entered Jiangxi from Fujian and occupied Ningdu and Shicheng in the southeast, then Guangxin-fu and Jianchang-fu in the northeast before surrendering in the tenth month of 1676. Qing forces recovered Ji'an-fu in the third month of 1677 and progressively pushed Wu's troops back to Hunan and beyond.

Genealogical information about immigrant families contained in some local gazetteers provides broad confirmation of the three waves of Pengmin migration. Unfortunately, such information is sparse and, moreover, pertains only to families that survived at the time of compilation, had not moved away, and remained unassimilated. The best data are those of Pingxiang county, which was administratively part of Yuanzhou prefecture in the Gan basin, but was physiographically on the Xiang side.[25] Of the 563 families and lineages (*shizu*) for whom the time of arrival is given, the first wave in the late Ming numbered 70, but possibly a few more if those who gave "Ming" as the time of arrival are included. The second wave, of 105 families, came after the Qing conquest but before the upheaval caused by the War of the Three Feudatories and associated Pengmin revolts. The third wave, totaling 146, arrived in the long peaceful era of the Kangxi, Yongzheng, and Qianlong reigns. The figures for the second and the third migrations would be slightly higher if account is taken of the 37 families who stated "Qing" as the time of arrival.

The 1989 gazetteer of Jing'an, farther to the north, lists the origin and time of arrival of 231 families; of the 47 listed as coming from Guangdong or Fujian (that is, probably Hakka), 9 arrived in the Ming. There is little sign of any arrivals in the third quarter of the seventeenth century, but 25 of the families traced their origins to the third wave from the late seventeenth to the late eighteenth centuries. Some families continued to arrive through the nineteenth century.[26]

Data on the establishment of villages indicate that the temporal pattern of migration differed even between contiguous counties, but that the late seventeenth and eighteenth centuries were in general the period of greatest migration. Thus, in Wanzai and Tonggu, the Shunzhi and Kangxi reigns (1644–1720) saw an average of around three villages a year established by migrants from Fujian and Guangdong, a rate that fell substantially from the mid-eighteenth century. On the other hand, in Xiushui and Fengxin the peak, though substantially lower than in the other counties at only between one and two villages a year, came in the mid- or late eighteenth century (Yongzheng and Qianlong reigns, 1720–96). In Xiushui, a much larger number of villages were established by migrants from Hubei, also mainly in the late eighteenth century, though the early nineteenth century saw a still fairly high level of village formation; the situation was similar in nearby Wuning.[27]

It is not possible to give even the roughest estimate of the numbers of migrants involved, seasonal and highly mobile as many of them were. Still less is it possible to quantify the size of the different waves. However, the sources leave us in no doubt that the numbers were substantial. In Wanzai, for example, Pengmin started arriving from 1524, at first in small numbers, later by the "hundreds of thousands."[28]

Economic Activities

Although some of the migrants had been driven out of their home areas by events such as the *wokou* raids in the late Ming or the early Qing ban on coastal inhabitation,[29] pull factors, notably the growth of commodity production throughout the southern Gan as well as on the Xiang-Gan border, seem to have been most important.

The type of commodities produced by the migrants varied by district as well as over time. In the southern Gan, indigo production expanded rapidly from the late Ming, and fed into the regional trading systems. On the supply side, this development was linked to the arrival of migrants from the Hakka area of Tingzhou (though also from non-Hakka areas of Fujian), from where they transplanted their knowledge of indigo production; on the demand side, it was linked to the popularization of cotton and cotton cloth throughout the country.[30] In the Qing, the big story was the emergence of much of the southern Gan Yangzi as a center of tobacco production. In Ruijin, this development was again linked to the arrival of Fujianese migrants with knowledge of tobacco production.[31] Also linked to the arrival of migrants from Fujian was the emergence of sugar production in the Yudu-Nankang area. Other, lesser products still indicate the high degree of market exposure of the Pengmin: for instance, orchids were shipped down the river to the Jiang-Huai region, making large profits for the Gan Yangzi.[32]

In the more remote and mountainous regions, economic crops also predominated, with the growth of markets for forest products. Tea oil, tung oil, and lacquer were all produced for the market, and all relied on migrants from Fujian and Guangdong. Indeed, such products grew to overtake in importance the more traditional commodities such as indigo.[33]

Since a growing population increased the demand for grain, migrants were also involved in the production of food crops and introduced new varieties such as yams and maize and promoted new techniques of rice production.[34] New strains of rice were developed to fit in with the needs of tobacco production, allowing further expansion of the production of that commodity.

Large numbers of Pengmin were also drawn to the Xiang-Gan border by its ready access to high-order commercial centers on either side of the border. In this area, too, there were some changes between the late Ming and the Qing in the crops grown. Thus, in the area encompassing Wanzai, Yichun, and Fenyi, together with Pingxiang, Liling, and Liuyang across the macroregional border, the main products of the late Ming were ramie and indigo. Migrants mainly from Fujian rented native-owned mountain land where they raised hemp, which they wove into linen of empire-wide fame. Sugar was another commodity produced in the area at this time. These products were produced for the market and fed into the trading system.[35]

By the early eighteenth century, however, the production of both ramie and indigo had gone into steep decline, and the center of remaining production shifted to Liling and Liuyang, while production also developed in Yining. The center of sugar production also seems to have moved to Yining. On the other hand, a new industry—papermaking—emerged in the Wanzai area, very much linked to migrant Hakka craftspeople and merchants. Tobacco cultivation was also important, as the governor of Jiangxi reported when analyzing the background of the Wen Shanggui rebellion of 1723.[36] It is clear that migrants in this area also grew rice, and introduced new techniques and new seeds that remained long afterwards influential in the area. Finally, tea oil was another commodity strongly developed in the area.[37]

The economic impact of Pengmin activities endured. The filling up of marginal agricultural land that began in the late Ming and intensified in the early and mid-Qing was important in the demographic explosion. A descendant of the Pengmin in Ninggang characterized their contributions to the local economy as follows: raw wilderness was laboriously cleared to make way for sundry crops, and the ground subsequently nurtured into paddy fields, to the extent that a mountainous county like Ninggang was able to produce a rice surplus for export.[38] But, as Ho Ping-ti points out, some areas suffered so much denudation of vegetation and soil erosion that they now support fewer people than before.[39]

Provenance

We now need to confront the key issue of the ethnic and linguistic nature of the Pengmin in the southern Gan Yangzi and the Xiang-Gan border region, and specifically the question of how far they were actually Hakka.[40] The available data on the provenance of the Pengmin present special difficulties. Rarely did the gazetteers specify provenance other than by province. Thus, nearly all the Pengmin of the Xiang-Gan border were identified as having come from Guangdong and Fujian. The problem is how to narrow their origin down, especially in relation to their ethnic identification.

Concerning migrants from Guangdong, there is no evidence whatsoever that they were other than Hakkas. The logical lines of advance for the Cantonese, in any case, were up the West River into Guangxi or overseas. Nor did the Hoklos migrate to the Gan Yangzi in any numbers: in the late Ming, the Chaozhou fu area experienced an influx (of Min speakers) rather than an exodus. From early Qing times, Hoklo emigrants from these parts generally moved down the coast or abroad, rather than to the Gan Yangzi or the interior.

The story of migrants from Fujian is more complex. Especially in the Ming era, not all migrants were Hakka. The congestion of the province by late Ming times is well known, and instances of destitute peasants from various ethnic groups moving in all directions are legion. In addition, the Qing government took the unusual step in 1669 of resettling some of the surrendered Zhangzhou units of Zheng Chenggong's forces in military colonies in Gan xian, Xingguo, and Longquan. These colonists chose not to farm the land themselves, but instead called in peasants from the Ting basin and from Guangdong. These peasants had attracted attention since their revolts coincided with the War of the Three Feudatories.[41] There is evidence also that Zhang-Quan people played an important role as providers of capital for enterprises that employed Pengmin. In Ruijin, for example, they financed tobacco factories in the mid-Qing; both the factory hands and the tobacco farmers came from Fujian and Guangdong, and outnumbered the native population as a whole.[42]

Non-Hakka migrants from the Southeast Coast also migrated to the Xiang-Gan border on the far side of the Gan Yangzi. However, only in Pingxiang is there firm evidence for their presence. The appearance of Zhangzhou and Longyan immigrants as Pengmin has been reported by Duan Congguang, himself a native of Pingxiang. In his brief study of the Pengmin and their anti-Qing uprisings, Duan states that the Pengmin of the Lushui basin comprised immigrants from the Zhangzhou-Longyan area as well as Hakkas from the Mei basin.[43] He mentions the existence of native associations for migrants from that area (*Zhang-Long hui*) in Pingxiang prior to 1949.[44] The county gazetteer of 1935 records the building of two temples by Fujianese to the goddess Mazu, a patron saint of these people.[45]

Nevertheless, there is much evidence to suggest that the Hakka cultural group was predominant among the Pengmin, especially from the Qing.[46] Broadly, two types of evidence support this contention: linguistic evidence from both the *Language Atlas of China* and recently published local gazetteers, and genealogical evidence from listings in local gazetteers of the origins of major local lineages.

Linguistically, the *Language Atlas of China* shows the whole of the southern Gan Yangzi region as Hakka speaking, stretching as far north as Ningdu and Shicheng, and close to Guangchang, in the east and almost to Ninggang in the west, with some Hakka-speaking areas stretching up beyond Lianhua toward Pingxiang (see Map 6.2).[47] Of course, in part this area comprises the Hakka homeland in the southeast Gan Yangzi (see Maps 1.2, p. 24, and 1.3, p. 25). In the southern Gan basin the presence of the Pengmin often went unnoted in the local gazetteers, perhaps because the local dialect, except in Ganzhou-fu city and some of the county capitals, closely resembled the speech of the immigrants although, as will be seen shortly, this affinity did not preclude native-immigrant hostility. Thus, for instance, the Shicheng gazetteer does not link the prevalence of the Hakka dialect in the county with any specific migration in the late imperial period.[48]

Especially in the north and west, however, as suggested in Maps 6.1 and 6.2, the predominance of this dialect dates from the immigration of the Pengmin in the late Ming or early Qing, and this is even more true for the counties along the central and northern parts of the Xiang-Gan border. In Nankang, for which fortunately we have information, the *keji* ("temporary residents") from the Mei basin formed more than half the population in the 1920s, speaking what the natives described as *Guanglao yin* (Guangdong speech). According to Wu Rongchi, a linguist and himself a native of Nankang, "the influence of such immigrants is apparent to everybody in the southern Gan counties; moreover, it is felt from Suichuan and Wan'an to as far north as Xiushui, Wuning, and some rural parts of Nanchang."[49] Nearby Chongyi is also a mainly Hakka-speaking area, and again the gazetteer distinguishes locals from Hakka-speaking migrants from northern Guangdong and western Fujian, who migrated from the sixteenth century onward; moreover in some districts of the county, a dialect close to that spoken in Mei xian in Guangdong is still prevalent.[50]

Toward the northern limits of the Yugui subgroup of the Hakka dialect; the proportion of Hakka speakers declines, but it is clear that their origins still lie in the immigration of the Pengmin. In Lianhua, most people speak the Gan dialect, but a few in the mountains speak Hakka, as a result of migration of Hakka people from northeast Guangdong in the early Qing.[51] On a recent visit to Ninggang, the author learned from the *keji* there that Hakka speech was found in that county as well as in Suichuan, Ling xian, You xian, and Chaling among the descendants of Pengmin who migrated there mainly from the Mei and Ting basins ten to thirteen generations earlier; in Ninggang some 40% of the present-day population is descended from these Hakka-speaking migrants.[52]

Farther north there remains a pocket of a different subgroup of the Hakka dialect: the Tonggu subgroup. In Tonggu, which is a basically Hakka-speaking county that gives its name to this subgroup, the gazetteer again contrasts locals with migrants: "By custom, inhabitants who arrived before the Tang or Song are called 'locals,' and speak the Gan dialect; those who migrated to the county in the Kangxi and Yongzheng reigns of the Qing dynasty are called 'Huaiyuan people' (that is, Hakkas), and speak the Hakka dialect."[53] In Wuning, part of which was excised to form Tonggu, the origin of the Hakka dialect still spoken in a minority of localities was the immigration of Guangdong and Fujian migrants some two or three centuries earlier.[54] In Wanzai the gazetteer is even more specific: "In the Ming and Qing dynasties, for reasons of wars and rebellions and other factors, many Hakka people came from Guangdong, Fujian, and southern Jiangxi to Wanzai, living throughout the county (but mainly in the peripheral mountain localities). Therefore, the Hakka dialect is spoken in Wanzai along with the local Wanzai dialect."[55] Finally, the Yichun gazetteer similarly links the Hakka dialect in the county with migrations of Hakka people from Fujian and Guangdong in the late Ming and early Qing.[56]

Genealogical information on the origins of local families provides further indication of the provenance of the immigrants. In Xiushui, according to Chen Yinke, the eminent historian of the Tang, who was a native of the county, the immigrants there were all from the Mei and the Ting basins.[57] Another writer, Wu Zongci, after examining Hakka genealogies of Pingxiang and Luling, re-

TABLE 6.2

Origins of Lineages in Liuyang, Xinchang, and Luling

Location and date	*Pure Hakka counties*	*Mixed Hakka counties*	*Guang-dong*	*Fujian*	*Unknown*	*Total*
Liuyang (ca. 1900)	17	7			2	26
Xinchang (ca. 1917)	4		1	6	1	12
Luling (ca. 1920)	23	6		1		30
TOTAL	44	13	1	7	3	68

SOURCES: Liuyang XTZ (1907), 85 ff; Xinchang XZ (1917), *juan* 2; Luling XZ (1920), *juan* 8–11.
NOTE: The units enumerated are *shizu*, loosely translated as lineages.

ports that "a survey of the lineage genealogies of the Xiang-Gan border reveals that the majority originated from Tingzhou fu in Fujian and Jiaying zhou in Guangdong."[58]

We also have gazetteer information of a more specific kind for Wanzai, Liuyang, Xinchang, and Luling. The Wanzai gazetteer of 1940 lists a total of 873 families and lineages in a total population of 270,453 (as of 1900, when the information was gathered).[59] Wanzai had suffered cruel devastation and depopulation during the Ming-Qing transition. The walled county capital was broken into and ransacked more than a dozen times during the revolt of the Pengmin in 1643–44; the county was twice occupied during Jin Shenghuan's rebellion in 1648–49, and it was hit yet again by Pengmin outlaws during the rebellion of Wu Sangui in 1674–78. These ravages left a deep demographic mark. In 1900 there were only 53 native families and lineages, compared to 820 immigrant ones; the native population totaled 101,480 (37.5 percent) as against 168,973 of immigrant descent. Of the latter, 79 percent had come from the purely Hakka counties of the Mei (29 percent), Ting (27.2 percent), upper Gan (18.9 percent), and East River (3.9 percent) basins. These figures would no doubt be higher if we take into account immigrants who said their ancestors had come from Guangdong (5.6 percent) or from mixed Hakka counties (4.4 percent). Figures for Yining zhou dating from the 1720s show much the same picture, with the great majority of migrants from Fujian and Guangdong coming from Hakka-speaking areas.[60] Table 6.2 summarizes the information for Liuyang, Xinchang, and Luling, and shows that in those counties, too, over two-thirds of the migrant lineages originated in Hakka areas.

The gazetteer of Jing'an, toward the northeast, also records an influx of Hakka people into the county, coming from Fujian and Guangdong. Lineages originating in those two provinces were basically concentrated in the more mountainous *xiang* of the county, and the gazetteer specifically identifies them as Hakkas.[61]

In the Gan Yangzi region, therefore, a majority of a broader category of migrants known as Pengmin appears to have been of the Hakka speech group. As we will see in the next chapter, the interaction of Pengmin with the native population led, as it had in Lingnan and the Southeast Coast, to the emergence of an ethnic consciousness among the immigrants. Nevertheless, there remained significant differences between the experience of the Gan Yangzi and that of the other two macroregions.

7. Ethnic Conflict in the Gan Yangzi

The Hakka-speaking Pengmin of the Gan Yangzi, like the Hakkas of Lingnan, were long embroiled in ethnic assertiveness and conflict. And, as in Lingnan, ethnic struggle emerged in conjunction with the downturn in the macroregional economy. Yet, Hakka ethnic consciousness first arose in Lingnan and did not stir the Pengmin of the Gan Yangzi before the twentieth century. In other words, the timing and course of the emergence of ethnic consciousness were region-specific phenomena.

Native–Pengmin Interactions Along the Xiang-Gan Border

Along the Xiang-Gan border, more than in any of the other concentrations of Pengmin, the immigrants were relatively ethnically homogeneous; in other words, they were mainly Hakka. This meant that the boundary between immigrants and natives was particularly sharply drawn. As the magistrate of Wanzai observed in 1870: "Although residing in the same county, the natives have always discriminated against the *keji* (immigrants), disdaining to live in the same area with them. In the city no intermarriage takes place, the rare instance calling down the wrath of the entire native lineage concerned. Consequently, the Pengmin have developed solidarity among themselves. The natives, on their part, maintain an attitude of separateness."[1]

Also contributing to a strong undercurrent of interethnic tension was the delicate demographic balance between the two groups. The destruction caused by warfare, though grimly depopulating in effect, never reduced the native elite to insignificance. They remained in possession of the richer, lower-lying land,

and sometimes the land farmed by the Pengmin as well. However reduced in numbers overall, individual native lineages were still always larger and stronger in organizational and material resources; this was so even in those counties where the immigrants outnumbered the natives.[2]

The natives' perceptions of the immigrants reveal all the cultural assumptions about being Chinese. The Pengmin were unorthodox in every respect. Their cultural exclusiveness was implied by the name Pengmin itself. It carried the opprobrium of vagrancy, a sign of moral deficiency. A Pengmin was perhaps a fugitive from the law, a potential rebel or bandit, an intruder threatening local peace. He failed to minister to the ancestors and lacked kinship or communal restraints. Perhaps he was racially not Chinese at all. He generally settled in the hills and mountains, as aborigines did.[3] In the best of times, therefore, assimilation was difficult. Indeed, down to modern times, the Pengmin were never allowed more than *keji* status by the natives. Only for economic gain did the natives avail themselves of immigrant labor to render their wasteland productive. Immigrants were needed to fill the tax quotas where warfare had reduced the taxpaying population.

The Pengmin arrived, as we have seen, first as seasonal migrants, coming in spring and departing in winter; only later did they come with families, carrying ancestral bones on their backs, intending to stay.[4] From the late Ming onward, at different times the Pengmin might be found in various states of transition from sojourning to permanent residence.[5] Fluidity of status must have been an essential characteristic, given the vulnerability of the Pengmin economy to market forces, the susceptibility of their habitat to natural disasters and crop failures, and the strategic advantage of their locale for banditry and rebellion. Moreover, armed interethnic conflict contributed to the uncertainties of these settlers.

For the authorities, interethnic conflict revolved around three issues relating to the attempts by the immigrants to gain the advantages of "native" status: the implementation of the *baojia* system of mutual control and surveillance; the establishment of territorial subdivisions for levying tax; and the key question of eligibility for examination quotas. In the *baojia*, where Pengmin units were part of larger units that included native households and were led by native headmen, interethnic animosity, in addition to the logistical problem of reaching the Pengmin communities, made it virtually impossible for headmen to verify immigrant household registration. The question of territorial units for taxation was important inasmuch as such registration was the first step toward the acquisition of native status and hence of the right to sit for the examinations.

It was the unwillingness of the natives to accept the immigrants as permanent residents, equivalent in status to themselves, especially in regard to the "usurpation" of their examination quotas, that was at the core of the sharpest conflict. Frequent uproar at the triennial examinations for the first degree (*shengyuan*), which was the qualifying threshold for the gentry status, caused particular problems. Government policy makers were particularly concerned with this issue, affecting as it did the whole basis of the gentry. As happened in Lingnan, one possible answer was to establish special quotas for the immigrants, and this was done in the 1720s or 1730s. Although these lapsed under the influence of the economic boom in the area in the late eighteenth century, the downturn in the nineteenth century brought new conflict over the issue, with the Pengmin now complaining about their inadequate representation in the quotas.

Government action to tackle some of these problems came in the aftermath of the last of a series of rebellions by the Gan Yangzi Pengmin. The recurrence of these rebellions in the seventeenth and early eighteenth centuries is one of the most puzzling aspects of Pengmin history.[6] Although they can easily be construed as anti-Qing political action, since they coincided every time with events of much greater import, it is more probable that interethnic conflict was the root cause. From the very end of the Ming to the mid-Qing at least four such uprisings occurred.

1643–44. As Qing troops sought to subjugate tens of thousands of Zhang Xianzhong's men occupying the Lushui basin, the Fujianese immigrant Qiu Yanghuan, a hemp grower of Wanzai, rallied over 10,000 Pengmin followers for an uprising. After establishing a base in Tianjingwo, deep in the Luoxiao Mountains, the rebels occupied the prefectural capital Yichun, and repeatedly plundered the Wanzai county seat.[7]

1648–49. On the occasion of Jin Shenghuan's rebellion, the hemp growers of Yichun united with those of Pingxiang and Wanzai under the leadership of the Guangdong immigrant Zhu Yiwu. They occupied the prefectural capital for three months and then sacked Wanzai before being suppressed.[8]

1674–78. Largest in scale and coinciding with the War of the Three Feudatories, this uprising was again led by Zhu Yiwu, who upon surrender earlier had received a pardon. After Wu Sangui seized Changsha, the Pengmin of Yichun rose together with those of Fenyi, Xinchang, and Pingxiang. Zhu's uprising eventually affected an area several hundred *li* square over seven xian and his forces were designated the "Fujian army of hemp-growing shack dwellers" by the authorities. Wanzai was razed yet again, with more than 7,700 casualties. Across the macroregional border, Pengmin in Liuyang and Liling rose in support.[9]

1723. The last of the Pengmin revolts, this was led by the failed tobacco grower Wen Shanggui, a Hakka from Shanghang. It seems to have started in Xinchang, then spread to Wanzai; after suffering a defeat in Wanzai, Wen fled back to Xinchang, where he was captured and turned over to the Wanzai authorities.[10]

In the local gazetteers these events were, of course, described from the native perspective. The Pengmin were portrayed in each case as unsubmissive subjects, the most damnable attribute in the eyes of the Qing authorities. Thus, Qiu Yanghuan and Zhu Yiwu were said to have been in league with Zhang Xianzhong and Jin Shenghuan respectively.[11] The Pengmin were also said to have risen in response to Zheng Chenggong's attack on Nanjing in 1659, although no details were given. They were said to have guided Wu Sangui's entry into the Gan basin.[12] Most bizarre of all was the allegation that Wen Shanggui was a fugitive from Taiwan where he had taken part in Zhu Yigui's rebellion (1721).[13]

Historians in the People's Republic of China have found this view of Pengmin revolts congenial, anxious as they are to fit them into the pattern of antifeudal class struggle directed against landlords and the Qing government.[14] Nevertheless, despite the uncanny coincidence of these revolts with anti-Qing struggles, it may be more appropriate to see them as native-Pengmin conflicts. The Pengmin may be viewed as capitalizing on the weakness of outside authority, whose policies invariably favored natives over immigrants, and seizing upon the vulnerability of their native exploiters, who had grown more rapacious at a time of shrinking commercial opportunities. As in Lingnan, at least the earlier of these conflicts took place during economic contraction in the macroregion.

Accounts of these revolts in the gazetteers suggest another dimension of the bitter interethnic relations. The predicament of the native landowners was that, once they had benefited from immigrant labor, they could not turn the tide.

Following each devastation, more Pengmin arrived because the natives themselves had neither the knowledge nor the incentive to work the mountain land, while the quota of taxes had to be met. The eminent Qing literatus-official Shi Runzhang, who served as prefect of Yuanzhou fu in 1664–67, captured this predicament in his writings. "The natives do not exert themselves in farming," he wrote in a preface to the prefectural gazetteer of 1667. "By a wave of the hand, they call in tenants and give away the profits to be made from hemp in the mountain valleys to Fujian and Guangdong vagrants."[15] In the poem "The Vagrants" he wrote:

> They grow sugar and hemp,
> From the land they accumulate cash.
> Gradually they become arrogant,
> Organized as a formidable force ready to aid one another.
> They abscond with the rent and humiliate the natives,
> Baring their arms to fight or quarrel.
> An uncontrolled force in hundreds and thousands,
> Killing oxen and burning houses,
> Impossible to expel;
> In time a rebellion ripens.
> Officals in this remote land
> Look on in silence, and dare not cry out.[16]

Forcible expulsion was the preferred response of the native population. As early as the end of the Ming, the local prefect attempted unsuccessfully to expel the Pengmin of Yichun. After the suppression of Zhu Yiwu's uprising in the late 1670s, the gentry of the locality declared the Pengmin "not of our kind" (*fei wo zulei*) and "intractable as wolf cubs." They argued that the Pengmin had been continually involved in uprisings and petitioned the government for their expulsion.[17] The local military officer argued that the Pengmin were all from Fujian and should be returned there. In 1678 forcible repatriation was carried out, a policy that was extended to all the counties of Yuanzhou prefecture. It was limited, however, to those known to have been involved in violence.[18] Those remaining were soon joined by new arrivals.

The Wen Shanggui Revolt prompted the newly established Yongzheng court to take energetic measures to deal with the Pengmin issue. The governor of Jiangxi expressed nervousness about the issue: he noted that good was mixed with bad among the Pengmin; although the rebel leaders had been captured, he was afraid trouble still loomed.[19] As shown in Chapter 5, a thorough census was ordered in 1725, with a view to bringing the Pengmin under the *baojia* system. At the same time, there was a major shift in official thinking toward these immigrants. The court adopted a new policy with the dual objectives of stemming the tide of immigrants and improving the status of those who had already immigrated.[20] Immigrant households were permitted, for the first time, to apply for permanent residence, and those who had twenty years or more of residence, and possessed land, houses, and ancestral graves, were given the right to sit for the civil service and military examinations. The court hoped that, if the natives were willing, this might lead ultimately to assimilation. Thus the edict of 1726 made no reference to the right of the permanent Pengmin residents to participate in the examinations because the right to sit for the examinations was implied in the possession of permanent residence.

The issue of examination quotas was, however, in this as in other native-immigrant disputes, a key flashpoint. In general, migrants had to sit for the examinations in their place of origin.[21] Yet the native elite was always suspicious of immigrants eroding their quota for examination success. Thus, as Zhang Tingyu's memorial had foreseen, to relieve interethnic tensions a separate quota had to be set aside for the immigrants. The matter was already under consideration in 1725 when Jabina, the Liangjiang governor-general, asked in a memorial for a special quota for the offspring of those Pengmin who had been resident for twenty years and also met the other requirements mentioned above. The court approved this in principle, leaving the specific quota to be fixed when the number of Pengmin candidates justified it. Meanwhile, the condition was laid down that Pengmin students should attend a charity school (*shexue*) for five years before being permitted to take part in the preliminary examination. This turned out to be a hardship because few of them could journey the distance to the county seat where such schools were normally located, and the condition was subsequently abolished.[22]

In 1730, at the request of the governor of Jiangxi, a separate quota was decided upon, whereby one place each was set aside for the Pengmin in the civil and military examinations if the candidates exceeded 50 in each category, two places if they exceeded 100, three if 200, and four if more than 200. Where the number was less than 50, the Pengmin candidates were to compete alongside the natives.[23] In the Yuanshui basin, where the Pengmin population was largest and the pressure to enter the gentry class strongest, a special quota was set aside for Pengmin candidates in each county. The Pengmin sat for separate examinations and their names appeared in a separate list.[24]

The practice worked for 30 years without complications, which emboldened the government in 1763 to abolish the separate quota altogether. Native and Pengmin candidates were to be examined on the native quota.[25] Over the next 40 years this caused no difficulty even with the natives of Wanzai, where the immigrants probably constituted more than half the population. This easy acceptance stemmed from the recognition by both groups of imperial parsimony in these matters, from the impressive authority of the regime, and from the more relaxed intercommunal relations in the context of eighteenth-century economic expansion.

When the Gan Yangzi developmental cycle went into a downturn early in the nineteenth century, however, conflict erupted again over the issue of the examinations. The increasing numbers and success of the Pengmin candidates excited native ill will. The natives of Wanzai successfully pressured the government in 1808 for the reinstatement of separate quotas, examinations, and lists.[26] But interethnic tensions continued to mount. In his call for communal harmony in 1811, the prefect expressed innocent incomprehension over the recurrent uproar attending each examination. There was no longer any possibility for one to encroach upon the other's quota, he reasoned, nor was there any difference in the rewards given to the successful candidates, native or Pengmin.[27] The cause of continuing conflict was not difficult to find: the native quota was twelve civil and twelve military places, compared with the four and one respectively for the Pengmin, a situation hardly congruent with demographic realities.[28]

A similar issue involved the question of the establishment of administrative subunits to encompass the immigrants, who would thus take a step toward acquiring "native" status. In Yichun, the *baojia*, which had been instituted as far back as the 1660s to control the immigrants, treated Pengmin strictly as temporary residents without any rights and to be tolerated only because they were too numerous to dislodge.[29] The practice was to enroll the dispersed and mobile immigrant households as addenda to the registers of the nearest subcounty units, called *tu*. As the immigrant households increased, they were grouped into units of roughly the size of a native *tu*. But unlike the native *tu*, which were discrete territorial entities, those of the Pengmin had no reference to any particular territory, and were kept distinct by the prefix *ke*.[30] Registration in and identification with a particular locale was the mark that defined a native, one who enjoyed the rights of full membership in a local community; this was denied to the immigrants, who were even listed separately as taxpayers.

In Yichun, as elsewhere, the conflict was manageable in times of cyclical upturn, but was exacerbated in the downturn of the economy in the nineteenth century. During the mid-Qing, interethnic relations in Yichun were relaxed, as they were in Wanzai. As an official observed, "the long period of peace induced many more Pengmin to come and open up more mountain land. Some achieved prosperity and established lineages, living in peace with the natives."[31] In Pingxiang in 1690, in Yining zhou in 1725, and in Fengxin county in 1735, territorial subunits specifically for the Pengmin were established.[32] In Yichun itself two such units were approved by the county government late in the Qianlong reign.

Soon after, however, in 1796, the natives rose in opposition, thus reflecting again the general trend toward exacerbation of conflict during cyclical downturns. A petition for the abolition of the subunits was addressed to the prefect, arguing that their continuing existence would lead to an inundation of immigrants and a perpetration of such malpractices as impersonations and fraudulent claims of requisite status at the examinations. The prefect bowed to the pressure and closed the opportunity for the immigrants to acquire native status.[33]

In 1842 the natives became agitated once more upon discovering that three territorial subunits had been created by the Pengmin with the connivance of functionaries of their kind in the county office. The county magistrate had apparently been persuaded that the subunits were needed to facilitate the collection of taxes. Once more the native gentry petitioned the prefect to have them abolished, and once more the prefect caved in; whereupon over 600 Pengmin families and lineages joined in an appeal to the governor-general in Nanjing. The natives on their part advertised the firmness of their resolve by declaring an examination strike. It was two years before a decision was handed down, and it was in favor of the natives.[34] The crux of the Pengmin question, as one investigator concluded, was the desire of the immigrants to shed the *keji* status. "By erasing the label *ketu* and registering in the same way as the natives, it would then be possible to merge with the natives."[35]

The gazetteers of other counties are more reticent on native-Pengmin interactions, although a similar rhythm of accommodation and conflict in line with the regional cycles may be assumed. Wu Zongci mentions, without giving his sources, the feud connected with the native destruction of a Hakka ancestral hall in Liuyang in the Qianlong period, and another native-Hakka feud in Pingxiang during the Tongzhi reign.[36]

We also have from Mao Zedong's writings a rare glimpse of the situation in the 1920s on the Xiang-Gan border region just south of the Yuanshui basin. Reporting on behalf of the Front Committee of Jinggangshan to the Central Committee of the Party on 25 November 1928, Mao highlighted the serious problem posed for the revolution by the "deep division" and "historically very strong antagonism" between the immigrants from Guangdong and Fujian on the one hand, and the natives on the other.

> From the area bordering on Guangdong to the Hunan-Jiangxi border and as far as southern Hubei, these *keji* number several millions. They occupy the highlands and are oppressed by the lowland natives, being denied all political rights. All the *keji* welcomed the National Revolution of 1926–27, seeing it as an opportunity to free themselves from oppression. It has turned into counterrevolution, however, and the *keji* continue to be oppressed.

According to Mao, the native-*keji* conflict could be found in all the 56 counties occupied by the Communists, especially Ninggang, Suichuan, Ling xian, and Chaling, but it was sharpest in Ninggang.[37] Mao recounted with some anxiety several episodes of how revolutionary class struggle was being distorted by interethnic conflict. In 1926–27, united under Communist Party leadership, native and *keji* revolutionaries overthrew native gentry power and exercised joint control of Ninggang. In June 1927, however, after the Jiangxi militarist Zhu Peide had declared his allegiance to the Nationalists, native gentry guided his troops in an attack on the county. When the border region was lost to the enemy in August 1928, the natives started the rumor that the *keji* were out to massacre them, whereupon most of the native peasants broke with the revolution, hoisted the white banner, and guided enemy troops burning down *keji* houses and searching out and destroying the *keji* in the mountains. After the Red Army defeated the enemy forces in October and November, native peasants fled while *keji* peasants helped themselves to the pigs, oxen, and other property of the natives. Finally, the Communists were to become embroiled in the tensions between the natives and the *keji*; the famous conflict between Mao and two Xiang-Gan bandit chiefs has to be seen partly in this context.[38]

More than 50 years after Mao wrote, a visitor to Ninggang could still find evidence everywhere of the once powerful ethnic separateness. The immigrants still cleaved to the mountain valleys, in contrast to the native lowlanders. Their houses were simpler in style, made of wood and thatch. They were shaped in the form of a row of rooms with extensions added on either side, and were quite unadorned. Native houses, on the other hand, were more likely to be built of bricks and tiles; additions were made at the back, and the high beam at both ends as well as the roof corners were decorated with ornate "phoenix claws" curving pretentiously upwards.

The *keji* I have met still speak the recognizable dialect of the Mei basin. They receive guests with cups of tea and small dishes of peanuts or corn crackers, not with wine and duck or dog meat as the natives reportedly still do; they prefer hot food to the cold food of the natives. They remember that the festival to the ghosts used to be observed on a different day from that of the natives, the fourteenth instead of the fifteenth day of the seventh month. Much pride is taken in personal and household cleanliness; the immigrants bathe daily except in winter, when they bathe every other day, whereas the natives, the *keji* say, may go unwashed for a whole month, and their homes are overrun by pigs and chickens. The Longjiang Academy in the county capital stands as testimony to the ethnic solidarity of the *keji* in the late Qing. It was built by contributions from the *keji* of Ninggang, Ling xian, and Chaling, and was open only to *keji* students. The academy is kept in perfect condition for altogether different reasons, however: to commemorate the place where Mao Zedong and Zhu De met in the spring of 1928 after separately fleeing earlier revolutionary disasters; it was also the place where Mao lived and worked as a guerrilla leader for a time.

Old men can recount vividly, if unspecifically as to dates, the incident of a native who erected an imposing grave to the memory of a dog that had been killed accidentally by an immigrant hunter. The grave was swept each year at Qingming to repledge enmity toward the immigrants. There was also the celebrated court case brought against a presumptuous *keji* lineage for building an unusually large ancestral hall with more than one set of doors; the case was dismissed by a magistrate who happened to be a native of Mei xian, the original home of many of the immigrants.[39]

Pengmin–Native Conflict in the Southern Gan

The rhythm of ethnic conflict emerging from the interaction between migration and regional economic cycles was visible even when both natives and immigrants were of the same linguistic group. The southern Gan highlands, in which lay the numerous tributaries of the Gan River and a strategic and commercial gateway to Lingnan, were populated by a people with a speech classified today as Hakka. But when Hakka immigrants, identified in the sources as primarily from Guangdong, began arriving in late Ming times and then in successive waves, native-immigrant conflict was no less extreme than on the Xiang-Gan border, although the immigrants spoke a dialect similar to that of the natives. This conflict was manifested in armed confrontations in the 1640s, 1650–51, and 1674–78. Both the population movement and the sporadic conflict conformed largely to the same rhythmic pattern as in the western Gan.

The headwaters of the Shangyou tributary in particular had had a long history of dissidence, going back to the beginning of the sixteenth century, when She refugees from drought entered from Guangdong and then engaged in a prolonged contest for land with local Han Chinese. In 1518 Wang Yangming launched an extensively coordinated pacification campaign to suppress the revolts of the She and their poor Han Chinese allies. The area was further stabilized by the creation of a new county, called Chongyi, and the establishment in it of a fortified military outpost at Yingqian, although peace in the whole southern Gan highlands would be shattered by local or invading outlaws again and again for more than 150 years.[40]

Disturbances by "Guangdong bandits" broke out in the region in the late 1620s and early 1630s. A group led by (the probably female) Su Yapo ravaged Xinfeng, Huichang, Anyuan, and Dingnan in 1628, and unrest continued for the next few years. At the very end of the Ming, rebel groups rose again under leaders such as Luo Rong, who went under the colorful title of Yanwangzong (Commanding King of Hell). Luo was first reported from Ruijin in 1642 and joined up on occasion with sect leaders. Other groups of rebels, many of whom were tobacco farmers, were also found in Xingguo and other places.[41]

By the Ming-Qing transition, several tens of thousands of rebels under Yanwangzong were pillaging across the two prefectures of Nan'an and Ganzhou.[42] In 1645 the Ming Grand Coordinator of Nan'an and Ganzhou (*Nan-Gan xunfu*) had sought to pacify the rebels by recruiting them into the Ming garrison at Yingqian.[43] In 1648–49 they resumed their rebellion in Dayu before finally surrendering to Qing authorities in 1651.[44] Years of turmoil and fighting had greatly reduced the local population. In 1659 Guangdong immigrants, including many ex-bandits, responded in strength to the government's call for settlers, and were accepted by the local authorities, anxious to bring the land back under cultivation and restore the tax base.[45] Hakka immigrants settled in large numbers in Shangyou and Chongyi, whence they spread to Nankang and Longquan.[46]

The revolt of 1674–78, as recounted in the Nan'an fu gazetteer of 1710, was led by two men, He Xing and Yu Xian, described as Guangdong vagrants from Shangyou. In May 1674, taking advantage of the War of the Three Feudatories, they overran the garrison at Yingqian and took it as their base, built fortresses in the mountains, and began plundering the surrounding counties. The entire immigrant population at Yingqian was swept into revolt. The large number of landlord gentry killed suggests a bitter landlord-tenant relationship was a major cause of conflict.[47]

In the spring of 1676, possibly in the context of the brief adherence to the rebel cause of Shang Zhixin in Guangdong, He and Yu with "tens of thousands of followers" made a thrust from Renhua and Lechang over the provincial border, and crossing the Dayu range they defeated the Qing garrison troops. Their depredations were not stopped until two years later, distracted as the Qing was by the Feudatories.

In the aftermath, the issue became one of the native population demanding the expulsion and repatriation of the immigrants. This posed a dilemma for the Qing government since forcible repatriation of so many illegal immigrants threatened to drive them once more to revolt. The government therefore adopted a policy of suasion after confiscating the rebels' arms: some of those who surrendered were recruited for garrison duty and the rest were permitted to settle and resume farming in the area where they had wreaked so much havoc. This policy, however, failed to assuage the intense hostility of the natives. Thus, in 1678, Magistrate Liu Zhenru of Shangyou county argued strenuously against leniency, reminding his superiors that in the space of 30 years (1645–78) the immigrants had become outlaws three times, and more than 10,000 natives had been killed and much of their property destroyed.

> Expelling the Guangdong people by force may seem extreme intolerance, but over the years they have killed the natives' fathers and brothers, dug up their ancestral graves, raped their wives and daughters, and seized young and old for sale to their own people in Guangdong. Now the natives are asked to accept them into their community. In rebellion they kill the natives' kith and kin, while in peace they usurp their land. There is no end to the natives' hatred.[48]

The former rebels, continued the magistrate, were now gathering once more in their old strongholds, building fortresses and training militia. But the harassed magistrate was equally concerned that the natives who had taken refuge elsewhere, among them landowning taxpayers, were hesitant to return to the county. He suggested that the garrison recruits be divided and dispersed, and the settlers scattered or repatriated.

The complaint led to a modification of policy that combined repatriation (for those willing) with resettlement elsewhere for the purpose of opening up new land. However, as Liu's successor, Magistrate Chen Yanjin, complained in 1682, little had been accomplished. The ex-rebels, regarded by natives as "not of our kind," were still occupying land in a troublesome border area. The call for agriculturalists had brought new settlers, all of them Guangdong Hakkas, who behaved "like tigers glaring at their prey." The natives were still unwilling to return, fearing to put themselves "in the tiger's mouth." Those immigrants who had been recruited into the garrison and given titles of command were refusing to submit to local jurisdiction, while those settled as agriculturalists were illegally occupying native land. The *baojia* was not working because "Guangdongese cleaved to one another," developed solidarity, and remained beyond the reach of native *baojia* heads. Moreover, the local administration was unable to keep track of these agriculturalists, as they were "gone before breakfast" and moved with shifting agriculture. The only viable policy, insisted Magistrate Chen, was repatriation, permitting only former natives back into the county.

Magistrate Chen's petition received strong endorsement by his superior, the prefect of Nan'an fu, who urged that the precedent of forcible repatriation, carried out in the Xiang-Gan border areas, such as Ning zhou (Yining zhou), Wuning, and Xinchang, be followed. The prefect's superior, the local circuit intendant, concurred after consulting with the garrison commander of Ganzhou, and commended the petition to the provincial governor, who then sought the views of the governor-general of Liangjiang in Nanjing. "Expelling the pacified masses may hinder their progress toward submitting to imperial rule (*xianghua*)," Governor Tong Kangnian anxiously observed, "and thereby cause a repetition of rebellion. Should public opinion be followed in this matter?" The governor-general sent a laconic reply, in which he approved repatriation, having in view the strength of native public opinion, but the extent to which the new policy was carried out is unrecorded. Probably, in time, the establishment of effective rule and the return of economic prosperity provided the environment for eventual accommodation, though not assimilation. This may account for the continuing presence of the Guangdong Hakkas as a large proportion of the southern Gan population into the twentieth century.

The gazetteers record one further revolt, in 1752. According to contemporary sources, this was a small affair posing little threat to the government. Both its leaders appear to have been Hakkas. He Yasi, from Xingning in Guangdong, was residing in Shangyou by 1752, tilling the land and making charcoal; he had a reputation for instability. Li Dexian, from Changle in Fujian, was making a living as a fortune-teller in Chongyi. According to a memorial of Acting Governor Erongan, He Yasi stumbled on a hoard of silver and Li developed various schemes to cheat him out of it. Li used the treasure to make flags, seals, and other paraphernalia of a possible rebellion. Those involved in the revolt seem to have numbered no more than a few dozen; armed with gongs, guns, and staves, they were no match for the government soldiers, who easily defeated and dispersed them. The incident is perhaps of little importance except that it illustrates the complex undercurrents running through eighteenth-century Chinese society, which could blow up a small affair into a major issue, a phenomenon expertly analyzed by Philip Kuhn in *Soulstealers*.[49] But the emperor, mindful that the leniency offered to two earlier rebels had backfired, imposed the most draconian precedent available in the Chinese penal tradition: the two leaders were sentenced to death by slicing, and their kinsmen exterminated.[50]

The authorities rounded up and executed He Yasi's father, wife, daughter-in-law, and grandson, all residing in Pingjiang (Middle Yangzi); his brother in Yongshun (Middle Yangzi); an uncle, his sons, and their wives and children in Renhua (Lingnan); and another uncle in Ling xian (Middle Yangzi). That this single family was scattered over three macroregions says much about the geographical mobility of the Hakkas in this period.

The lesser leaders, eight in all, were seized and decapitated, and their followers were banished as slaves. The severity of the Qing regime's response to the rebellion appears to have modified whatever tradition of rebelliousness the immigrants might have had, for there was no report of their resorting to arms again.

Conclusion

Thus in the Gan region, the hypothesis outlined in Chapter 1 receives remarkable confirmation from the data on the migration of the Pengmin. The Pengmin migrated in three separate waves during the cyclical upturns of the Gan Yangzi in the late Ming, early Qing, and mid-Qing, and ethnic self-consciousness was salient at each downturn. The absence of any connection between the Pengmin and Hakkas elsewhere emphasizes the relative lack of integration of the Gan Yangzi region with Lingnan or the Southeast Coast.

There seems little doubt that the same Hakka cultural group, largely of the Mei, the Ting, and the upper Gan basins, was involved for the most part in the population movements discussed above. Yet the Pengmin were separated from the Hakkas elsewhere by regional structure and regional cycles. The differences between the developmental cycles of the Southeast Coast and of Lingnan have already been noted. Compared with Lingnan, the Gan Yangzi cycles differed in two important respects. The Gan basin recovered more quickly from the Ming-Qing transition and enjoyed a quarter of a century of peace and development before Lingnan began its upturn in the early 1680s. Thus the second wave of Pengmin immigration occurred in the third quarter of the seventeenth century, whereas the second phase of the Hakka advance in Lingnan occurred in the last quarter. Second, the sharpest ethnic conflict and mobilization occurred in the Gan region in the seventeenth century, but in Lingnan in the nineteenth century. There was also nothing in Lingnan to compare with the destructiveness of the Taiping wars in the Gan and Xiang basins in the mid-nineteenth century.

For these and possibly other reasons, there was a distinct absence of contact between the ethnic groups of the two regions. Though the Pengmin periodically visited their native place (well into the present century, the author was told), the two groups differed even in the ethnic labels they chose for themselves. The term "Hakka," though not unknown in the Gan basin, seems never to have been adopted by the Pengmin. Instead, they referred to themselves as *kebian ren* (literally "*ke*-side persons"), and on more formal occasion as *keji*. The "side" or boundary implied in the label, as explained to the author, refers to that between highland and lowland. Thus, though Hakka in culture, it seems doubtful that these people were ever part of the Hakka ethnic group of Lingnan or the Southeast Coast.

In the twentieth century, however, Hakka-speaking people from this area, like those from Lingnan, participated in national politics, especially in the Communist soviet in southern Jiangxi and its aftermath.[51] After the failed Nanchang uprising in August 1927, some Communist units, led by Mao Zedong and Zhu De, headed for the hills in the Hunan-Jiangxi border area, while the main force moved south. The latter cut their way along the Jiangxi side of the Wuyi Mountains, then crossed over to Fujian and continued on through southwestern Fujian to Guangdong, sowing the seeds of class warfare all along the way. When the Communist movement finally assumed a rural character in the early 1930s, most soviets came to be based in heavily Hakka-populated areas. Thus, when the Western Fujian Revolutionary Base Government was set up in March 1929, it held sway over ten counties. Culturally, five of them—Changting, Shanghang, Wuping, Yongding, and Ninghua—were exclusively Hakka, while the rest—Qingliu, Guihua (Mingxi), Liancheng, Longyan, and Jianning—had a substantial Hakka population.[52] By the time the Central Soviet Government was proclaimed at Ruijin (a purely Hakka county) in 1931, the central soviet base area was formed by twenty counties on both sides of the Wuyi Mountains. Those on the Jiangxi side comprised the four purely Hakka counties of Ruijin, Huichang, Anyuan, and Xunwu, and the heavily Hakka-populated counties of Yudu, Xingguo, Ningdu, Shicheng, and Guangchang.[53] Only Nanfeng and Lichuan fell outside the Hakka linguistic boundary. On the Hunan-Jiangxi border, the four counties that formed the soviet base in the

Jinggangshan area—Ninggang, Suichuan, Yongxin, and Chaling—also had a strong Hakka presence.

That these soviets came to be based in a predominantly Hakka population had to do with strategic considerations rather than any qualities inherent in the Hakka cultural group itself. These strategic considerations, which drove the Communists out of the core agricultural areas into the peripheries and the upland areas, mirrored closely the logic of the Hakka migration and settlement strategies, which also targeted such areas. Once the soviets were established, they also owed their initial success to the Hakka tradition of female field labor, important for the soviet economy since it enabled the menfolk to be mobilized for warfare. A problem for the Communist revolution in some of these areas was the control of interethnic conflict, as one of Mao's reports shows.[54]

Even after the expulsion of the Communists from the Hakka areas and their sojourn in the north, members of the Hakka cultural group still occupied many senior positions in the Communist movement. Indeed, this has continued to be true in the post-1949 regime. Had the soviets not ended in failure, it is conceivable that the Hakkas would have played an even more prominent role.[55]

8. Environmental Degradation: The Pengmin in the Lower Yangzi

A major concentration of Pengmin was found on the periphery of the Lower Yangzi macroregion, mainly toward the west and south, straddling the borders with the Gan Yangzi and the Southeast Coast.[1] Map 8.1 and Table 8.1 lay out the information we have on the distribution, origins, and activities of the Pengmin in the Lower Yangzi macroregion and along its borders with the Gan Yangzi and the Southeast Coast. Except for a few outlying groups as far north as the border with the North China macroregion, the main body of Pengmin settlement was on the highlands south of the Yangzi.[2] There appears to have been a more or less continuous band of settlement stretching from Guangde in the north to Nanping in the south. Settlement was, however, concentrated in the uplands in the Huangshan-Tianmushan range in the north, separating the Yangzi basin from the Qiantang basin, and on the hills dividing the Qiantang, Gan, Ou, and Min river basins in the south. This southern area stood astride the frontiers of the Lower Yangzi, Gan Yangzi, and Southeast Coast macroregions.

Both the provenance and the temporal and geographical distribution of these Pengmin relative to the regional market systems broadly conform to the pattern suggested in the model in Chapter 1 and outlined for the Gan Yangzi: migrants from the peripheries of adjoining macroregions gravitated to higher-level market systems in times of economic upturn. The Lower Yangzi was the most commercialized of all regions, and one of the most stable during the period 1500–1850. As such, it was the destination of many of the key commodities

TABLE 8.1

Pengmin In-migration Within the Lower Yangzi and Adjacent Sectors of the Gan Yangzi and Southeast Coast Regions, 1650–1850

Destination	*Macro-region*	*Time of Migration*	*Provenance*	*Economic Activities*	*Source*
OUTLYING DESTINATIONS TO THE NORTH IN THE LOWER YANGZI					
Lai'an, AN	LY	DG			Tao Zhu, 26: 18b
Quanjiao, AN	LY	post-Taiping	Hefei, Yanshan, (Anhui)		XZ (1920) 4: 1b
Jurong, JS	LY	DG, TZ, GX	Anqing, Wenzhou, Taizhou, Hubei, Henan		XZ (1904) 6: 4a–5b, 16b–17b, 23b
Jiashan, ZJ	LY		Wenzhou, Taizhou	sweet potatoes	XZ (1894) 12: 21b
Tongling, AN	LY				Tao Zhu, 26: 5b
DESTINATIONS IN THE HUANGSHAN-TIANMUSHAN RANGES TO THE NORTH OF THE QIANTANG BASIN					
Shouchang, ZJ	LY		Fujian, Anhui	maize, paper, indigo, ramie	XZ (1930) 3: 11b, 10: 9a–b, 10: 22a
Fenshui, ZJ	LY	QL	Fujian, She, Jiangxi	indigo, ramie, maize	XZ (1906) 1: 42b–43a, 3: 42a
Changhua, ZJ	LY	JQ	Jiangxi	maize	XZ (1823) 3: 6a–b
Yuqian, ZJ	LY	QL	Anqing	maize	XZ (1906) *juan* 18
Yuhang, ZJ	LY	QL	Fujian, Guangdong	ramie, sweet potatoes	XZ (1808) 38: 5b, 8a
Deqing, ZJ	LY			maize, indigo, sweet potatoes	XZ (1808) 4: 2a–b
Wukang, ZJ	LY	JQ		sweet potatoes	XZ (1829) *juan* 4
Anji, ZJ	LY	1730s	Fujian, Jiangxi, Ning-Shao-Wen-Tai		ZZ (1750) 8: 22b; XZ (1874) 7: 11b, 8: 13b
Guangde zhou, AN	LY				Tao Zhu, 26: 5b
Xuancheng, AN	LY			maize, potatoes, indigo, ramie, tobacco	XZ (1888) *juan* 2; Mei Zengliang, 10: 5a–b
Ningguo, AN	LY		Anqing	maize	Ningguo FZ (1815) 18: 1b; XZ (1869) 1: 23b, (1936) 4: 23b; Tao Zhu, 26: 5b

TABLE 8.1 (*cont.*)

Destination	Macro-region	Time of Migration	Provenance	Economic Activities	Source
Jingde, AN	LY		Fujian, Jiangxi, Zhejiang, Anqing	maize	XZ (1808) 5: 46a
Jixi, AN	LY	1760s	Anqing	maize	XZ (1810) pp. 350–51; Tao Zhu, 26: 5b
She xian, AN	LY	late Ming, QL	She, Huaining, Yanshan, Taihu, Tongcheng, Jiangxi, Zhejiang	maize	Gu Yanwu, 9: 78b; Tao Zhu, 26: 5b
Xiuning, AN	LY	JQ			Tao Zhu, 26: 5b; Gao Tingyao, pt. 1: 32b
Yi xian, AN	LY				XZ (1812) *juan* 11; Tao Zhu, 26: 5b
Qimen, AN	GY/LY	mid-Qing	Anqing (Anhui)	maize	XZ (1827) 12: 3b, 11b–12a
Jiande (Zhide), AN	LY		Jiangxi, Wenzhou, Taizhou, Chuzhou		Tao Zhu, 26: 5b
Poyang, JX	GY		Taihe (Anhui)	maize	XZ (1824) 12: 1b
Fuliang, JX	GY	mid-Qing		ramie	XZ (1783) 5: 32a
Wuyuan, AN	GY			maize	Huizhou FZ (1827) 4.2: 42b
Kaihua, ZJ	LY	late Ming	Jiangxi, Fujian	indigo, ramie, paper, iron ore, maize	Chuzhou FZ (1711) preface; XZ (1896) *juan* 2
		DESTINATIONS SOUTHEAST OF THE QIANTANG ALONG MACROREGIONAL DIVIDES			
Changshan, ZJ	LY	late Ming	Jiangxi, Fujian	charcoal, mushrooms, ramie	Chuzhou FZ (1711) preface; XZ (1723) *juan* 11–12; Cao (2), p. 31
Xi'an (Qu xian), ZJ	LY			maize	XZ (1811) 21: 2b–3a
Longyou, ZJ	LY	post-1676	Fujian (Ting and She)		XZ (1925) 2: 17b, *juan* 3–4, 4: 42b–43a
Tangxi, ZJ	LY		Fujian	indigo	XZ (1931) *juan* 3
Suichang, ZJ	SEC/LY	late Ming	Fujian (Ting)	indigo, ramie, sugar, iron ore	XZ (1765) 1: 12b, 16b–17b, 18b–19b, 8: 8b–9b
Songyang, ZJ	SEC		Fujian (Ting), She		XZ (1926) 6: 24a–b

(*cont.*)

TABLE 8.1 (*cont.*)

Destination	*Macro-region*	*Time of Migration*	*Provenance*	*Economic Activities*	*Source*
Xuanping, ZJ	SEC/LY	SZ, QL	Fujian, Jiangxi, She, Anhui	ramie, indigo, maize, tobacco	XZ (1656) 1: 6a, (1753) 9: 3a; Chuzhou FZ (1877) 24: 20b; XZ (1878) 5: 2b
Lishui, ZJ	SEC	late Ming	Jiangxi, Fujian, She	ramie, indigo	Chuzhou FZ (1635) 1: 16b–17a; XZ (1874) 13: 18a, 15: 14a, (1906) 12: 16b
Xinchang, ZJ	LY	KX			XZ (1671) 8: 6b
Qingtian, ZJ	SEC	KX	Jiangxi, Fujian, Guangdong	ramie, indigo, charcoal	XZ (1876) 4: 6a–b, 14: 25a
Yunhe, ZJ	SEC		Fujian (Ting), Jiangxi, She	ramie, indigo, tobacco, iron ore	XZ (1864) 15: 12b, 15a–16a, 30a–31b
Jingning, ZJ	SEC		Fujian, She	ramie, indigo	Chuzhou FZ (1877) 24: 21b; XZ (1873) 12: 3a
Taishun, ZJ	SEC	KX, YZ, QL	Fujian (Ting), Pingyang	indigo	XZ (1879) 2: 20a–b
Longquan, ZJ	SEC/LY		Fujian, She, Jiangxi	ramie, indigo, mushrooms, timber	XZ (1762) 11: 2a–b; Chuzhou FZ (1877) 24: 15a
Songxi, FJ	SEC	KX		ramie, mushrooms	XZ (1700) 6: 6a
Ouning (Jian'ou), FJ	SEC		Fujian	tea	TZ (1868–71) 57: 11b
Nanping, FJ	SEC		Ting, Zhangzhou, Quanzhou, She, Zhejiang	indigo, ramie, tea, timber, lacquer, mushrooms	XZ (1810) 8: 10a–11b
Jianyang, FJ	SEC		Jiangxi	tea	XZ (1832) 2: 36a–38b; Chen Shengshao, 1: 1a–b
Pucheng, FJ	SEC			maize	XZ (1811) 6: 11b–12a
Yanshan, JX	GY		Fujian	sweet potatoes, paper, ramie, sugar	XZ (1873) 5: 25a, 30: 45b–46a; Cao (2), pp. 30, 31
Jiangshan, ZJ	LY	late Ming, QL	Jiangxi, Fujian	ramie, indigo	XZ (1713) *juan* 1 and 72, (1873) 1: 6b

TABLE 8.1 (*cont.*)

Destination	*Macro-region*	*Time of Migration*	*Provenance*	*Economic Activities*	*Source*
Yushan, JX	GY	early and mid-Qing	Fujian, Guangdong	ramie, tobacco	XZ (1823) 12: 1b–2a, (1873) 1: 24b; Cao (2), p. 28
Shangrao, JX	GY	mid- and late Qing	Jiangxi, Fujian, Guangdong	ramie, tree oil, sweet potatoes, sugar	Guangxin FZ (1783) 2: 68b, (1873) 1.2: 99a; Cao (2), pp. 28, 31
Xing'an (Hengfeng), JX	GY		Fujian	tree oil	Cao (2), p. 32
Yiyang, JX	GY	early and mid-Qing	N Fujian		Cao (2), p. 35
Guixi, JX	GY	Qing	N Fujian	sweet potatoes	Cao (2), pp. 31, 32, 35

NOTE: For conventions and abbreviations used in the tables, see p. xvii. The destinations can be identified on Map 8.1: basically, apart from the outlyers, the list here goes counterclockwise from Shouchang in the northern concentration of settlement, and clockwise from Changshan around the southern concentration.

of the Pengmin economy. Furthermore, within the Lower Yangzi itself, the Pengmin were concentrated in the area south of the river; this was both more directly in their line of advance, which was from the south, and closer to the rich Lower Yangzi core, which also lay south of the river. (Similarly, in the Gan Yangzi, Pengmin settlements were concentrated more in the richer western basin than in the east.)

Pengmin Migration to the Lower Yangzi Periphery

Pengmin migration to the Lower Yangzi and surrounding peripheries in the Southeast Coast and Gan Yangzi began, like that to the rest of the Gan Yangzi, in the early sixteenth century. Gu Yanwu reports that some She people, moving apparently on their own, entered She xian, where they were identified by their preferred self-designation *shanke* (sojourners of the mountains).[3] Farther north, in Fengyang on the Lower Yangzi–North China boundary, other She—valued as specialists in mountain agriculture—arrived as "invited settlers" (*zhaolai*). In Fengyang, we have one of the most graphic descriptions of late Ming social disintegration. The 1621 edition of the county gazetteer reports that state func-

Fengyang-fu
Tianchang
Yangzhou-fu
Shou-zhou
Dingyuan
Lai'an
Luhe
Tong-zhou
Haimen-ting
Chu-zhou
Zhenjiang-fu
Jiangning-fu
(Nanjing)
Quanjiao
Jiangpu
Jurong
Changzhou-fu
Jintan
JIANGSU
Taicang-zhou
Luzhou-fu
He-zhou
Hanshan
Lishui
Liyang
Yixing
Lu'an-zhou
Taiping-fu
Gaochun
Suzhou-fu
Shanghai
Songjiang-fu
Shucheng
Lujiang
Wuhu
Wuwei-zhou
Huoshan
Jianping
Changxing
Jiashan
Huzhou-fu
Jiaxing-fu
Fanchang
Ningguo-fu
Xuancheng
Guangde-zhou
Tongcheng
Tongling
Nanling
ANHUI
Anji
Deqing
Ningguo
Wukang
Qingyang
Jing-xian
Xiaofeng
Hangzhou-fu
Qianshan
Guichi-fu
Lin'an
Yuyao
Cixi
Yuhang
Xiaoshan
Anqing-fu
Huaining
Changhua
Yuqian
Shaoxing-fu
Shangyu
Ningbo-fu
Taihu
Shili
Taiping
Jingde
Fuyang
Xincheng
Donglu
Jixi
Fenshui
Fenghua
Tonglu
Zhuji
Wangjiang
Jiande
Yi-xian
Huizhou-fu
She-xian
Sheng-xian
Xiangshan
ZHEJIANG
Qimen
Yanzhou-fu
Jiande
Xinchang
Chun'an
Ninghai
Pengze
Xiuning
Sui'an
Pujiang
Hukou
Shouchang
Yiwu
Dongyang
Tiantai
Lanxi
Fuliang
Jinhua-fu
Taizhou-fu
Linhai
Kaihua
Tangxi
Wuyuan
Quzhou-fu
Xi'an
Longyou
Yongkang
Xianju
Duchang
Wuyi
Huangyan
Dexing
Changshan
Xuanping
Jinyun
Leping
Taiping
Suichang
Raozhou-fu
Poyang
Yushan
Jiangshan
Chuzhou-fu
Lishui
Yugan
Guangxin-fu
Shangrao
Songyang
Leqing
Wannian
Yuhuan-ting
Xing'an
Guangfeng
Yunhe
Qingtian
Wenzhou-fu
Anren
Yiyang
Jinxian
Dongxiang
Guixi
Yanshan
Longquan
Jingning
Rui'an
JIANGXI
Pucheng
Pingyang
Fuzhou-fu
Jinxi
Chong'an
Qingyuan
Taishun
Luxi
Songxi
Shouning
Fuding
Chongren
Guangze
Jianyang
Zhenghe
Yihuang
Jianchang-fu
Shaowu-fu
Fu'an
Funing-fu
Xincheng
FUJIAN
Pingnan
Nanfeng
Jianning-fu
Jian'an
Ouning
East China Sea
Taining
Shunchang
Ningde
Yanping-fu
Nanping
Guangchang
Jianning
Jiangle
Gutian
Luoyuan
Areas of Pengmin in-migration
Limits of physiographic regions
Provincial boundaries
Provincial capital
Prefectural-level capital
County-level capital
0
50
100
150 Km

tionaries held the first-grade land and rich private families the medium grade, while the poor were left with the lowest grade. Land that had been improved by the poor soon ended up in the hands of the rich. Burdened with growing taxes and corvée ("palanquin bearers in the morning, porters during the day, and lantern bearers at night"), the poor took flight, and thus in extreme cases "the tithing unit (*li*) contains no more than one or two *jia* [instead of ten], and 90 percent of the land lies in waste."[4]

Elsewhere in the Lower Yangzi, as in the counties of Kaihua, Changshan, Jiangshan, and Suichang, immigrants from Fujian were joined by those from Jiangxi, the former specializing in indigo farming, the latter in ramie. Both groups also engaged in iron-ore mining and smelting as well as papermaking.[5] These immigrants were involved in uprisings in the mid-seventeenth century, some of which coincided with the more serious rebellions mounted by the Pengmin in the western Gan Yangzi.[6]

The data on later immigration into the northern Southeast Coast and the Lower Yangzi do not, however, permit detailed temporal analysis. In the Southeast Coast, the sources suggest that after the late Ming wave new arrivals from "Fujian" and "Jiangxi" came during the eighteenth century. The contiguity of the Ouling subregion to the economically flourishing Lower Yangzi was apparently sufficient to offset the prolonged depression in the Southeast Coast from the early seventeenth to the mid-nineteenth century.

In the Lower Yangzi, movement into the highlands was probably fairly continuous until the massive devastation of the Taiping Rebellion in the mid-nineteenth century.[7] Migrants filled in upland areas south of the Yangzi to the west of Hangzhou and Huzhou in Zhejiang and around Huizhou, Ningguo,

MAP 8.1 (opposite). Areas of Pengmin in-migration within the Lower Yangzi and adjacent sectors of the Gan Yangzi and Southeast Coast regions, 1650–1850, showing administrative capitals as of 1820. In general, we have assumed that Pengmin settlement was limited to the upland areas of counties around the rim of the irregular shaded polygon. Since county capitals were often sited in riverine lowlands, many capitals of counties for which Pengmin in-migration is documented lie outside the area of putative Pengmin settlement, that is, outside the shaded area. Pengmin settlement is documented for each of the counties neighboring Lin'an xian (in Zhejiang, west of Hangzhou) but not for Lin'an itself: we assume that county had its Pengmin population even though the gazetteer is silent on this point.

and Guangde in Anhui. Smaller numbers gathered in Chuzhou to the north of the river.[8] But the region was rapidly approaching the limits of its demographic potential through natural increases during the eighteenth century, leaving only the most marginal hill land to be exploited; the resulting problems became more evident in the last two decades of the eighteenth century and through the nineteenth.[9]

After the initial late Ming phase, the evidence suggests the highland economy became a mixture of commercial farming by the Pengmin and subsistence agriculture by refugees fleeing overpopulation and natural calamities. Most of these refugees were from counties north of the Yangzi and from the lower-lying counties of the northern Southeast Coast.[10] Maize figured prominently, often as the sole crop, because of its suitability to poor highland soil, but also because it was produced as a food crop to meet the needs of the teeming rural and urban poor.

It would appear that Hakkas made up a much smaller proportion of the Pengmin around the Lower Yangzi peripheries than they did in the west and south of the Gan Yangzi. Certainly, Hakkas were present: as Xiong Renlin pointed out, many of the indigo growers arriving in southern Zhejiang in the late Ming were from Tingzhou.[11] Again, over the border, Pengmin migrants to Nanping explicitly included those from Tingzhou (who were, therefore, almost certainly Hakkas).[12] Nevertheless, linguistic data show virtually no Hakka-speaking population in the area, with the exception of a few villagers who are identified as She.[13] Gazetteers indicate that the migrants came predominantly from non-Hakka areas: in Yushan, Guangfeng, and Shangrao, most came from Fujian or from Nanfeng in Jiangxi and a few from Zhejiang or Anhui. Those from Fujian came mainly, though not exclusively, from coastal areas speaking *minnanhua* (the dialect of southern Fujian). Pengmin in Yiyang, Guixi, Yanshan, and Xing'an also came mainly from Fujian, but from the nearer mountainous regions in the north of the province.[14]

As outlined in Chapter 6, the overpopulation of the Southeast Coast set in motion pressures for poor peasants to move in all directions in search of a livelihood. Reference has already been made to the migration of Hokkien peasants from Zhangzhou and Quanzhou (Zhang-Quan) and from Yanping toward Fuzhou as indigo farmers, and of Zhang-Quan people to the Ou basin in the north in the late Ming and early Qing.[15] The Yanping fu area, long linked with the northeastern Gan basin by overland trade, had a concentration of Pengmin drawn from the Zhang-Quan subregion, including Yongchun, as well as from the Ting basin, although the time of their arrival is unclear.[16]

There was also movement across the Wuyi mountain passes, especially of people close to the Southeast Coast regional boundary. In the mid-Qing the highlands of the Gan basin in the northeast received "Fujianese" migrants who produced *tongzi* and *muzi* varnish, hemp, and tobacco.[17] The presence of Fujianese peasant tenants in the southeast corner of the Gan basin since Ming times has already been mentioned; in the mid-Qing more Fujianese arrived, leasing mountain land to produce oil from *tongzi* and tea trees.[18]

As is true in other regions, in the Lower Yangzi also precise details of the economic organization of Pengmin enterprises are lacking. Officials observed that the Pengmin-landlord relationship could take various forms, ranging from sharecropping by solitary immigrant families to payment of a sizable cash rent in advance—often for the entire lease period—by a large group of families led by those of means. With regard to leasing arrangements, some contracts stipulated the amount of rent, the length of the lease, and the surrender of the land upon the expiry of the agreement; others specified no time limit, and the land was returned only after its complete exhaustion.[19] An official commented in amazement: "One hundred *mu* [a *mu* is about one-sixth of an acre] of mountain wasteland is worth very little, yet the Pengmin are willing to pay up to a thousand taels in rent. After turning the virgin forests into mature land, the Pengmin plant it with maize, reaping a two- to fivefold profit. . . . They stay ten, fifteen, twenty, or thirty years until the soil is exhausted and then lease another hill."[20] In a case for which we have concrete detail, a group of sixteen families pooled 4,000 taels of silver as advance payment of rent and enlisted 800 laboring hands (*banggong*); together with women and children, a community of over 4,000 people came into existence.[21]

Although, as we shall see, the cultivation of dry-land crops generated many of the problems discussed in this chapter, many Pengmin also grew cash crops to feed into the expanding Lower Yangzi market. As elsewhere in the Gan Yangzi, the most important cash crops included ramie, indigo, and tobacco, as well as commercialized forest products. Of the handicraft industries, papermaking, which was centered on Yanshan, was the most important.[22]

Environmental Degradation and Social Conflict

As Map 8.1 shows, the concentration of Pengmin straddled both sides of the border between the Lower Yangzi, on the one hand, and the Southeast Coast and Gan Yangzi macroregions, on the other. Conditions differed somewhat on either side, and social conflict was much more prevalent in the Lower Yangzi.

The Pengmin resident to the south of the macroregional border, that is in the highlands of the northern Southeast Coast, experienced less social conflict. In some respects their history resembled that of Pengmin in the west and south Gan Yangzi more than those in the Lower Yangzi. They began arriving at the same time—in the latter part of the sixteenth century. The same cultural group was involved, though in this case there were more immigrants from the Ting basin than from the Mei, and these were subsequently joined by many from the eastern Gan basin. The same cash crops were dominant in both areas: ramie and indigo.

Nevertheless, the Southeast Coast experienced little of the interethnic tension that characterized the west and south Gan Yangzi, or the Lower Yangzi. The Pengmin of the northern Southeast Coast experienced no difficulty in establishing permanent residence; and no separate examination quota was ever necessary, even for aboriginal She candidates, who were first permitted to sit for the examinations in 1804. Although there existed large pockets of people of the Ting speech down to the twentieth century, relaxed intercommunal relations, evidenced by intermarriage, no doubt facilitated assimilation. The very proximity of the Ouling subregion of the Southeast Coast to the Lower Yangzi was a major reason for this lack of conflict since, as Skinner points out, the latter region experienced a long cycle of uninterrupted economic development from the sixteenth to the mid-nineteenth century, associated with the rise of Suzhou as the regional metropolis.[23] The lack of ethnic conflict in a situation of economic upturn is again consistent with the hypothesis outlined in Chapter 1.

The level of social conflict over the border in the Lower Yangzi was, however, very much greater. During the Jiaqing reign at the very beginning of the nineteenth century the government found itself facing a crisis associated with soil erosion and floods.[24] The early Pengmin had been joined by countless destitute peasants, fleeing famine and population pressures from across the Yangzi and from the lower-lying counties of the northern Southeast Coast. Unlike anywhere else, the Pengmin in the Lower Yangzi were subject to a systematic restriction on the growth of their numbers, if not outright expulsion. The premier position of the region as a source of revenue and of sociopolitical support for the state, and the nature of Pengmin agriculture itself, heavily influenced government policy. The Lower Yangzi furnished the central government with more tax revenue than any other region, including the all-important tribute grain shipped to feed the capital. This alone required the government to be concerned about damage to irrigated agriculture and to the interests of the landlord gentry, who were disproportionately represented in the highest echelons of the bureaucracy.

The predominance of maize in the Lower Yangzi Pengmin economy proved particularly disastrous. As Zhejiang governor Ruan Yuan observed in 1802 when he imposed a ban on it, the plant had long roots so that, for the best results, the forests had to be cleared by fire, the tree roots dug up, and the soil loosened before planting.[25] Mountain land was not measured by the *mu* in relation to the amount of rent charged, and this freed tenants from the need for careful husbandry; the normal practice, indeed, was to exhaust the fertility of a hill until nothing would grow on it, at which point the tenant would lease another. Owners of mountain land were unconcerned, as they reaped huge benefits: the mountain land was tax-exempt, the rents were high in relation to the value of the land and, if owners possessed fields in the foothills, these were fertilized by the rich mountain soil washed down by the rain.[26]

Everywhere the damage reported was the same. The Qimen county gazetteer of 1826 summed it up as follows:

> Fields down below are inundated by sand and rocks when the rain falls, and the streams are dry when the rain ceases. Everywhere the fields are laid waste. Gradually the sediment silts up the larger streams, making it impossible to store water for drought, or discharge it during a flood while much land remains submerged. Since the Pengmin began opening up the mountain land, the riverbeds have been rising daily, making them unnavigable. When rain fails for but ten days, goods cannot be brought in by water, overland transport costs rise, and every village is reduced to desperate straits.[27]

The alarm of the native elite was reflected in their writings. Mei Zengliang, a Daoguang *jinshi*, native of Xuancheng and senior secretary of the Board of Revenue, while preparing a biography of the Qing official Dong Jiaozeng, ironically discovered that the latter, while governor of Anhui, had strenuously petitioned the throne for the Pengmin to be permitted to enter and open up the hills. Dong had criticized native opponents for geomantic superstition and for allowing a natural resource to go to waste.[28] After seeing the consequences of soil erosion in his native county, Mei was moved to write: "This is tantamount to opening up wasteland at the cost of harming rice-producing fields, and giving employment to people who pay no taxes at the cost of impoverishing taxpaying households."[29]

Another scholar-official, Zhang Jian (1768–1850), a *juren* from Wucheng with a special academic interest in water control, provided the background to various measures concerning the Pengmin taken by Ruan Yuan in 1802 as governor of Zhejiang. In Zhang's view, the Pengmin had caused much intercommunal conflict with the damage they had done to rice fields. Moreover, because the Pengmin were difficult to keep track of, they had caused confusion in the household registration system. It was greed alone, he believed, that had prompted gentry and commoner owners of hill land to invite them in.[30] Fang Chun, another *juren* and a native of She xian, agreed with Zhang and added to the list of grievances: the Pengmin were disturbing the ancestral tombs of the natives, causing shortages of firewood through deforestation, and engaging in predation.[31]

Given these pressures, the provincial authorities of Zhejiang and Anhui were compelled to act. In January 1802 Governor Ruan Yuan proclaimed detailed procedures under which:

1. The Pengmin already in the province were permitted to remain, but would be enrolled in the *baojia* registers only after a careful survey and enumeration with the view of preventing further arrivals. Any yamen functionary found extorting money during the survey was to be beaten to death with the rod.
2. Those Pengmin who invited more of their kind to join them were liable for punishment.
3. Gentry landowners found leasing more land to their Pengmin tenants would thenceforth be deprived of their gentry status and subject to other forms of punishment.
4. Landowners were enjoined to reclaim the land when the existing contracts

expired and would be punished if they extended the contract or leased more land to the Pengmin.

5. At the end of each year, each county magistrate was to investigate and report to his superiors on any reduction or increase of Pengmin.
6. Maize was banned as a crop on hill land. Landlords were to instruct their tenants to switch to indigo, tea, or sweet potatoes.
7. Landlords were encouraged to redeem land already leased by compensating the Pengmin.

In 1815 the court issued a comprehensive edict concerning the Pengmin of Zhejiang. This edict shows that the issues addressed by the Yongzheng policy on Pengmin in the Gan Yangzi (see Chapter 7) were still very much alive in Zhejiang in the 1810s; the range and problematic nature of the solutions also show striking similarities with the earlier period. Those who had resided in the province for at least twenty years, possessed land, homes, and ancestral tombs, and were married were permitted to establish permanent residence, that is to acquire native status. Those who had resided for less time, but had satisfied all the other requirements, were allowed to become permanent residents when the temporal requirement was satisfied. Those who were unmarried, or rented on the basis of a short-term lease, or had rental contracts not specifying a definite period, were considered temporary residents. They were to return the land when the lease expired, or for indefinite leases, in five years. Meanwhile, temporary residents were required to enroll themselves in the *baojia* registers. Each unit of 30 households was to have a headman (*pengzhang*), who would make checks periodically, tying the constituent households to a system of joint responsibility and mutual surveillance. Finally, those who were not registered were to be expelled and repatriated.[32] The policy in Zhejiang sought therefore to stagger the expulsion and repatriation of those not qualified to acquire permanent resident status. How far this succeeded cannot be gauged from the records.

In Anhui, the policy was much the same and was governed by the same fear that precipitous expulsion would provoke disorder. As early as 1789 the governor had ordered expulsion, but had been disobeyed. In Huizhou prefecture, from 1802 onward, bloody native-Pengmin feuds erupted over damage to fields. Landlords who had leased land to the Pengmin joined in the clamor for expulsion, so that they could pocket the rent their tenants had paid in advance and repossess land that had been rendered productive by Pengmin labor. As an official observed: "Most of the mountain land leased to the Pengmin is lineage land with multiple shareholders. The poorer members leased it to the Pengmin with the connivance of the lineage elders who, upon the lease being signed and the advance rent received, would lay charges before the magistrate. They would ask for the Pengmin to be expelled, thereby swindling the Pengmin of the rent."[33] Sometimes the Pengmin responded violently. In retaliation, gangs of natives raided Pengmin farms, hoping to drive the immigrants out.[34]

Finally, in 1807, the government was prompted to issue regulations after a most bizarre case involving a landowner and his tenants in Xiuning county. The well-connected gentry landlord, a village elder, had journeyed to the imperial capital to lay the charge that his tenants of four years had committed murder and rape and consorted with bandits. The petition continued: "Of late they have assembled 10,000 men, and are engaged in building fortresses, digging trenches, and making weapons in preparation for an uprising." The imperial court instructed the governor of Anhui to dispatch posthaste troops under senior civil and military officials to nip the rebellion in the bud. In the normal course of events, the appearance of the troops would have sent such putative rebels into a panic, forcing them to take up arms in self-defense and to call for help; the result would have been yet another gang of bandits or rebels suppressed, or an uncontrolled revolt.

In this case, however, the presence of mind of one official, Gao Tingyao, averted what might have turned into a major slaughter of the innocent or prompted a large-scale revolt by people who initially had no intention of revolting. Restraining his colleague, the *daotai* of Wuhu, from sending in a large force, Gao volunteered to visit the scene with a small escort to assess the allegation, while having troops close by in case of need. He discovered soon enough that the accuser had perpetrated a hoax for selfish gain.[35]

In the course of dealing with the case, *daotai* Yang Maotian investigated the Pengmin problem in Huizhou prefecture, where the immigrants were most numerous. On the basis of his report, Governor Chu Pengling obtained imperial assent for the promulgation of a set of procedures. As in Zhejiang, these procedures permitted those who met the requirements to enroll as permanent residents, and required those on contract to withdraw and repatriate on the expiry of their contracts. Where no time period was stipulated in the tenancy contracts, and when the Pengmin had had use of the land for ten years or more, two years of grace were given. Where the contracts were still valid and landlords were willing to return part of the advance rent, local authorities were to determine a fair compensation. The cultivation of maize was to be banned when the owners recovered the mountain land. Landlords who continued after 1807 to call in non-natives to open up land were to be banished to the frontiers for military servitude if the land leased exceeded 50 *mu*; if it was less, they forfeited the rent to the government. Tenants were to suffer the penalty set out in the penal code for "usurping state or private land."[36]

One glaring omission from these provisions concerned *baojia* registration. The last order for *baojia* registration of the Pengmin had been issued in 1739 but, in this as in other areas, because the *baojia* was not designed for a scattered and mobile population, it had been difficult to implement. *Daotai* Yang made the revealing observation that self-policing by means of *baojia* could not be enforced. The settlers were scattered deep in the mountains, and were unable to carry out mutual surveillance. Vast numbers of the Pengmin were seasonal farmhands, arriving in spring and leaving in autumn. Thus, although he was able to enumerate only 1,563 farms with 8,661 Pengmin in Huizhou prefecture, Gao Tingyao estimated that at the height of the farming season, possibly as many as 200,000 were working in the hills.[37] Furthermore, there was the worry that the Pengmin, once enrolled in the *baojia* registers, would "usurp the land as their own and even insist on participating in the examinations," causing difficulties with the natives.[38] An official later reported that the procedures for repatriation were not being followed because the Pengmin found various pretexts for delay and landlords were braving the rod by leasing more land.[39]

The issue was thus stalemated: the lenient method of encouraging the Pengmin to leave in stages and preventing new ones from arriving had not worked, but the government was not prepared to risk the consquences of forcible expulsion. The court repeatedly demanded substance, not "mere formality," in the implementation of *baojia* registration. Yet, in practice implementation remained nominal.

These dilemmas are graphically revealed in the memorials of Tao Zhu, a man of great administrative experience, who was governor of Anhui in 1823–25 and of Jiangsu in 1825–30, and governor-general of Liangjiang (Jiangsu,

Anhui, and Jiangxi) in 1830–39.[40] In 1815, just after an influx of lowland poor from the northern Southeast Coast and from across the Yangzi, the court had ordered provincial officials to conduct yet another survey of the Pengmin, with the additional injunction that each year after the harvest, when hired hands had departed, the *baojia* registration should be checked to prevent concealment of criminals.[41] In 1824 Censor Lang Baochen, a native of Anji, one of the counties affected by soil erosion, asked the throne for a fresh investigation, whereupon the court demanded a new *baojia* registration.

In his memorials, Governor Tao proposed that the hill people in Anhui be grouped in such a way that ten households form a *pai* and ten *pai* a *peng*. In addition, each hill would have a headman, called *pengtou*. Commenting on Tao's intention to carry out the order of *baojia* registration, the Daoguang emperor commanded, "Investigate seriously so that it is not a mere formality (*you ming wu shi*)."[42] Tao subsequently reported that the investigation had discovered 2,751 households in the province. Tao revealed that 136 *pengtou* had been designated and, to discourage further immigration, that landlords had been warned not to lease more land to immigrants.[43]

In 1837, however, another censor, Tao Shilin, a native of Anhui (Nanling county), informed the throne that the Pengmin were damaging irrigated agriculture and concealing criminals. He urged that the immigrants be given a period of grace and then be asked to return to their native areas, and that no new hill land be made available to them. Once again, Tao Zhu, who was then serving as governor-general of Liangjiang, was instructed to investigate and report. Once more he assured the emperor that the *baojia* apparatus was working, and that no criminals had been detected. As for repatriation and withholding new land, he pleaded: "Because of recurrent famines, refugees from elsewhere have come to eke out a living here. It is impossible to expel them, for otherwise they will be deprived of a livelihood."

The result of expulsion would have been, of course, to drive the immigrants to crime. Tao advised instead the imposition of a ban on selected hills, where cultivation was likely to affect rice fields below, and a prohibition on landlords leasing more land to the immigrants. Recognizing the dilemma, the Daoguang emperor accepted Tao's argument against repatriation. The emperor's shrill warning to the governor-general that he would be held personally responsible for any disorder was a tacit admission that there was no alternative.[44]

9. Frontier Society: The Pengmin in the Hanshui Basin

The upper Hanshui basin, along with the highlands that formed the boundaries of the Northwest and Upper Yangzi macroregions, was not fully opened up until the eighteenth century.[1] The delay in part resulted from the past turbulence of the area. Here in 1464–66 and again in 1470–71 the well-known Yunyang uprisings occurred. Some two million fugitives from oppressive taxation and landlord exactions joined with refugees from natural disasters. The attempt of the Ming government to dislodge them from an area officially banned to settlers and forcibly to repatriate them turned into a financially crippling campaign and involved casualties in the hundreds of thousands.[2] The ban (*jinshan*) remained in force while the imperial administration progressively absorbed the near periphery. This was achieved by the establishment of Yunyang prefecture in 1476. Together with five other adjacent prefectures straddling the provinces of Hubei, Henan, and Shaanxi, it was placed under a governor of its own in order to strengthen its defense.[3] Subsequently, the highlands were, in James Parsons's words, the "epicenter" of the late Ming rebellions of 1634–41, and the scene of the last battles fought by the remnants of Li Zicheng's forces in 1647–64.[4] A decade later, this area was again the site of warfare as it was engulfed in the revolt of the Three Feudatories.

Up to the early eighteenth century, the ravages of war and the continued ban on settlement of some areas had kept the highlands undeveloped and sparsely populated. Their opening up during the eighteenth century was related to the lifting of the ban in mid-century, during the campaigns against the Jinchuan aboriginal rebels.[5] But, more importantly, it derived from the economic development associated with the emergence of Wuhan as the integrating metropolis of the Middle Yangzi region.[6]

Map 9.1 and its accompanying Table 9.1 provide a broad overview of Pengmin settlement in this region. Here the Pengmin settled in two more or less continuous bands: one to the north of the Hanshui basin, on the Qinling highlands separating the Hanshui from the Wei River basin, and the other (connected to the northern band through settlement in Mian xian, which was to the west) to the south, on the Dabashan, separating the Hanshui from the Yangzi River drainage. Settlement almost exactly followed the northern, western, and southern frontiers of the arm of the Middle Yangzi macroregion stretching west along the Hanshui.

Migration to this region generally took place a little later than in the Gan Yangzi. As we have seen, in some parts of the Gan Yangzi the peak of migration came early in the eighteenth century. It may well be that the land in the Hanshui basin was more difficult to till, the living poorer. In any case, although there is evidence of some early migration after the mid-seventeenth century devastation, it was the mid- to late eighteenth century (Qianlong period) before the majority of the migrants arrived.[7]

Because local officials despaired of meeting the fixed tax quotas imposed on a reduced population, the first wave of settlers was officially encouraged. If the events in Xixiang county are any guide, at the call for settlers by the governor-general of Shaanxi and Sichuan in 1709, immigrants, coming from Hunan, Hubei, Jiangxi, and as far as Guangdong, in groups of hundreds and thousands appeared "like a wind rising on all sides. Traversing several thousand *li* over mountains and rivers, they came with wives and children, bearing hoes and spades." Hostels were constructed to house them temporarily. They were given calves and shacks and, because the best land had been claimed by the rich and powerful, they undertook to meet the tax shortfall in exchange for "the rocky wastes."[8] Thereafter, fresh calls for settlers were issued from time to time.[9] The

MAP 9.1 (opposite). Areas of Pengmin in-migration along the Dabashan and Qinling frontiers, upper Hanshui basin, 1650–1850, showing administrative capitals as of 1820. The seat of Chengkou ting is plotted for reference even though that subprefecture had not yet been established as of 1820.

NORTHWEST CHINA
HENAN
GANSU
SHAANXI
QINLING
MIDDLE YANGZI
UPPER YANGZI
DABA SHAN
HUBEI
SICHUAN
Qin-zhou
Shancha-ting
Fengxiang-fu
Qian-zhou
Gaoling
Weinan
Hua-zhou
Baoji
Fufeng
Xingping
Wugong
Xianyang
Lintong
Mei-xian
Wei R.
Zhouzhi
Hu-xian
Xi'an-fu
Chang'an
Xianning
Lantian
Luonan
Lushi
Shang-zhou
Liangdang
Feng-xian
Hui-xian
Cheng-xian
Liuba-ting
Xiaoyi-ting
Shanyang
Shangnan
Zhen'an
Lueyang
Yang-xian
Ningshan-ting
Baocheng
Chenggu
Shiquan
Mian-xian
Hanzhong-fu
Nanzheng
Xixiang
Yunxi
Yunyang-fu
Yun-xian
Hanyin-ting
Ningqiang-zhou
Xunyang
Baihe
Han shui
Jun-zhou
Hanshui
Xing'an-fu
Ankang
Dingyuan-ting
Ziyang
Guangyuan
Pingli
Zhuxi
Zhushan
Zhaohua
Nanjiang
Fang-xian
Taiping-ting
Tongjiang
(Chengkou-ting)
Ba-zhou
Areas of Pengmin in-migration
Limits of physiographic regions
Provincial boundaries
Prefectural-level capital
County-level capital
0
50
100 Km
Daning
Xingshan
Dongxiang
Suiding-fu
Da-xian
Kai-xian
Kuizhou-fu
Fengjie
Gui-zhou
Wushan
Badong
Xinning
Yunyang
Yangzi R.

TABLE 9.1

Pengmin In-migration Along the Dabashan and Qinling Frontiers, Upper Hanshui Basin, 1650–1850

Destination	*Macro-region*	*Time of Migration*	*Provenance*	*Economic Activities*	*Source*
		NORTH OF THE HANSHUI: QINLING FRONTIER			
Luonan, SA	N/MY	1778–79 famine	Anhui, Hunan, Hubei		XZ (GX ed.), p. 97
Shang zhou, SA	MY	1741			Zhen'an XTZ (1908) pt 1: 32b
Xiaoyi ting (Zhashui), SA	MY		Hubei, Jiangxi	Irish potatoes	TZ (1883) 3: 12a
Zhen'an, SA	MY	1741		iron ore	XTZ (1908) pt 1: 32b; Yan Ruyi, 9: 4b
Xunyang, SA	MY		Jiangxi, Hubei	maize, ramie, tree oil, tree fungi, medicine, lumber, charcoal, iron	XZ (1783) 11: 13b, (1902) 5: 14a–b; Yan Ruyi, 9: 4b
Ankang, SA	MY	1772–73 famine	Hubei, Sichuan, Henan, Anhui, Jiangxi		XZ (1815) 17: 4b–5a
Hanyin ting, SA	MY	YZ, QL			Sun Daren, p. 137
Shiquan, SA	MY	1772–73 famine	Sichuan, Hubei, Henan, Jiangxi, Anhui	maize	XZ (1849) 2: 35b–36a, 4: 66a
Ningshan ting, SA	MY			lumber	Yan Ruyi, 6: 26b–27a
Zhouzhi, SA	NW			lumber	Yan Ruyi, 9: 3b
Yang xian, SA	MY			lumber, paper, iron ore, mushrooms, tree fungi	XZ (1898) 4: 1b
Chenggu, SA	MY			gold mining	Yan Ruyi, 9: 16b
Liuba ting, SA	MY			iron ore	Yan Ruyi, 9: 4b
Feng xian, SA	UY/MY	1710, JQ, DG, GX		maize, buckwheat	XZ (1892) 1: 14a, 3: 1a, 8: 1a

TABLE 9.1 (*cont.*)

Destination	Macro-region	Time of Migration	Provenance	Economic Activities	Source
Liangdang, GS	UY		Hubei, Sichuan	iron ore, mining, smelting	Yan Ruyi, 3: 2b, 9: 4b
Mian xian, SA	UY/MY			lumber, iron ore, maize, Irish potatoes	Yan Ruyi, 6: 19a–b, 9: 2b, 4b
			SOUTH OF THE HANSHUI: DABASHAN		
Ningqiang zhou, SA	UY/MY	late Ming, early Qing	Hubei, Sichuan, Jiangxi	iron ore	Yan Ruyi, 9: 4b; XTZ (GX ed.), p. 47
Nanzheng, SA	MY		Sichuan, Hubei	gold mining	XZ (1794) 2: 18b–19a; Yan Ruyi, 9: 16b; XZ (1921) 5: 1b
Xixiang, SA	UY/MY	1710	Hunan, Hubei, Guangdong, Jiangxi	paper	Yan Ruyi, 9: 5b; XZ (DG ed.), p. 49
Dingyuan ting (Zhenba), SA	UY/MY			maize, Irish potatoes, paper, iron ore	Yan Ruyi, 9: 4b, 5b; TZ (1879) 4: 8b, 5: 4a, 8: 1b, 3b
Taiping ting (Wanyuan), SC	UY/MY			salt	Yan Ruyi, 3: 22a, 9: 7b, 8a
Kai xian, SC	UY			salt	Yan Ruyi, 9: 7b–8a
Yunyang, SC	UY			salt	Yan Ruyi, 9: 7b
(Chengkou ting), SC	UY/MY			salt	Yan Ruyi, 9: 8a
Pingli, SA	MY	pre-1754	Hubei	Irish potatoes, ramie, paint, tree oil, tree fungi, medicine	XZ (1756) 2: 46b, 3: 28b, (1897) 8: 26b
Daning (Wuqi), SC	UY		Hunan, Hubei	salt	XZ (1885) 1: 1a; Yan Ruyi, 3: 27a, 8: 9b–10a, 9: 7b
Xingshan, HB	MY			iron ore, paper	Yan Ruyi, 3: 14b

NOTE: For conventions and abbreviations used in the tables, see p. xvii.

highland population was greatly augmented in 1772–73 by refugees from famine in Sichuan and Hubei, and again in 1778–79 by immigrants from Anhui, Hunan, and Hubei.[10]

The majority of the Pengmin immigrants would appear not to have been Hakkas. First, there is no evidence of surviving pockets of Hakka speakers in southern Shaanxi; even in Sichuan, the nearest scattered pockets of Hakka speakers lie to the south or west of the counties in which we have identified Pengmin.[11] Second, the gazetteers identify the majority of the migrants as coming from Sichuan, Hubei, or Hunan. Only a very few seem to have come from Guangdong. There is no evidence of migration of Hakkas from Sichuan or Hunan, and the likelihood remains that most immigrants were not Hakkas.

As Ho Ping-ti has pointed out, the delay in the development of these highlands perhaps also arose from a lack of suitable crops. The introduction of maize and the sweet potato and, after 1800, the Irish potato in the loftier terrain made the difference.[12] The Shiquan county gazetteer of 1849 records that millet had been the chief crop before 1765, but thereafter maize, which was introduced by immigrants from Sichuan and Hubei, became most prevalent. "Though millet yields less than corn, it has the advantage of being easier to preserve."[13] The Dingyuan gazetteer of 1879 noted: "Irish potatoes (*yangyu*) . . . are suited for lofty mountain land because they prefer a dry climate. . . . Corn yields more than rice, but cannot be kept for long. People in the highest terrain rely only on Irish potatoes."[14]

These food crops provided the basis for a complex economy. Rice cultivation, it is estimated, occupied but a fraction of the land;[15] in any case, rice was not considered as filling as maize by the hardworking lumberjacks and haulers, iron-ore miners and foundry workers, paper-mill workmen, salt porters, and firewood and charcoal peddlers. Enterprises that employed these men closed down whenever the crops failed, or the price of food was deemed excessive, thereby throwing hundreds of thousands out of work. This was a recurring nightmare for the local authorities.[16]

The immigrants found land abundant and cheap. Few natives would brave the primeval forests (*laolin*), infested by wild beasts and invariably described as "unfrequented, dark, and eerie." Hence there was an abundance of "wasteland." Immigrants entered into an agreement with the local government specifying the location and extent of the wasteland they were to cultivate as well as the amount of tax due when the land became productive.[17] As for titled land, large tracts could be leased for a few taels of silver. The land could then be opened up by hired farmhands or, alternatively, it could be sublet to others.[18] The subcontracting could occur as many as seven or eight times, making it impossible for the owner to recover the land without indemnifying the successive layers of tenants.[19] Illiterate landowners, it is reported, often signed away permanent tenancy and the tenant's right to sublet.[20] As late as 1821, an official reported that "in the old forest area, upon payment of a few strings of cash to the owners, immigrants can lease several slopes or ravines; the unemployed of Jiangxi, Guangdong, Guizhou, Hubei, Sichuan, and Shaanxi sojourn there in their millions. Relying on kinsmen and friends, they open up the virgin land, put up shacks for shelter, and move away when the harvest becomes lean."[21] Yan Ruyi vividly describes how the hill land was opened: "The opening of a hill involves scores of people concerting their physical strength. Long ropes are fastened on the tall trees and pulled by heavy rocks, while the men assist with axes and saws until the tree is felled. The branches are lopped off as fuel, the leaves and twigs dried and burned to provide fertilizer. Consequently, the soil is rich without adding fertilizer, and often the yield is a hundredfold."[22]

In addition to farming, a range of industries also flourished. Largest was lumbering, which developed an elaborate organization and innovative technology. Merchant-investors in Xi'an, Zhouzhi, and Hanzhong entrusted their business to a general manager (*zhanggui*), assisted by a "scribe manager" (*shuban*) who handled contracts and invoices. Below them were headmen in charge of river banks (*ling'an*) and labor contractors (*baotou*) for land and water transport. Timber was transported from deep in the forest to concentration points on the water, along pathways constructed from logs and where necessary put in place using "sky trolleys" (*tianche*) to cope with the most difficult terrain. The muscle power in each case was provided by oxen, mules, horses, or a team of twenty to thirty haulers. The largest lumber businesses hired 3,000–5,000 workers, organized into battalions and commanded in military fashion. Valuable timber (such as was used for priceless coffins), weighing 300 lbs. per piece, was carried by men called "mules," at a rate of ten to fifteen miles per day.[23]

The enterprises next in size were iron-ore mining and smelting. "Red hills" were mined where trees were available for charcoal to fuel the furnaces. Several thousand men were employed to mine the ore and supply the fuel. In the foundries, each furnace was manned by one master smith and more than ten hired hands who operated the bellows in day and night shifts. A large foundry with half a dozen furnaces could employ as many as two to three thousand workers. Another thousand transported the iron ingots to workshops that produced farm implements and kitchen utensils.[24]

A host of other enterprises—charcoal burning and papermaking, and the collection of bamboo shoots, edible tree fungi (*muer*), and mushrooms—employed smaller numbers of men.[25] People in the remotest parts of the forests made a living by gathering medicinal ingredients, such as *danggui* and *huanglian*. Merchants leased large areas to Pengmin households to plant *huanglian* trees, which took ten years to mature.[26]

By the end of the eighteenth century there had emerged in these hills and mountains a rough-and-tumble frontier society, made up of immigrants of varied provenance who were, in many of the counties, more numerous than the natives.[27] Moreover, the immigrants were rootless and, in the eyes of the administration, lawless. The immigrants sorted themselves out and formed solidarities based on bonds such as those of shared provenance, speech, or surname. In some cases, for mutual protection people of several, even scores, of surnames cohabited within one household. People adopted sons of different surnames, and widows brazenly "called in" men as husbands. All of this the orthodoxy-conscious officials and natives heartily disapproved of.[28] Yan Ruyi summed up the situation thus: "In the Sichuan-Shaanxi border, only one or two in ten are native. Five are from Hunan and Hubei, while three or four are from Guangdong, Anhui, and Jiangxi. These people from all directions are not bound by any lineage ties or constraints of propriety or education. They seek out their own kind and group together on the basis of sworn brotherhood, marriage ties, and other bonds. . . . Crimes are committed daily."[29]

The upper Hanshui basin and the surrounding highlands posed graver problems of security and defense than any other area occupied by the Pengmin. This was one of the more remote peripheries, and the task of administration was greatly complicated by the large and volatile immigrant population. Mobile of necessity, given their shifting agriculture, and insecure by virtue of the dependence of their various enterprises on a regular supply of affordable food, the immigrants were prone to predation. The White Lotus Rebellion of 1796–1805 spectacularly demonstrated the loss of control by the Qing administration. But even before the rebellion, the turbulent history of the upper Hanshui highlands, never far from the minds of the administrators, had underlined the vulnerability of the empire in this peripheral region.

Government Responses to a Frontier Society

The Pengmin immigrants in the upper Hanshui basin and other highlands bordering on it presented different administrative problems from those in the other macroregions. Unlike in the Xiang-Gan highlands, native-immigrant conflict was muted by the numerical superiority of the Pengmin over the natives.[30] This is not to say that, at the local level, the ethnic boundary was absent; gazetteers draw a clear distinction between natives (*bendi*) and newcomers. Although enrolled as permanent residents, the latter were called "new subjects" (*xinmin*), as in Xixiang and other counties, or "people from downstream" (*xiahebang*), as in Zhen'an.[31] Still, many gazetteers of the nineteenth century reported that the immigrants had "all become native, peaceably pursuing their livelihood."[32] It was far easier here than anywhere else for the immigrant to acquire native status. As Yan Ruyi stated, "the people opening up wasteland in the mountains obtain permission in writing [from the local yamen]; in three to four years when the wasteland is made productive, the sojourners (*liuyu*) change to native status."[33]

Damage from soil erosion was reported in a few counties, but the impact on lowland agriculture was less than on the water-control works of the Hanshui itself.[34] The well-known official Wei Yuan wrote: "The opening of the primeval forests by the Pengmin on the Shaanxi-Sichuan border causes soil and sand to be washed down by rain, turning the Hanshui muddy. However, the increasing population, thanks to a long period of peace, makes it impossible to ban cultivation upstream." The result was the need for greater vigilance in maintaining dikes because of the rise in the river bed, a problem compounded by polder construction.[35]

The principal administrative problem stemmed from the character of the periphery itself and from the government's superficial penetration of the vast and inaccessible highlands, which had but recently been settled. This frontier immigrant society, volatile and mobile, easily became a hotbed of illicit activities. Counterfeiters, many of whom were attached to government mints, took advantage of the increasing monetization of the economy.[36] Salt smugglers seized on the opportunity of supplying illicit salt from the Upper Yangzi at a lower price than the legal salt coming from the Lower Yangzi wells.[37] The *guolu*, bandit gangs organized as armed militia, floated from market town to market town, preying on communities; their method of class warfare was "feeding off rich families" (*chidahu*, literally, "eating rich households").[38] Following a government crackdown, their ranks became swollen by counterfeiters and salt smugglers. The *guolu* bandits specialized in racketeering, extortion, and kidnapping. They operated gambling rackets as a form of extortion, often appearing uninvited at funerals and weddings where they pressured the guests into a game of chance and then held the hapless host responsible for his guests' losses.[39] Other riffraff, called *xiandalang*, when not in league with the *guolu*, offered themselves to the government as mercenaries when recruits were needed.[40]

Even more enigmatic was the way in which the *guolu* came to be associated with the White Lotus religious sect. Unlike the *guolu*, who were clandestine and hated as troublemakers, the White Lotus was open and popular. In normal times, the sect ministered to the religious needs of rich and poor alike, including yamen personnel. It also provided some modest welfare services. The sect was capable, however, of being swept into an eschatological frenzy, as when provoked by a government crackdown it joined forces with the *guolu*, counterfeiters, salt smugglers, and other malcontents.[41] An oppressive and extortionist local administration helped to direct the sect's fury against the state itself, even though, as in the White Lotus Rebellion, the sect formed but a small part of the rebels, and the uprising began without an organizing center or political pretensions.[42]

The dynasty survived the rebellion but at an enormous cost to its coffers—it spent an estimated 120 million taels, exhausting most of the surplus accumulated up to the late Qianlong period.[43] The suppression of rebellion, however, did not root out the outlaws or alter the moral climate of highland society. The problem of gaining control over the immigrant and native populations remained. How the Qing administration tackled this problem may best be studied with reference to the unusually rich but hitherto little tapped collection, *Sansheng bianfang beilan* (Guide to frontier defense in three provinces), compiled by Yan Ruyi from his own and other officials' writings on the border region. Yan was one of those mid-ranking Qing officials, like Gao Tingyao, notable for their assiduity and abiding faith in the system; they gave substance to the principle of governance based on the personal merit of the people who made up officialdom.

Acknowledged as an expert on border affairs, Yan served as the Shan'an military circuit intendant from 1821 until his death in 1826. He intended his collection to be a helpful reference for other officials, who would find useful details on the physiography of the mountainous terrain as well as information on strategic passes, distances between points, and the kinds of settlements found in various parts. Much of this information Yan had personally gathered on an inspection tour. One chapter gives concrete details of various economic enterprises, including their organization and techniques; another outlines the manners and customs of the immigrants. A concluding chapter assembles Yan's own analysis as well as official communications, all of which sheds invaluable light on how the government machinery in this region had evolved.

As a first principle, according to Yan, "the securing of the highlands consists primarily in settling the displaced people (*liumin*) in peace." The war against the heterodox elements could only be won by winning over the immigrants, by ensuring for them a secure livelihood, and by giving them a stake in peace and order.[44] Never short of ideas, Yan outlined a host of concrete measures. Taxation, in his view, was a leading cause of popular disaffection. "Though the quota for a county may not exceed one thousand taels," he observed, "the actual amount collected is tens of thousands." Middlemen and government runners were able to take a cut because the yamen was too far away for the mountain folk to make the journey to deliver the equivalent of a few copper coins of tax in person. Yan suggested that officials should visit the communities instead, collect the taxes on the spot, and accept copper coins instead of insisting on their equivalent in silver.[45]

For defense against banditry, he suggested the time-honored measures of building walls and forts and training militia, but also advocated relying on game hunters and guards employed by the Pengmin enterprises.[46] Apart from asking the local communities to depend on themselves for defense, Yan felt government funds were needed to strengthen, equip, and house the military posts (*yingxun*). These were scattered deep in the mountains and, as things stood, "the guards panic and flee pell-mell upon hearing a cry in the dark."[47]

As for self-policing by means of the *baojia*, the current method in the highlands was to hold landowners (*zhaozhu*) and headmen of enterprises responsible.[48] The *baojia*, however, was only practical in towns. In the rural areas, the Pengmin had no fixed abode and they were too scattered to watch over one another; enrolling them would only provide an opportunity for yamen personnel to engage in extortion.[49]

As a Confucian official, Yan ultimately saw the task of government to be the civilizing of the turbulent highland society. "Increasing the number of military posts is less desirable than subdividing [the area] into administrative units," he wrote. The introduction of civil administration would not only facilitate the dispensing of justice, the collection of taxes, and the development of commercial centers, but would also encourage agriculture, promote learning, and improve moral standards.[50] In this proposal, Yan identified the key problems for the government: to overcome the superficiality of the administrative machinery by subdividing the inordinately large administrative units into more manageable counties and ordinary subprefectures, to establish additional supervisory units over the counties and subprefectures so created, and, finally, to increase the number of military posts. According to another writer, the larger counties had a perimeter as large as 1,000–2,000 *li*, and the smaller ones 500–600 *li*.[51] Ankang county, in one of the more densely populated areas, for example, was 400 *li* from end to end; the perimeter of the Taiping subprefecture in Sichuan was 3,000 *li*, and parts of the Hubei-Sichuan-Shaanxi border were 600 *li* from any administrative center. Yunyang prefecture in Hubei, with six counties in it, was as large as Anhui province.[52]

The proposed intensification of administration, however, had implications for both revenue and central control. The government had been reluctant to create additional administrative units even before the White Lotus Rebellion; now its financial straits increased that reluctance. Shaanxi and Sichuan, the provinces where subdivision was most urgent, already depended on contributions from revenue-surplus provinces to make up their budgetary deficit.[53] Yet there was also clearly a cost in the failure to squeeze other provinces harder to fund a more adequate administrative machinery.

To relieve the burden on the magistrate, many of the existing administrative units were in need of additional subordinate officials (*zuoza*), such as submagistrates of various grades and jail wardens. The creation of additional administrative units was even more costly than adding officials to existing administrative units. On four separate occasions, in 1782, 1802, 1821, and 1824, eight new ordinary subprefectures (*ting*) were created and one was converted from an existing *xian*.[54] As Skinner has shown, *ting* were concentrated on the periphery of peripheral prefectures, since this unit of organization allowed the prefectural yamen to exercise the closest supervision of security and defense.[55] For these additional units to have any value, the posts had to be designated "important," and filled under the "preferment" category by personnel appointed by governors and governors-general. Such upgrading of posts was, as Watt notes, "an important concession to decentralization."[56] Only appointees who already had five years' administrative experience and whose salary carried a supplement for serving in a frontier post (*bianfeng*) were considered adequate to the task. An inexperienced person, said one memorialist, would be "too fainthearted to venture into the forested mountains."[57]

Ostensibly for reasons of finance, but no doubt also of centralized control, regulations allowed provincial governors and governors-general only to propose transfers, but not additions.[58] The memorials show graphically how provincial leaders responded to this restriction. Each additional post, whether within an existing unit or in a new one, involved reduction and reclassification elsewhere in the province in order to maintain the predetermined number of posts and their designations. Only by the most strenuous pleas were additions and waivers for reduction and reclassification granted.

There was one concession to decentralization that the throne was even more loathe to make. This involved the "temporary" establishment of a high-ranking office to coordinate the defense of the prefectures straddling the three provinces, a proposal consciously modeled on Ming practice. The memorialists saw this as a way of overcoming the inertia among officials that led them to ignore what happened beyond their own jurisdiction. The proposal was contained in a memorial of 1821 by the Hanlin academician Zhuo Bingtian, probably written at the urging of Yan Ruyi himself.[59] It was ignored, threatening as it did the finely tuned system of checks and balances built into the administration.

Conclusion

Part Two of this book has sought to shed light on the subject of internal migration through an examination of the Pengmin, and on how the Qing administration handled the problems associated with population movement. Although the data, drawn from a survey of the local gazetteers, official documents, and writings by scholar-officials, are fragmentary and incomplete, they highlight the significant exploitation of marginal land both before and during the period of population explosion. Because of the shifting and seasonal nature of Pengmin migration, it is impossible to give even the most general estimate of the number of people involved. Nevertheless, examination of the Pengmin in a regional context allows us to elucidate many key variables in their migration and economy.

Differences of space and history shaped the degrees and kinds of mobility and permanence of the Pengmin, the ease with which they achieved native status and local acceptance, and the economic activities they pursued. Thus, in the Lower Yangzi, the region's leading economic position and its long and relatively undisturbed cycle of economic development from the sixteenth to the eighteenth century led to the maintenance of a powerful landowning class, which owned practically every parcel of hill and mountain land, and which often held such land for ritual purposes only. Here it was less common for immigrants to buy land outright, and no "wasteland" existed for the newcomers to open up and take possession of. Capitalist farming, dominated by maize production, was the result of the high degree of commercialization in the region. Such farming may also account for the seasonal character of population movement.

The character of Pengmin migration to the Gan Yangzi region falls halfway between that of the Lower Yangzi and that of the upper Hanshui basin. Here the situation was shaped by the additional factor that the main body of immigrants was of a specific subcultural group. The immigrants tended to be far less involved in organized capitalist enterprises. Their settlement was more permanent because land was available for purchase, even though only after a period of tenancy. Moreover, there still existed some "wasteland" over which the settlers could claim ownership upon rendering it productive and assuming the tax quota.

The particular history of the Gan Yangzi in part springs from the dislocation and depopulation that occurred in this area during the Ming-Qing transition. But the persistence of a strong, if reduced, landowning elite together with the relative cultural homogeneity of the immigrant population shaped an inter-communal relationship that alternated between the "open" and "shut" patterns in rhythm with the regional cycles. Access to lowland marketing systems, where textile and other handicraft industries were flourishing, accounted for the types of crops and products of the Pengmin economy.

In the upper Hanshui basin, an area that was, because of its turbulent past, far from approaching its population potential, the immigrants outnumbered the natives. The abundance of "wasteland" and land for long-tem tenancy as well as a favorable demographic balance facilitated permanent settlement.

The role of Pengmin migration in relieving growing population pressure seems clear, even if hard to quantify. Through the opening up of marginal land and the introduction of new food crops, the Pengmin also made important contributions to regional economic development. More difficult to assess, however, is the damaging long-term impact of deforestation; Ho Ping-ti has noted that some of these highlands now support smaller populations than in the past.[60]

Concerning the Qing administration, this study reveals a wide range of dilemmas thrown up by internal migration, which the administrative system was hard-pressed to cope with. Still, one cannot fail to be impressed by the tenacity and diligence of Qing officialdom in dealing with such problems, and by the flexibility and innovative ideas they brought to bear on them. At the same time, one is left with the overwhelming impression that the capacity of the Qing government for social control was being rapidly attenuated by the inappropriateness of the *baojia* self-policing apparatus itself.

Reference Matter

Notes

Notes, references, and other material enclosed in brackets have been added by the editor.

INTRODUCTION

1. Averill, p. 87
2. Segawa Masahisa, pp. 201–2.
3. Wolf and Huang, pp. 350–53.
4. Ibid., chap. 27.
5. Ibid.
6. Ibid.; Pasternak, chap. 3.
7. American Board of Commissioners for Foreign Missions Papers, 16.3.5, vol. 22, Walker to Clark, May 8, 1873.
8. Baker, pp. 27–28.
9. Segawa Masahisa.

1. ORIGINS AND HISTORIOGRAPHY

1. Skinner, "Regional Urbanization"; Skinner, "Presidential Address"; Skinner, "Regional Systems." As an approach of broad social science application, see Smith.
2. Patterson, pp. 305–6.
3. Abner Cohen, p. xi.
4. Barth, pp. 9–38.
5. On the situational aspect of ethnicity, see Ronald Cohen.
6. Patterson, p. 306.
7. Ibid., pp. 309–10.
8. Rhoads, pp. 12–13; Lamley, pp. 282–83; Skinner, *Chinese Society*, p. 35. Parish and Whyte, pp. 23–26, use "sub-ethnic."
9. Among the sparse literature on the subject, the following works are outstanding: Tan Qixiang, "Zhongguo neidi yimin shi"; Ho, chap. 7; Robert H. G. Lee; James Lee; Entenmann.
10. Skinner, "Regional Urbanization," pp. 211–20; Skinner, "Presidential Address." The most sustained analysis of long-term regional cycles is Hartwell.

11. Kuhn, "Origins of the Taiping Vision."
12. Roberts.
13. Rhoads, pp. 102–3.
14. The major English-language treatment to date of the Pengmin is Averill.
15. The Han River running south through Hubei to the Yangzi River is referred to as the Hanshui, in order to distinguish it from the Han River running through eastern Guangdong into the sea at Shantou, which is referred to as the Hanjiang.
16. Luo Xianglin, *Kejia yanjiu daolun*, chap. 2. For a critique of Luo's work, see Char, pp. 56 ff. [For a recent treatment of many of the problems, see Chen Zhiping and also Li Mo, where it is stressed that these five waves of migration were by no means restricted to Hakkas, but formed the origins of the Cantonese, Teochiu, and Hokkien groups as well.] Luo's treatment of the geographical distribution of the Hakkas also leaves much to be desired. Instead of local gazetteers, he relies on the recollections of relatives and acquaintances for information as to which of the counties of Jiangxi and Fujian were all or partly Hakka in population. For Guangdong, except for a few cases where he draws on the unpublished draft gazetteer of the province, he gives no sources at all, as he considers areas of Hakka settlement to be common knowledge. Luo Xianglin, *Kejia yanjiu daolun*, pp. 114–21.
17. Luo Xianglin, *Kejia yanjiu daolun*, p. 71.
18. Myron L. Cohen.
19. Char.
20. [Japanese scholarship on the Hakkas is represented by Nakagawa Manabu, whose work makes considerable use of Luo Xianglin's book. See especially Nakagawa Manabu, *Kyakka ron no gendaiteki kōzu*. His work is introduced in English in Nakagawa Manabu, "Studies on the History of the Hakkas."]
21. [Jiang Bingzhao, "Lun kejia," p. 108. See also Segawa Masahisa, pp. 186–87.]
22. Xu Songshi, pp. 143–45; Rao Zongyi, pp. 101–19. The conventional view of the She people as a branch of Yao is the subject of much inconclusive debate among Chinese scholars. See *Shezu jianshi*. [See also Huang Zanfa, pp. 93–96.]
23. Tan Qixiang, "Zhongguo neidi yimin shi." [Chen Zhiping, chaps. 4–5, stresses that these southward migrations were in no way exclusive to the Hakkas.]
24. Han migration to the Upper Yangzi slightly predated the start of this first southward migration.
25. Bielenstein.
26. *Shezu jianshi*, pp. 11, 17–19.
27. Tan Qixiang, "Zhongguo neidi yimin shi," pp. 75–77.
28. [The material on dialects has mainly been added by the editor, using Norman, esp. chap. 9. This book—which was not available to Professor Leong when he worked on the original manuscript—embodies the results of a great deal of recent

scholarship on Chinese dialects, and necessitates the revision of some of the statements made in the original manuscript on the basis of earlier scholarship. Much of that earlier scholarship is well summarized in Forrest.]

29. *Yongle dadian*, 7893: 17.
30. *Xingning zhi* (1518) 3: unpag.
31. [Norman, p. 210.]
32. [Ibid., p. 222.]
33. *Yongle dadian*, 5343: 47.
34. [Norman, p. 222.]
35. [Ibid., pp. 214, 221.]
36. [Chen Zhiping, chaps. 4–6.]
37. [Nakagawa Manabu, *Kyakka ron no gendaiteki kōzu*, p. 41.]
38. The views of Song Xiang are contained in Xu Xuzeng, appended to the genealogy of the Xu lineage of Heping and reproduced in Luo Xianglin, *Kejia shiliao huipian*, pp. 297–99; for Wen Zhonghe's views, see *Jiaying ZZ* (1898) 7: 85b–86a.
39. Skinner, "Introduction," p. 27.
40. Skinner, "Regional Systems," pp. 34–35.
41. [Li Mo, p. 126. See also Segawa Masahisa, p. 196.]
42. [Jiang Bingzhao, "Lun kejia," p. 110; of course, there could have been various reasons for this change.]
43. [Li Mo, p. 124.]
44. [Segawa Masahisa, p. 195.]
45. [Zeng Weicai, p. 36.]
46. Cited in Wang Yangming, 2: 53.
47. [See Jiang Bingzhao, "Lun kejia," p. 107 for an argument that this was the origin of the term *kejia* (Hakka).]
48. Wang Yangming, 1: 10–12. [Li Mo, p. 127.]
49. Skinner, "Regional Systems," pp. 32–33.
50. The scholar is Xu Xuzeng; see Luo Xianglin, *Kejia shiliao huipian*, p. 298. Early Qing edicts against footbinding are mentioned in Qu Xuanying, 1: 98–99.

2. HAKKA MIGRATIONS

1. Thus the Hoklos of eastern Guangdong migrated within the Southeast Coast macroregion mainly from the Zhang-Quan subregion in Fujian, starting to arrive probably around the ninth century. To this day, they maintain a strong linguistic affinity with that area. They occupied the fertile lower basin of the Hanjiang and other coastal areas as far as Haifeng. See Yang Chengzhi, p. 99; Fuson, p. 9.
2. Hashimoto, pp. 1–7.
3. Eberhard, pp. 60–67. [Chen Zhiping, chaps. 3–4, stresses the similarity of the origin myths of the Hakkas, the Cantonese, and the non-Hakka inhabitants of Fujian.]
4. [Chen Zhiping.]
5. [See Huang Zanfa.]
6. [I am indebted to G. William Skinner for drafting Figure 2.1 to illustrate his understanding of the relevant regional cycles.]

7. Skinner, "Presidential Address," pp. 275–79.
8. Elvin, chap. 14.
9. Skinner, "Presidential Address," pp. 285–86.
10. Quan Hansheng, *Zhongguo jingji shi luncong*, 1: 417–50.
11. Rawski, *Agricultural Change*, chap. 4.
12. Quan Hansheng, *Zhongguo jingji shi yanjiu*, 2: 85–158.
13. Qu Dajun, pp. 371, 626, 632–34.
14. Ibid., pp. 57–58.
15. On the deflation in the early nineteenth century, see Wang Yeh-chien, *Land Taxation*, p. 114.
16. [Map 2.1 was compiled by G. William Skinner largely on the basis of the research conducted by Leong. While not all the routes shown on this map and on Map 2.2 can be clearly documented, they represent the most likely scenarios given our current state of knowledge. In particular, it should not be assumed that the absence of an indication of Hakka migration on the map means that there was no such migration.]
17. [Chen Zhiping, p. 87.]
18. *Yongfu XZ* (1612), 1: 42b–43a.
19. Ibid.
20. *Ming Shenzong shilu*, 211: 8a (vol. 105).
21. *Yongfu XZ* (1612), 1: 29b.
22. *Yongfu XZ* (1748), 1: 19a–b.
23. American Board of Commissioners for Foreign Missions Papers, 16.3.5, vol. 22, Walker to Clark, May 8, 1873.
24. [See also Fu Yiling, *Ming-Qing fengjian shehui tudi suoyouzhi lungang*, p. 129.]
25. For *liaozhu* and *shanzhu*, see also Averill, p. 94, though the character for *liao* is different in his usage.
26. Xiong Renlin, pp. 23–27. This rare work is apparently available only at the Beijing Metropolitan Library. A biography of Xiong Renlin is found in Sun Yiwen, 58: 21b.
27. [Wurm, map B9.]
28. *Songyang XZ* (1926), 6: 24a–b; *Taishun XZ* (1879), 2: 20a–b; *Yunhe XZ* (1864), 15: 12b; Stubel and Li, p. 2. [See Segawa Masahisa for an argument that outside Hakka areas She people were distinguished at least partly by cultural characteristics shared by the Hakkas.]
29. *Huizhou FZ* (1595), 2: 55a–b.
30. *Yongle dadian*, 5343: 47.
31. Ibid.
32. *Boluo XZ* (1631), 1: 45b; *Huizhou FZ* (1595), 2: 51a.
33. Yang Kaidao, pp. 159–60.

34. *Huizhou FZ* (1881), 17: 44a; Watt, pp. 148–50.
35. *Huizhou FZ* (1881), 17: 45a.
36. *Huizhou FZ* (1688), 5: 14a–b.
37. *Longmen XZ* (1936), 17: 210.
38. *Conghua XZ* (1730), 2: 104a.
39. Ibid., 104b–5a.
40. *Ming-Qing shiliao, yibian*, 8: 784.
41. *He XZ* (1890), 7: 13a, (1934), 2: 4b.
42. *Sanjiang XZ* (1946), 2: 1a–9a.
43. *Rong XZ* (1897), 4: 26a.
44. *Luoding zhili ZZ* (1687), 1: 22b–23b, 36a–b, 37b–38a, 9: 9b; *Zhaoping XZ* (1934), 7: 2a, 5b.
45. *Tongzheng XZ* (1933), 7: 1b–2a.
46. *Zhaoqing FZ* (1673), 4: 7a–b, 32b–33a, 5: 8b, 21: 4b–5a. [Although there is no documentation on this point, the likely route taken by these migrants is shown on maps 2.1 and 2.2, as coming from the west.]
47. [Chen Zhiping, chap. 7, suggests that some migration might have taken place, but that the Hakkas were assimilated by the dominant Hoklos or people of Fuzhou. Most (though not all) of the examples he gives are, however, of an earlier date.]
48. *Taishun XZ* (1879), 2: 20a–b.
49. [This section on Taiwan has mostly been added by the editor, on the basis of some recently published work in Taiwan, notably: Chen Yundong, *Taiwan de kejiaren*, esp. pp. 95–112; Lin Zaifu, esp. pp. 26–37; and Yin Zhangyi, esp. pp. 349–80. Important earlier sources include Lamley and Lian Wenxi.]
50. [Chen Yundong, *Taiwan de kejiaren*, p. 96; Lian Wenxi, p. 1. There appears to be some problem with the analysis of the late seventeenth century, as Jiaying zhou was at the time part of Chaozhou prefecture.]
51. [Ng, p. 105.]
52. [Wang Yeh-chien, "Food Supply," p. 91; Ng, pp. 126–36.]
53. [Skinner, "Presidential Address," pp. 278–79.]
54. [Lamley, p. 292.]
55. [Chen Yundong, *Taiwan de kejiaren*, pp. 177, 196.
56. [Shepherd, p. 314.]
57. [Lian Wenxi, pp. 2–3.]
58. [This is the predominant interpretation in Lian Wenxi.]
59. [Yin Zhangyi, pp. 358, 362. Of course, the three explanations are by no means mutually exclusive, and all no doubt played a part in some areas.]
60. [Lamley, pp. 284, 309.]
61. [Yin Zhangyi, pp. 366–75.]
62. [Ibid., p. 376.]
63. *Zengcheng XZ* (1686), 1: 21a, (1754), 3: 10a–b.
64. *Dongguan XZ* (1689), 2.4.
65. *Xin'an XZ* (1688), 3: 15b.

66. *Hua XZ* (1687), 1: 36a–b.
67. *Heshan XZ* (1754), 12: unpag.; *Guangzhou FZ* (1759), 60: 28b.
68. *Zhupi yuzhi*, 52: 19b–20a. [Because it is not at all clear what route these migrants were taking when they were diverted to Xinning and other counties, this migration is not shown on Map 2.2; it is possible, but by no means certain, that this group was directed across the Lingnan core. It is unlikely that other groups took that route.]
69. *Xinning XZ* (1738/1804), 2: 38a.
70. Ibid., 44b.
71. Ibid., 38a–39b.
72. Ibid., 44b.
73. *Zengcheng XZ* (1754), 3: 9b–11b.
74. Ibid., 1: 14b–20b.
75. Luo Xianglin, *Kejia yanjiu daolun*, p. 297.
76. *Xinning XZ* (1738/1804), 2: 38b.
77. Myron L. Cohen; Lo Wan; Roberts.
78. *Kaiping XZ* (1823), 6: 23b–24a; *Xin'an XZ* (1819), 9: 12a–b; *Xinning XZ* (1839), 6: 33b, (1893), 267–68; *Guangdong tong zhi* (1822), *juan* 171.
79. Stauffer, p. 351; MacIver, introduction to first edition.
80. Skinner, "Regional Systems," p. 37.
81. Gu Zhi and Luo Xianglin both believe that the name *kejia* derived from *jike zhidu* of the Eastern Jin. Luo Xianglin, "Kejia yuanliu kao," pp. 61–62, 69 n. 106. In fact, as a Japanese scholar has shown, *ke* refers to serf-like tenants attached to the salary land of officials, granted in accordance with rank. Kusano Yasushi.
82. *Jiaying ZZ* (1898), 7: 86b.
83. Chen Yundong, *Kejiaren*, p. 12.
84. *Chixi XZ* (1920), pp. 51–52.
85. Huang Zanfa, p. 106.
86. *Jieyang XZ* (1779), 7: 7a–b, 9b.
87. *Yong'an XCZ* (1687), 14: unpag. The 1586 edition in manuscript was consulted at the Shanghai Library; the 1687 edition at the Zhongshan (Guangdong Provincial) Library in Guangzhou.
88. Ibid.
89. (Guangdong) *Changning XZ* (1756), 8: 5a–b, (1839), 8: 7a. These two editions were consulted at the Zhongshan Library. Two earlier editions were compiled in 1672 and 1731, neither of which seem to be extant. "Shuiyuan" was the name of a subsection of a county also called Changning (later Xunwu), which lay at the source of the East River on the Jiangxi side of the border. (Jiangxi) *Changning XZ* (1876), 1: 3b–4a.
90. (Guangdong) *Changning XZ* (1756), 8: 5a–b, (1839), 8: 7a.
91. *Dongguan XZ* (1689), 2.4: 3b; the 1720 edition is cited in *Guangzhou FZ* (1759), 60: 29a–b. In the latter, the natives condemned the Hakka tenants for violence toward rent collectors, for stealthily burying ancestral bones in another's grave to gain geomantic benefits, and for setting fire to forests in order to cause an artificial shortage of fuel and thereby drive up the price. "At the slightest provocation, the

conch shell is blown, summoning from far and near a great force of men armed with knives."

92. Qu Dajun, p. 337.
93. On the *baojia* system see, among others, Hsiao, chap. 3.
94. *Xinchang XZ* (1683), 2: 124b; *Xingguo XZ* (1711), 13: 9a–10b.
95. [Jiang Bingzhao, "Lun kejia," p. 107.]
96. [Li Mo, p. 121; Segawa Masahisa, p. 187.]
97. *Xunzhou FZ* (1874), 4: 14a–b, (1897), 56: 15a.
98. For a stimulating structural interpretation of how the social context of the "Guangxi Hakkas" made them receptive to the Christian message of Hong Xiuquan, see Kuhn, "Origins of the Taiping Vision," pp. 363–66.

3. FORMATION OF HAKKA ETHOS

1. [Chapters 3 and 4 are an edited version of Leong, "The Hakka Chinese of Lingnan." In his notes to the latter, Professor Leong thanked the participants in the "China in Transformation" workshop and Jerome Ch'en, David Pong, G. William Skinner, Alexander Woodside, and Tim Wright for their comments, and the Australian Research Grant Scheme for financial help. I am grateful to the University Press of America for permission to reprint a revised version of "The Hakka Chinese of Lingnan."]
2. This is noted by Lamley, p. 286. I have examined the records of the English Presbyterian Mission, which was active on the Hakka-Hoklo isogloss during the latter half of the nineteenth century.
3. *Yuanzhou FZ* (1760), 13: 14b–15b.
4. *Guangdong tong zhi* (1822), pp. 3094–96, 3098; *Xinning XZ* (1893), pp. 267–69; *Xin'an XZ* (1819), 9: 12a–b; *Kaiping XZ* (1823), 6: 23b–24a.
5. Eitel, "Ethnographical Sketches," p. 50.
6. Myron L. Cohen, pp. 252–57.
7. See, for example, the description of Hakka settlements in *Xin'an XZ* (1819), *juan* 2; *Zengcheng XZ* (1754), *juan* 3; *Xiangshan XZ* (1923), *juan* 3; *Gaoyao XZ* (1948), pp. 107–249; *Yangchun XZ* (1821).
8. *Zhupi yuzhi*, 4: 51b, Shiliha memorial.
9. Eitel, "Ethnographical Sketches," p. 50.
10. Fang Junyi, 12: 3b–4a.
11. Hsiao, pp. 184–205.
12. Kuhn, *Rebellion and Its Enemies*, pp. 136–37.
13. [The Taiping aspects of Map 3.1 were compiled by G. William Skinner from Laai, Michael, and Sherman. This brief section on the Taipings has been added by the editor mainly on the basis of secondary works and with the aid of Map 3.1.]

14. Michael, 3: 1200–1201.
15. Ibid., 1: 39.
16. Jen Yu-wen, pp. 10–11, 41.
17. Kuhn, "Origins of the Taiping Vision," pp. 363–65.
18. Michael, 1: 179.
19. Fang Junyi, 12: 3b; Roberts.
20. Fang Junyi, 12: 3a.
21. Eitel, "Ethnographical Sketches," p. 81.
22. Ibid., p. 82.
23. Eitel, "Outline History," p. 163.
24. Lo Wan.
25. Mayer's notes as incorporated in Eitel, "Outline History," p. 164.
26. Skinner, "Chinese Peasants," p. 280.
27. Barth, pp. 9–38.
28. Eitel, "Ethnographical Sketches," p. 13.
29. Gu Zhi, 2: 13a.
30. Campbell, p. 472.
31. Luo Xianglin, *Kejia shiliao huipian*, pp. 297–99. The following paragraphs, including the quotation, all come from this source.
32. Ibid., p. 299.
33. [See also Chen Zhiping, chap. 4.]
34. Luo Xianglin, *Zhongguo zupu yanjiu*, pp. 157–70; *Pinghe XZ* (1719), 12: 37a–b, 38b–39a; *Chenghai XZ* (1815), 6: 14.
35. Eberhard, pp. 61–63; Huang Foyi. [See also *Nanxiong XZ* (1991), pp. 906–13, and Chen Zhiping, p. 30.]
36. Eberhard, pp. 66–67, Piton; Luo Xianglin, *Kejia shiliao huipian*, pp. 377–87. [See also Chen Zhiping, pp. 36–37, 40, 65, 78, and *passim* for examples of lineages claiming origins in Shibicun.]
37. Qu Xuanying, 1: 98–99; Li Youning and Zhang Yufa, p. 1515.
38. Luo Xianglin, *Kejia shiliao huipian*, p. 298.
39. Ibid., p. 297.
40. Lo Wan, p. 98.
41. Luo Xianglin, *Kejia yanjiu daolun*, pp. 5, 27 n. 19.
42. Lin Daquan, pp. 131–35.
43. *Gaoyao XZ* (1863), 2: 29b–30b; *Xinhui XXZ* (1870), 10: 7; *Xinning XZ* (1893), 8: 6b.
44. *Gaoyao XZ* (Xuantong), 25: 39b.
45. *Yangjiang XZ* (1925), 7: 4, 20, 21: 94b–100a.
46. *Enping XZ* (1934), 22: 32b, 34b–35a.
47. *Zhenping XZ* (1880), pp. 331–400.

48. [But note the discussion in Chapter 1, which indicates that this is not now the consensus of modern scholarship.]
49. *Jiaying ZZ* (1898), 7: 84b–91a.

4. ETHNICITY AND NATIONALISM

1. *Meishui shizhuan*, preface by Huang Zunxian.
2. Luo Xianglin, *Kejia yanjiu daolun*, pp. 5–6, 28.
3. Campbell, pp. 471–72.
4. Luo Xianglin, *Kejia yanjiu daolun*, p. 6.
5. Qiu Fengjia's foreword is preserved in Weng Huidong, 4: 182–83. I have not been able to consult the pamphlet itself.
6. According to Zhong Yonghe, the Yue people were descendants of the Yue king Gou Jian, who in turn was descended from the great ruler Yu of antiquity. The essay, originally entitled *Tu ke yuanliu kao* (Origins of natives and Hakkas), was begun in 1900, prompted by the author's discovery of a racial slur on Hakkas in the county gazetteer of Sihui. It was first published in a Hong Kong newspaper, and then in 1905, on the occasion of the school text controversy, a revised version was published in Swatow and Canton newspapers. It was reissued in 1921 under a new title, *Yuesheng minzu kaoyuan* (Origins of the peoples of Guangdong province), during another textbook controversy. The 1921 edition was consulted at the Zhongshan Provincial Library of Guangdong.
7. Sun Yat-sen's Hakka origin was first asserted in 1933 in Luo Xianglin, *Kejia yanjiu daolun*, pp. 263–65; for a challenge to this long-accepted view, see Tan Bi'an. [The issue has reemerged, for instance in Yang Qingping; it should be noted that Sun Yat-sen did not speak Hakka as his native tongue and thus an identification of any Hakka ancestry becomes somewhat academic.]
8. Rhoads, pp. 101–4.
9. Gu Zhi, 2: 18b.
10. Rhoads, pp. 182, 186.
11. Ibid., pp. 235–36; United States, Department of State, Decimal File 893.00/954, Bergholz to U.S. Minister in Peking, 15 Dec. 1911.
12. United States, Department of State, Decimal File 893.00/891, Tours to U.S. Minister in Peking, 16 Nov. 1911.
13. Ibid.
14. Rhoads, pp. 237–38, 248–49.
15. Friedman, pp. 292–93.
16. Luo Xianglin, *Kejia yanjiu daolun*, p. 6.
17. Rhoads, p. 251.
18. Luo Xianglin, *Kejia yanjiu daolun*, p. 29.

19. Ibid., p. 7.
20. "Kanton kyakka minzoku no kenkyū," p. 357.
21. Ibid., pp. 346–47.
22. For a biography of Chen Jitang, see Boorman, 1: 160–63.
23. Ibid., pp. 213–17.
24. Ibid., pp. 56–61.
25. "Kanton kyakka minzoku no kenkyū," p. 315.
26. Ibid., pp. 348–49.
27. Ibid.
28. Ibid., p. 343.
29. Ibid., p. 344.
30. Luo Xianglin, *Kejia yanjiu daolun*, pp. 10, 31. The incident was followed by another spurt of Hakka ethnic affirmation. Gu Zhi, a Mei xian Hakka and professor at Zhongshan University, penned a spirited "Hakka reply" with the view of correcting Cantonese misconceptions. It was the most complete catalog to date of Hakka cultural and historical greatness, their impeccable ancestry, prestigious language, academic achievements, and famous personalities, and a proud record of patriotic antiforeignism.

5. POLICIES TOWARD MIGRATION

1. The Pengmin have only recently received detailed attention. The most sophisticated treatment to date is the substantial article by Averill. The Pengmin role in the opening of the Middle Yangzi highlands, first highlighted by Ho Ping-ti, is also dealt with in a work by Sun Lung-kee on the upper Hanshui basin. On the mainland, the chief investigator has been Fu Yiling, who in the 1960s included the Pengmin in his studies of tenant revolts; Fu has also examined the Pengmin in relation to the sprouts of capitalism. Fu Yiling, *Ming-Qing nongcun shehui jingji* and *Ming-Qing shehui jingji shi lunwen ji*, pp. 3–102.
2. Xiong Renlin, pp. 23–27; *Nanping XZ* (1810), 8: 10a–11b. The Japanese scholar Tajiri Minoru examines the economics of the indigo industry of Jiangxi, in which the Pengmin figured prominently.
3. *Hubu zeli*, 3: 9b–10a.
4. *Yichun XZ* (1683), 6: 3a.
5. *Chuzhou FZ* (1635), 1: 16b–17a.
6. Ibid., 21b.
7. For another classification, see Averill, p. 98.
8. Ibid., p. 93. [See also Cao (1), p. 25, though only on occasion does Cao highlight the term "Pengmin" or the issue of Hakka identity.]
9. Counties in which Hakka migrants were described as Pengmin included Guishan (Huiyang), Dongguan, Boluo, Longhua, Conghua, and Haifeng. To the north and west, the four counties on the Lingnan–Middle Yangzi frontier (Guiyang zhou, Linwu, Lanshan, and Jianghua), as well as other counties in the northern and western regions of Lingnan (He xian, Rong xian, and Xiang zhou) also

reported the in-migration of Pengmin, who were almost certainly Hakka. See sources listed in Table 2.2.

10. Skinner, "Introduction," pp. 19–23, and "Cities and the Hierarchy of Local Systems," pp. 301–44.
11. Liu Min, "Shilun Ming-Qing shiqi huji zhidu."
12. Ibid., p. 221.
13. Ibid., p. 223.
14. Ibid., p. 225.
15. Ibid., p. 227.
16. Kwang-Ching Liu, pp. 202–3.
17. Ho, p. 34.
18. *Zhupi yuzhi*, 7: 5b; Terada Takanobu, p. 138.
19. Zhang Tingyu, 4: 4a–5a; *Gongzhong dang Yongzheng chao zouzhe*, 2: 439.
20. See Chapter 7.
21. Liu Min, "Shilun Ming-Qing shiqi huji zhidu," p. 225.
22. Liu Min, "Lun Qingdai pengmin de huji," p. 20; on "preferment" posts, see Watt, p. 46.
23. *Qinding da Qing huidian shili*, 158: 3b–4a.
24. Chang Chung-li, pp. 80–81, 82.
25. On separate examination quotas for the Lingnan Hakkas, see Chapter 2.
26. Morita Akira.
27. Hoang, p. 102, as quoted in Taiwan Sōtokufu, 2: 107.
28. *Huangchao tongzhi*, p. 7251.
29. Terada Takanobu.
30. For a more recent discussion, based on more limited sources but arriving at much the same conclusion as my own, see Liu Min, "Lun Qingdai pengmin de huji."
31. *Zhupi yuzhi*, 7: 8b.
32. Ibid., 39: 24b–25b.
33. Cited in Hsiao, pp. 46–47.
34. *Qinding da Qing huidian shili*, 158: 4a–b.
35. *Zhupi yuzhi*, 57: 61b.
36. *Qinding da Qing huidian shili*, 158: 2a.
37. Ibid., 5b.

6. MIGRATION TO THE GAN YANGZI

1. Satake Yasuhiko, p. 102. In his earlier model, Skinner had the Gan Yangzi area as part of the Middle Yangzi macroregion. There is more material on the development of the Middle Yangzi; see, for example, Tan Qixiang, "Zhongguo neidi yimin shi," pp. 58, 82; Rawski, *Agricultural Change*, pp. 101–38; Ho, pp. 143–53.
2. Skinner, "Introduction," p. 11.
3. Elvin, pp. 131, 133.
4. Shiba Yoshinobu, pp. 66–67.
5. Ibid., pp. 64–65.

6. Ibid., pp. 100–101, 104, 121, 125. [Zhu Cishou, p. 479.]
7. Shiba Yoshinobu, pp. 100, 198.
8. Ibid. p. 13.
9. Ibid. pp. 93, 98.
10. Wang Yeh-chien, *Land Taxation*, p. 114.
11. Rawski, *Agricultural Change*, p. 104.
12. Perkins, p. 154.
13. [This pattern, and those in Maps and Tables 8.1 and 9.1, became clearer after the compilation of the maps by G. William Skinner. These remarks have, therefore, been added by the editor.]
14. [This last type of information is mainly taken from Cao (2). However, the data are grouped by reign periods, with Shunzhi and Kangxi listed together, so that it is impossible to distinguish between the second and third waves outlined below.]
15. Ho, p. 145.
16. *Ming Muzong shilu*, 26: 3a (vol. 183). [Cao (1), p. 25.]
17. [Cao (1), p. 25.]
18. *Xinchang XZ* (1683), 2: 107a–b.
19. *Yichun XZ* (1683), 6: 23a, (1871), 5: 17b–18a.
20. *Ganzhou FZ* (1621), 7: 35a. A similar immigration occurred in the neighboring prefecture of Nan'an; see *Nan'an FZ* (1609), 13: 12b, 15: 17a.
21. Wei Li, 8: 100b. *Ningdu XZ* (1592), 3: 11b speaks of all the land in the county being farmed by outsiders.
22. *Shicheng XZ* (1660), 8: 8b–9a; Fu Yiling, *Ming-Qing nongcun shehui jingji*, p. 107. [Oh Kem-sung, pp. 1090–91.]
23. [*Shicheng XZ* (1990), p. 504.]
24. *Da Qing Shengzu Ren (Kangxi) huangdi shilu*, pp. 670, 677, 680, 814–15, 841, 862, 898.
25. *Pingxiang XZ* (1935), *juan* 3–4. Besides Pingxiang, the gazetteers of Yifeng, Luling, and Liuyang contain similar information, but the picture given is much less clear. In Yifeng, of the twelve families and lineages recorded in the 1917 edition, six had arrived in the early Qing, six in the mid-Qing, there being no trace left of late Ming immigrants. *Xinchang XXZ* (1917) (*Yansheng*), *juan* 2. In Luling, of the thirty recorded in 1920, three had arrived in the Ming, twelve at some unspecified time in the Qing, three in the early Qing, nine in the mid-Qing, one in the late Qing, and two were unknown. *Luling XZ* (1920), *juan* 8–11. In Liuyang, of the twenty-six recorded in 1907, six had arrived in the early Qing, nineteen in the mid-Qing, and one was unknown. *Liuyang XTZ* (1907), p. 89 ff.
26. [*Jing'an XZ* (1989), pp. 113–17.]
27. [Cao (2), pp. 34–35.]

28. [*Wanzai XZ* (1988), p. 66. The number should not be taken literally.]
29. [*Jing'an XZ* (1989), p. 112.]
30. [Cao (1), pp. 25–26.]
31. [Ibid., p. 32.]
32. [Ibid., pp. 33–34.]
33. [Ibid., p. 35.]
34. [Ibid., pp. 36–37.]
35. [Cao (2), p. 17.]
36. *Gongzhong dang Yongzheng chao zouzhe*, 1: 199.
37. [Cao (2), pp. 22–26.]
38. Personal interview, Aug. 1982.
39. Ho, p. 148. [See also Zhang Jianmin, p. 71.]
40. See also Averill, pp. 90–91.
41. *Ganzhou FZ* (1873), 33: 1a; *Xingguo XZ* (1711), 17: 2a, 14: 15a–21a; *Longquan XZ* (1824), 18: 13a–b.
42. *Ruijin XZ* (1683), 2: 7b–8b, (1710), 2: 9a–10b, 4: 52a, (1753), *juan* 2. Ruijin is now a purely Hakka county. Liu Shengkui.
43. Duan Congguang, pp. 33–34. [Cao Shuji, "Ming-Qing shiqi de liumin he Gan-nan shanqu de kaifa," p. 28.]
44. Duan Congguang, pp. 35–36.
45. *Pingxiang XZ* (1935), 2: 30b.
46. [See also Cao Shuji, "Ming-Qing shiqi de liumin he Gan-nan shanqu de kaifa," p. 38].
47. [Wurm, map B15.]
48. [*Shicheng XZ* (1990), p. 504.]
49. Wu Rongchi, p. 32.
50. [*Chongyi XZ* (1989), p. 568.]
51. [*Lianhua XZ* (1989), p. 693.]
52. [Cao (1), p. 31, says that 70–80% of the population of Longquan were Hakka, and that the situation was similar in Chongyi and Shangrao; see also Benton, p. 380.]
53. [*Tonggu XZ* (1989), p. 654.]
54. [*Wuning XZ* (1990), p. 726.]
55. [*Wanzai XZ* (1988), p. 63.]
56. [*Yichun SZ* (1990), p. 873.]
57. Luo Xianglin, *Kejia yanjiu daolun*, p. 115 n. 3.
58. Wu Zongci, p. 32b. (Seen in the Jiangxi Provincial Library, Nanchang.)
59. *Wanzai XZ* (1940), *juan* 3–4.
60. [Cao (2), p. 36.]
61. [*Jing'an XZ* (1989), pp. 112–17, 731.]

7. ETHNIC CONFLICT IN THE GAN YANGZI

1. *Wanzai XZ* (1872), 7: 38b.
2. For example, see the *shizu* chapters in *Pingxiang XZ* (1935), chaps. 3–4.
3. The term *shanpeng* ("mountain shack people") appeared as far back as Tang times and referred to mountain dwellers in Henan province. They lived by hunting and trading in animal skins and medicinal herbs. Han Chinese lowlanders

regarded them as non-Chinese, and therefore despised them. Hino Kaizaburō, 1: 493–516.

4. *Yichun XZ* (1683), 6: 23a.
5. *Zhupi yuzhi*, 7: 8a.
6. See Averill, pp. 118–22.
7. *Yuanzhou FZ* (1760), 9: 26a, 15: 13a–14b; *Wanzai XZ* (1872), 3: 11a–b, (1940), 7.2: 5b.
8. *Yuanzhou FZ* (1760), 15: 15b–18a; *Yichun XZ* (1871), 5: 10a; *Pingxiang XZ* (1683), 1: 18a–b. [See also Watanabe Osamu; Xie Guozhen, *Qingchu nongmin qiyi*, p. 354.]
9. *Yuanzhou FZ* (1760), 15: 18b; *Yichun XZ* (1871), 5: 10a–11b; *Fenyi XZ* (1822), 14: 11a–b, (1940), 15: 4b–5a; *Wanzai XZ* (1872), 14: 6b–7b, (1940), 7.2: 6b–8a; *Pingxiang XZ* (1683), 1: 19a–b, 6: 16a–17b. [Fu Yiling, *Ming-Qing fengjian shehui tudi suoyouzhi*, p. 133; Xie Guozhen, *Qingchu nongmin qiyi*, pp. 352–54.]
10. *Yuanzhou FZ* (1760), 15: 19a–20a; *Wanzai XZ* (1773), 12: 11b–12a; *Xinchang XZ* (1683), 2: 8b, 10a; *Gongzhong dang Yongzheng chao zouzhe*, 1: 199. [Xie Guozhen, *Qingchu nongmin qiyi*, p. 355.]
11. *Yuanzhou FZ* (1760), 15: 15a, 17a, 18a.
12. *Yichun XZ* (1683), 6: 18a, (1871), 5: 17b–18b.
13. *Yuanzhou FZ* (1760), 15: 19a–b, (1871), 14: 8a. The authorities gave no credence to this view, being in possession of depositions from Wen and his associates. *Gongzhong dang Yongzheng chao zouzhe*, 1: 199.
14. Xie Guozhen, *Ming-Qing biji*, pp. 97–98; Duan Congguang, pp. 33–34. [For a more recent interpretation, see Fu Yiling, *Ming-Qing fengjian shehui tudi suoyouzhi*, pp. 129–31.]
15. Shi Runzhang, 2: 1a–b.
16. Ibid., 8: 7a–b.
17. *Yichun XZ* (1683), 6: 23a–26a. [Xie Guozhen, *Qingchu nongmin qiyi*, p. 356.]
18. *Fenyi XZ* (1822), 14: 11a–b, (1940), 15: 4b–5a; *Wanzai XZ* (1872), 10: 37b; *Pingxiang XZ* (1683), 6: 16a, (1935), 7: 7b. [Xie Guozhen, *Qingchu nongmin qiyi*, p. 356.]
19. *Gongzhong dang Yongzheng chao zouzhe*, 1: 199.
20. The new policy was the result of a memorial by Zhang Tingyu, president of the Board of Revenue. See Zhang Tingyu, 4: 4b–5b. On its implementation, see *Zhupi yuzhi*, 7: 8a–b.
21. The example of the mainly immigrant city of Hankou is discussed in Rowe, pp. 236–41.
22. *Yuanzhou FZ* (1760), 13: 14b–15b.
23. Ibid., 13: 15b–16b. This gazetteer also reports that the separate quota was used for the first time in Wanzai in 1731, in Pingxiang in 1742, and in Yichun in 1744.
24. *Yuanzhou FZ* (1760), 13: 14b–15b. See Chapter 5 for a discussion of these issues in relation to the social status of the Pengmin.
25. *Wanzai XZ* (1872), 7: 35b–37a.

26. Ibid., 7: 37a–39b.
27. An original leaflet distributed by the prefect, kindly loaned to the author by Mr. Wang Zichen of the history department, Jaingxi Teachers College, Nanchang.
28. *Wanzai XZ* (1872), 7: 38b.
29. Shi Runzhang, 2: 3b–4a.
30. *Yichun XZ* (1871), 1: 11b–12a.
31. Ibid., 11b.
32. *Pingxiang XZ* (1872), 1: 7a; *Fengxin XZ* (1826), 1: 8b; *Yining ZZ* (1824), 2: 3a.
33. *Yichun XZ* (1871), 1: 4b–7b.
34. Ibid., 9a–15a.
35. Ibid., 13a.
36. Wu Zongci, p. 32a.
37. Mao Zedong, *Mao Zedong ji*, 2: 54–55.
38. [Benton, pp. 382–83.]
39. Information gathered on a field trip in August 1982.
40. *Shangyou XZ* (1881), 15: 1a–b, 16: 46b; *Nan'an FZ* (1710), 16: 12b–13a, 15a–16b.
41. [Oh Kem-sung, pp. 1088–89; Xie Guozhen, *Qingchu nongmin qiyi*, p. 286.]
42. [Xie Guozhen, *Qingchu nongmin qiyi*, p. 287.]
43. *Shangyou XZ* (1881), 15: 1a–b, 16: 46b.
44. Ibid., 1b.
45. Ibid., 2a.
46. Ibid.
47. Ibid., 16: 15a–16b; *Nankang XZ* (1823), 7: 6b; *Nan'an FZ* (1710), 16: 12b–13a, 15a–16b.
48. This information and that below is from *Shangyou XZ* (1881), *juan* 15.
49. [Kuhn, *Soulstealers*.]
50. [In addition to the material in *Shangyou XZ* (1881), *juan* 15, a detailed account, originating in the *Zhupi yuzhi*, of this incident can be found in Zhongguo renmin daxue Qingshi yanjiu suo, 2: 664–65.]
51. [For a recent analysis of the role of Hakkas in the Chinese Communist movement both before and after 1949, see Erbaugh.]
52. Kong Yongsong and Qiu Songqing, pp. 105–9.
53. Ibid., p. 112.
54. Mao Zedong, *Mao Zedong xuanji*, 1: 73–74. [See also Benton, pp. 380–81.]
55. The following are some of the Hakkas for whom biographical data are available (see Klein and Clark, pp. 54–58, 201–2, 285–86, 485–87, 632–34, 917–19, 968–70) whose careers began in the Jiangxi Soviet period:

    Fu Lianzhang: native of Changting, Fujian; joined the Red Army as a doctor in 1927 in Fujian; president of the Chinese Medical Association from 1950.

    Li Jingquan: native of Huichang, Jiangxi; political commissar in the First Front Army in 1931; chairman of the Chengdu Military Control Commission and deputy political commissar of the Southwest Military Region under Deng Xiaoping in 1950.

    Liu Yalou: native of Wuping, Fujian; joined the Red Army and the CCP in 1929; commander of the PLA airforce in 1949–50.

    Liu Yongsheng: native of Shanghang, Fujian; leader of a guerrilla band in western Fujian in 1931; deputy PLA commander of the Fujian Military District in 1950;

chairman of the Fujian Provincial Revolutionary Committee in 1968. See *Who's Who in Communist China*, pp. 468–69.

Qiu Chuangcheng: native of Ruijin, Jiangxi; joined the Red Army during the Jiangxi Soviet period; deputy commander of the PLA artillery force in 1952.

Wang Ping: native of Ruijin, Jiangxi; participated in the Long March; chairman of the Military Control Commission in Datong, Chahar, 1949–52.

Yang Chengwu: native of Changting, Fujian; participated in the western Fujian revolt of 1929; political commissar in the Red Army First Corps in 1932; vice-commander of the PLA Beijing-Tianjin Garrison Command in 1950; acting chief of staff in 1966; garrison commander of Beijing in 1968; commander of the Fuzhou military district in 1982.

Zhang Dingcheng: native of Yongding, Fujian; chairman of the Western Fujian Soviet Government and member of the CCP Sixth Central Committee in 1930; PLA commander of the Central China Military District in 1946; chairman of Fujian in 1949–54; subsequently chief procurator.

[Erbaugh also argues that prominent leaders such as Deng Xiaoping, Yang Shangkun, Zhu De, Zhang Guotao, Chen Yi, Wang Zhen, and Hu Yaobang were Hakkas, though she stresses the problems of identification.]

8. PENGMIN IN THE LOWER YANGZI

1. [Major new contributions to the study of this area have been Osborne, "Barren Mountains" and "The Local Politics of Land Reclamation." Osborne both builds on and supplements (and occasionally corrects) Sow-Theng Leong's manuscript that forms the basis of this chapter; she also brings a somewhat, though not totally, different set of concerns and questions to the material. I have left the author's manuscript basically as it was, making only a few minor corrections and amendments on the basis of Osborne's dissertation.]
2. [Editor's remarks added after compilation of the maps by G. William Skinner.]
3. Gu Yanwu, 9: 9b–11a.
4. Ibid., excerpts from *Fengshu* (1621).
5. See Table 8.1 and Map 8.1.
6. [Fu Yiling, *Ming-Qing fengjian shehui tudi suoyouzhi*, p. 133.]
7. After the Taiping Rebellion, population movement of a different kind and scale occurred in the extensively depopulated Lower Yangzi. Immigrants called *kemin*, coming from other congested provinces, repopulated the lowland core itself, in a free-for-all atmosphere, giving rise to ethnic organization and interethnic conflict on a variegated and massive scale. See Wang Tianjiang. However, there is no evidence to suggest that most, or even a substantial portion, of these migrants were Hakkas. Ironically, in some parts of the Lower Yangzi, such as the counties of Yanzhou prefecture, which were not in the line of direct advance of new settlers,

officials suggested inviting the Pengmin down from the hills to bring waste lowland back under cultivation. Dai Pan, 1a–4a.

8. See Table 8.1. [See also Osborne, "The Local Politics of Land Reclamation," p. 6.]
9. [Osborne, "The Local Politics of Land Reclamation," pp. 6–7.]
10. Refugees from north of the Yangzi were identified as coming from Tongcheng, Qianshan, Susong, Taihu, Shucheng, Huoshan, and Anqing. Those from the northern Southeast Coast originated from the prefectures of Wenzhou, Taizhou, and Chuzhou. Tao Zhu, 26: 4a, 11b.
11. [Xiong Renlin, pp. 23–27. See Chapter 2; also, Liu Xiusheng, p. 54; Lin Renchuan, p. 202.]
12. *Nanping XZ* (1810), 8: 10a–11b.
13. [Wurm, map B15; *Yanshan XZ* (1990), p. 625.]
14. [Cao (2), pp. 28–30.]
15. See Chapter 2.
16. *Nanping XZ* (1810), 8: 10a–11b.
17. *Guangxin FZ* (1783), 2: 68b; *Yushan XZ* (1823), 12: 1b–2a, (1873), 1: 21b.
18. *Shicheng XZ* (1745), 3: 24a–b.
19. It is this contractual relationship with a cash nexus that has attracted the attention of Chinese Marxist historians. See Feng Erkang; Fu Yiling, "Capitalism in Chinese Agriculture."
20. *Huizhou FZ* (1827), 4.2: 42a.
21. Gao Tingyao, 1: 33b–34a.
22. [See Cao (2), pp. 30–33.]
23. Skinner, "Introduction," p. 17.
24. [Osborne, "The Local Politics of Land Reclamation," provides further case studies and analysis of these issues.]
25. *Deqing XZ* (1808), 4: 2a–b.
26. *Qimen XZ* (1873), 12: 3b, 11b–12a; *Jurong XZ* (1904), 6, pt. 1: 16b–17a; *Huizhou FZ* (1827), 4.2: 43a.
27. Cited in *Qimen XZ* (1873), 12: 1a–b; reports of damage to agriculture are found in *Jixi XZ* (1810), pp. 350–51; *Xuancheng XZ* (1888), 2; *She XZ* (1812), *juan* 11; *Huizhou FZ* (1827), 4.2: 39b–46a; *Jingde XZ* (1808), 5: 46a; *Changhua XZ* (1823), 3: 6a–b; *Xi'an XZ* (1811), 21: 2b–3a; *Jurong XZ* (1904), 6, pt. 1: 16b.
28. [See Osborne, "Barren Mountains," p. 217 for correction of the original identification of this official.]
29. Mei Zengliang, 10: 3a–b.
30. Zhang Jian, 2: 8b–9a.
31. Fang Chun, *Chusong shanfang zazhu* cited in *Huizhou FZ* (1827), 4.2: 45b–46a.
32. *Qinding da Qing huidian shili*, 158: 8a.
33. *Huizhou FZ* (1827), 4.2: 42b.
34. Ibid.
35. The episode is recounted with some pride in Gao Tingyao, 1: 32b–35a.

36. *Huizhou FZ* (1827), 4.2: 43a–45a; Tao Zhu, 26: 7b–8a.
37. *Huizhou FZ* (1827), 4.2: 42a, 43a; Gao Tingyao, 1: 34b.
38. *Huizhou FZ* (1827), 4.2: 43a.
39. Ibid., 39a.
40. Tao Zhu, 26: 1a–10b.
41. Ibid., 4a.
42. Ibid., 1a–3a.
43. Ibid., 5a–6a.
44. Ibid., 7a–10b.

9. PENGMIN IN THE HANSHUI BASIN

1. Ho, pp. 149–53; Rawski, "Agricultural Development"; Sun Lung-kee.
2. Fan Shuzhi; Lai Jiadu. [See also Huang Guoqiang.]
3. Lai Jiadu, pp. 53–54; Yan Ruyi, 11: 30b.
4. Parsons, p. 46.
5. Liu Min, "Lun Qingdai pengmin de huji," p. 21.
6. Skinner, "Introduction," p. 16; see also Rowe.
7. [See Sun Daren, p. 135; Xu Dixin and Wu Chengming, p. 444.]
8. *Xixiang XZ* (1828), pp. 50–52; Yan Ruyi, 11: 28a.
9. *Zhen'an XZ* (1755), 3: 3b, 12a.
10. *Luonan XZ* (Guangxu ed.), 3: 1a–b; *Shiquan XZ* (1849), 2: 25b–26a.
11. [Wurm, map B15.]
12. Ho, p. 149.
13. *Shiquan XZ* (1849), 4: 66a.
14. *Dingyuan TZ* (1879), 8: 1b, 3b.
15. Rawski, "Agricultural Development," pp. 65–66.
16. Yan Ruyi, 5: 15a, 14: 49a.
17. Ibid., 14: 54b; *Feng XZ* (1892), 8: 5a.
18. *Xunyang XZ* (1870), 11: 15a–16a.
19. Yan Ruyi, 11: 18b–19a.
20. *Xunyang XZ* (1870), 11: 16a.
21. *Da Qing Xuanzong Cheng (Daoguang) huangdi shilu*, 10: 20b–22a; *Qing shi liezhuan*, 40: 5b–10a.
22. Yan Ruyi, 11: 19b.
23. Ibid., 9: 1a–4b; see also Xu Dixin and Wu Chengming, pp. 433–51.
24. Yan Ruyi, 9: 4b–5b.
25. Ibid., 4b, 5b–7b, 15b–17a.
26. Ibid., 15b.
27. On the frontier-like society of regional peripheries, see Skinner, "Cities and the Hierarchy of Local Systems," p. 322.
28. Yan Ruyi, 11: 19a; *Dingyuan TZ* (1879), 4: 8b.
29. Yan Ruyi, 11: 31a–b.
30. *Feng XZ* (1892), 8: 1b–2a; *Ningqiang zhou XTZ* (late Qing ed.), pp. 46–49.
31. Yan Ruyi, 11: 19a–b; *Xixiang XZ* (1828), p. 31.
32. *Shiquan XZ* (1849), 2: 26a; *Pingli XZ* (1756), 3: 28a; Yan Ruyi, 14: 54b.
33. Yan Ruyi, 14: 54b.

34. *Feng XZ* (1892), 1: 14a; *Xiaoyi TZ* (1883), 3: 2b; *Xixiang XZ* (1828), p. 66.
35. Wei Yuan, 6: 5b, 11b.
36. Sun Lung-kee, pp. 19–21.
37. Yan Ruyi, 9: 9a–14b.
38. Ibid., 14: 17b.
39. Ibid., 11: 23b–24a.
40. A recent study identifies the *guolu* as the Gelao secret society and argues a common origin with the Triads of South China. The author puts forward the hypothesis that Hakka immigrants from Guangdong to Sichuan, where the *guolu* were mainly active, provided the link between the Tiandi (Heaven and Earth) and Gelao (Elder Brothers) societies. He adduces some evidence to show that the names of these societies were linked in Hakka speech. Tiandi appears in some documents as "T'iam-t'ai" (Hakka, meaning "adding younger brothers"), which bears an obvious relation to Gelao. *Guolu*, according to the author, is a local corruption of "Gelao." See Hu Zhusheng.
41. Yan Ruyi, 11: 21b–22a, 42a.
42. Jones and Kuhn, pp. 136–44; Sun Lung-kee, p. 32.
43. Jones and Kuhn, p. 144.
44. Yan Ruyi, 11: 24b–25a.
45. Ibid., 28b–29a.
46. Ibid., 26a, 31a–32b, 33a–34a, 37a.
47. Ibid., 37a.
48. Ibid., 14: 54b–55a.
49. Ibid., 11: 25a–b.
50. Ibid., 41a.
51. Ibid., 14: 17b.
52. Ibid., 22b, 24a, 25b, 26b.
53. Wang Yeh-chien, *Land Taxation*, p. 18.
54. Extracted from Yan Ruyi, 14: 3a–69b. The relevant *ting* and their dates of creation are as follows: Ningxia, Xiaoyi, Liuba, and Hanyin (the last converted from a *xian*) in 1782; Dingyuan in 1802; Zhuanping, Chengkou, and Baihe in 1821; Foping in 1824.
55. Skinner, "Cities and the Hierarchy of Local Systems," pp. 309–10.
56. Watt, p. 47.
57. Yan Ruyi, 14: 55a.
58. Ibid., 6a, 12a.
59. Ibid., 16a–19a for Zhuo Bingtian's memorial of 1821. It shows a notable similarity of phrasing to Yan's essay. The latter is not included in the collection but is found in He Changling, 82: 9a–b.
60. Ho, p. 148; Chen Qiaoyi.

Publications by Sow-Theng Leong

Books

Sino-Soviet Relations: The First Phase, 1917–1920. Contemporary China Centre Papers, no. 1. Canberra: Australian National University Press, 1971. Translated into Japanese as "Shoki Chū-Sō kankei no ichi kyokumen" 初期中蘇關系の一局面. *Aziya kenkyū* アジア研究 (Asiatic Studies) 17.3/4 (Jan. 1971): 51–88.

Sino-Soviet Diplomatic Relations, 1917–1926. Canberra and Honolulu: Australian National University Press and University of Hawaii Press, 1976.

Articles

"Wang T'ao and Self-Strengthening and Reform in the Late Ch'ing Period." *Papers on China* 17 (Dec. 1963): 101–130.

"Sun Yat-sen and the Bolsheviks." *Transactions of the International Conference of Orientalists in Japan* 14 (1969): 39–53.

Biographies of Chang T'ai-lei, Ch'en Kung-po, Ch'en Tu-hsiu, Ch'ü Ch'iu-pai, Li Ta-chao, P'eng P'ai, Su Chao-cheng, Teng Chung-hsia, and Yang Ming-chai. In Donald Klein and Anne B. Clark, eds., *Biographic Dictionary of Chinese Communism.* Cambridge, Mass: Harvard University Press, 1971.

"The Tsarist Legacy in North Manchuria, 1895–1917." *Papers on Far Eastern History* 6 (Sept. 1972): 63–90.

"China and the Siberian Intervention." *Papers on Far Eastern History* 7 (Mar. 1973): 101–44.

"Chinese Scholarship on Sino-Russian Relations: A Bibliographical Essay." *Papers on Far Eastern History* 14 (Sept. 1976): 91–122.

"Traditional Issues in Contemporary Sino-Soviet Relations Since 1949." In Ngok Lee and Leung Chi-keung eds, *China: Issues and Challenges,* vol. 1, pp. 117–143. Hong Kong: Centre for Asian Studies, University of Hong Kong, 1979.

"Kejia lishi xintan" 客家歷史新談 (Hakka history reinterpreted). *Zhongguo shehui jingji shi yanjiu* 中國社會經濟史研究 (Studies in Chinese social and economic history) 1.1 (1982): 101–5.

"The Sino-Soviet Border." *Obozrenie* 3 (Feb. 1983): 8–11.

"The Hakka Chinese of Lingnan: Ethnicity and Social Change in Modern China." In David Pong and Edmund Fung, eds., *Ideal and Reality: Social and Political Change in Modern China, 1860–1949*, pp. 287–326. Lanham, Md.: University Press of America, 1985.

"Sun Yat-sen's International Orientation: The Soviet Phase, 1917–1925." In J. Y. Wong, ed., *Sun Yat-sen: His International Ideas and International Connections, with Special Emphasis on Their Relevance Today*, pp. 53–90. Sydney: Wild Peony, 1987.

Translations

Previously untranslated writings of Mao Zedong. In Stuart R. Schram, *The Political Thought of Mao Tse-tung*. New York: Praeger, 1969.

Fu Yiling. "On the Laws of Development of Capitalism in Chinese Agriculture." *Modern China* 6.4 (Oct. 1982): 311–316.

Bibliography

Where possible, dates of local gazetteers have been given to accord with those in Zhongguo kexue yuan Beijing tianwen tai 中國科學院北京天文臺, *Zhongguo difang zhi lianhe mulu* 中國地方志聯合目錄 (Union catalog of Chinese local histories). Beijing: Zhonghua shuju, 1985.

American Board of Commissioners for Foreign Missions Papers. Houghton Library, Harvard University.

Anji xian zhi 安吉縣志 (Gazetteer of Anji county). 1874.

Anji zhou zhi 安縣州志 (Gazetteer of Anji department). 1750.

Ankang xian zhi 安康縣志 (Gazetteer of Ankang county). 1815, rep. 1853.

Anyuan xian zhi 安原縣志 (Gazetteer of Anyuan county). 1751.

Averill, Stephen C. "The Shed People and the Opening of the Yangzi Highlands." *Modern China* 9.1 (Jan. 1983): 84–126.

Baker, Hugh D. R. *A Chinese Lineage Village: Sheung Shui.* Stanford, Calif.: Stanford University Press, 1968.

Barth, Frederik. "Introduction." In Frederik Barth, ed., *Ethnic Groups and Boundaries: The Social Organization of Cultural Difference*, pp. 9–38. Boston: Little, Brown, 1969.

Benton, Gregor. *Mountain Fires: The Red Army's Three-Year War in South China, 1934–1938.* Berkeley: University of California Press, 1992.

Bielenstein, Hans. "The Chinese Colonization of Fukien Until the End of T'ang." In *Studia Serica Bernhard Karlgren Dedicata*, pp. 98–122. Copenhagen: E. Munksgaard, 1959.

Boluo xian zhi 博羅縣志 (Gazetteer of Boluo county). 1631.

Boorman, Howard L., ed. *Biographical Dictionary of Republican China.* 4 vols. New York: Columbia University Press, 1967–71.

Campbell, George. "Origin and Migrations of the Hakkas." *Chinese Student Monthly* 9.6 (Apr. 1914).
Cao Shuji 曹樹基. "Ming-Qing shiqi de liumin he Gan-bei shanqu de kaifa" 明清時期的流民和贛北山區的開發 (The development of the mountain areas of northern Jiangxi and the displaced people in the Ming and Qing periods). *Zhongguo nong shi* 中國農史 (History of Chinese agriculture) 1986.2 (1986): 12–37.
———. "Ming-Qing shiqi de liumin he Gan-nan shanqu de kaifa" 明清時期的流民和贛南山區的開發 (The development of the mountain areas of southern Jiangxi and the displaced people in the Ming and Qing periods). *Zhongguo nong shi* 中國農史 (History of Chinese agriculture) 1985.4 (1985): 19–40.
Chaling zhou zhi 茶陵州志 (Gazetteer of Chaling department). 1695; 1871.
Chang Chung-li. *The Chinese Gentry*. Seattle: University of Washington Press, 1955.
Changhua xian zhi 昌化縣志 (Gazetteer of Changhua county). 1823.
Changning xian zhi 長寧縣志 (Gazetteer of Changning county [Guangdong]). 1756; 1839.
Changning xian zhi 長寧縣志 (Gazetteer of Changning county [Jiangxi]). 1876.
Changsha fu zhi 長沙府志 (Gazetteer of Changsha prefecture). 1685; 1747.
Changshan xian zhi 常山縣志 (Gazetteer of Changshan county). 1723.
Char, Andrew. "Social Origins of Ethnicity: The Hakka in Central Kwangtung." *Stone Lion Review* 9 (Harvard University, Spring 1982): 53–78.
Chen Qiaoyi 陳橋驛. "Lishi shang Zhejiang-sheng de shandi kenzhi yu shanlin pohuai" 歷史上浙江省的山地墾殖與山林破壞 (The opening of mountain land and destruction of forests in the history of Zhejiang province). *Zhongguo shehui kexue* 中國社會科學 (Social sciences in China) 1983.4 (July 1983): 207–17.
Chen Shengshao 陳盛韶. *Wensu lu* 問俗錄 (Record of asking about customs). 1827.
Chen Yundong 陳運棟. *Kejiaren* 客家人 (The Hakkas). Taibei: Lianya chubanshe, 1978.
———. *Taiwan de kejiaren* 台灣的客家人 (The Hakkas in Taiwan). Taibei: Taiyuan chubanshe, 1989.
Chen Zhiping 陳支平. *Kejia yuanliu xinlun* 客家源流新論 (A new discussion of the origins of the Hakkas). Nanning: Guangxi jiaoyu chubanshe, 1995.
Chenghai xian zhi 澄海縣志 (Gazetteer of Chenghai county). 1815.
Chixi xian zhi 赤谿縣志 (Gazetteer of Chixi county). 1920.
Chongyi xian zhi 崇義縣志 (Gazetteer of Chongyi county). 1710; 1867; 1989.
Chuzhou fu zhi 處州府志 (Gazetteer of Chuzhou prefecture). 1635; 1711; 1877.
Cohen, Abner, ed. *Urban Ethnicity*. London: Tavistock, 1974.
Cohen, Myron L. "The Hakka or 'Guest People': Dialect as a Sociocultural Variable in Southeastern China." *Ethnohistory* 15.3 (Summer 1968): 237–92.
Cohen, Ronald. "Ethnicity: Problem and Focus in Anthropology." *Annual Review of Anthropology* 7 (1978): 379–403.

Conghua xian zhi 從化縣志 (Gazetteer of Conghua county). 1730.

Da Qing Shengzu Ren (Kangxi) huangdi shilu 大清聖祖仁(康熙)黃帝實錄 (Veritable records of the Kangxi period of the Qing dynasty). Rep. Taibei: Huawen shuju, 1964.

Da Qing Xuanzong Cheng (Daoguang) huangdi shilu 大清宣宗成(道光)黃帝實錄 (Veritable records of the Daoguang period of the Qing dynasty). Rep. Taibei: Huawen shuju, 1964.

Dai Pan 戴槃. *Yanling jilüe* 嚴陵紀略 (Records from Yanling). 1868.

Daning xian zhi 大寧縣志 (Gazetteer of Daning county). 1885.

Deqing xian zhi 德清縣志 (Gazetteer of Deqing county). 1808.

Dingnan ting zhi 定南廳志 (Gazetteer of Dingnan subprefecture). 1779.

Dingyuan ting zhi 定遠廳志 (Gazetteer of Dingyuan subprefecture). 1879.

Dongguan xian zhi 東莞縣志 (Gazetteer of Dongguan county). 1689.

Duan Congguang 段從廣. "Gan-xi pengmin de kang Qing douzheng" 贛西棚民的抗清鬥爭 (Anti-Qing resistance of the Pengmin of western Jiangxi). *Lishi jiaoxue* 歷史教學 (Historical education) 1955.1 (Jan. 1955): 33–36.

Eberhard, Wolfram. *Social Mobility in Traditional China.* Leiden: E. J. Brill, 1962.

Eitel, E. J. "Ethnographical Sketches of the Hakka Chinese." *Notes and Queries on China and Japan* 1.5 (31 May 1867), 1.6 (29 June 1867), 1.7 (31 July 1867).

———. "An Outline History of the Hakkas." *China Review* 2 (July 1873–June 1874): 160–64.

Elvin, Mark. *The Pattern of the Chinese Past.* Stanford, Calif.: Stanford Univ. Press, 1973.

Enping xian zhi 恩平縣志 (Gazetteer of Enping county). 1934.

Entenmann, Robert E. "Sichuan and Qing Migration Policy." Paper presented at the 32d annual meeting of the Association of Asian Studies, Washington, D.C., 22 Mar. 1980.

Erbaugh, Mary S. "The Secret History of the Hakkas: The Chinese Revolution as a Hakka Enterprise." *China Quarterly* 132 (Dec. 1992): 937–68.

Fan Shuzhi 樊澍志. "Mingdai Jing-Xiang liumin yu pengmin" 明代荆襄流民與棚民 (The displaced people and the Pengmin in the Jing-Xiang region in the Ming period). *Zhongguo shi yanjiu* 中國史研究 (Studies in Chinese history) 1980.3 (Sept. 1980): 119–28.

Fang Junyi 方濬頤. "He tu ke shuo" 和土客說 (Mediation between natives and Hakkas). In *Erzhi xuan wencun* 二知軒文存 (Collected works of Fang Junyi). n.p. 1878.

Feng Erkang 馮爾康. "Shilun Qing zhongye Wannan fuyu pengmin de jingying fangshi" 試論清中葉皖南富裕棚民的經營方式 (A preliminary exploration of the mode of production of the rich Pengmin of southern Anhui in mid-Qing times). *Nankai daxue xuebao* 南開大學學報 (Journal of Nankai university). 1978.2 (Apr. 1978): 92–96.

Feng xian zhi 鳳縣志 (Gazetteer of Feng county). 1892.
Fengxin xian zhi 奉新縣志 (Gazetteer of Fengxin county). 1826.
Fenshui xian zhi 分水縣志 (Gazetteer of Fenshui county). 1906.
Fenyi xian zhi 分宜縣志 (Gazetteer of Fenyi county). 1683; 1822; 1940.
Forrest, Robert A. D. *The Chinese Language*. 2d rev. ed. London: Faber & Faber, 1965.
Friedman, Edward. "Revolution or Just Another Bloody Cycle: Swatow and the 1911 Revolution." *Journal of Asian Studies* 29.2 (Feb. 1970): 289–308.
Fu Yiling 傅衣凌. "Capitalism in Chinese Agriculture: On the Laws Governing Its Development." *Modern China* 6.3 (July 1980): 311–16.
———. *Ming-Qing fengjian shehui tudi suoyouzhi lungang* 明清封建社會土地所有制論綱 (An outline of the landownership system in the feudal society of the Ming and Qing dynasties). Shanghai: Shanghai renmin chubanshe, 1992.
———. *Ming-Qing nongcun shehui jingji* 明清農村社會經濟 (Rural society and economy of the Ming-Qing period). Beijing: Sanlian shudian, 1961.
———. *Ming-Qing shehui jingji shi lunwen ji* 明清社會經濟史論文集 (Collected essays on Ming-Qing socioeconomic history). Beijing: Renmin chubanshe, 1982.
Fuliang xian zhi 浮梁縣志 (Gazetteer of Fuliang county). 1783.
Fuson, Chester Garfield. "The Peoples of Kwangtung." *Lingnan Science Journal* 7 (1929): 5–22.
Gan xian zhi 贛縣志 (Gazetteer of Gan county). 1756.
Ganzhou fu zhi 贛州府志 (Gazetteer of Ganzhou prefecture). 1621; 1782; 1873.
Gao Tingyao 高廷瑤. *Huanyou jilüe* 宦游紀略 (Records of a roaming official). Henan, 1908.
Gaoming xian zhi 高明縣志 (Gazetteer of Gaoming county). 1895.
Gaoyao xian zhi 高要縣志 (Gazetteer of Gaoyao county). Xuantong period, printed 1938; 1948.
(Xuxiu) Gaoyao xian zhi 續修高要縣志 (Revised gazetteer of Gaoyao county). 1863.
Gongzhong dang Yongzheng chao zouzhe 宮中檔雍正朝奏摺 (Palace memorials of the Yongzheng reign). Taibei: Guoli gugong bowuguan, 1977.
Gu Yanwu 顧炎武. *Tianxia junguo libing shu* 天下郡國利病書 (Characteristics of each province in the empire). Preface 1662; Sibu congkan ed.
Gu Zhi 古直. *Keren dui* 客人對 (Hakka reply). Shanghai: Longmen, 1930.
Guangdong tong zhi 廣東通志(General gazetteer of Guangdong). 1822, rep. 1934.
Guangxin fu zhi 廣信府志 (Gazetteer of Guangxin prefecture). 1783; 1873.
(Xuxiu) Guangzhou fu zhi 續修廣州府志 (Revised gazetteer of Guangzhou prefecture). 1759.
(Zhili) Guiyang zhou zhi 直隸桂陽州志 (Gazetteer of Guiyang independent department). 1818.
Guo Shouhua 郭壽華. *Kejia yuanliu xinzhi* 客家源流新志 (A new discussion of the origins of the Hakkas). Taibei: the author, 1964.

Haifeng xian zhi 海豐縣志 (Gazetteer of Haifeng county). 1750.

Hartwell, Robert. "Demographic, Political and Social Transformations of China, 750–1550." *Harvard Journal of Asiatic Studies* 42.2 (Dec. 1982): 365–442.

Hashimoto, Oi-kan Yue. *Phonology of Cantonese.* Cambridge, Eng.: Cambridge University Press, 1972.

He Changling. 賀長齡. *Huangchao jingshi wenbian* 皇朝經世文編 (Essays on statecraft from the present dynasty). Photographic rep. Taibei, 1963.

He xian zhi 賀縣志 (Gazetteer of He county). 1890; 1934.

Heshan xian zhi 鶴山縣志 (Gazetteer of Heshan county). 1754.

Hino Kaizaburō 日野開三郎. *Tōyō shigaku ronshū* 東洋史學論集 (Essays in Oriental history). Tokyo: San'ichi shobo, 1980.

Ho Ping-ti. *Studies on the Population of China, 1368–1953.* Cambridge, Mass.: Harvard University Press, 1959.

Hoang, Pierre. *Mélanges sur l'Administration.* Shanghai: la Mission Catholique, 1902.

Hsiao, Kung-chuan. *Rural China: Imperial Control in the Nineteenth Century.* Seattle: University of Washington Press, 1960.

Hu Zhusheng 胡珠生. "Tiandi hui qiyuan chutan" 天地會起源初探 (Preliminary investigation of the origins of the Tiandi hui). *Lishi xue* 歷史學 (History) 1979.4 (1979): 62–76.

Hua xian zhi 花縣志 (Gazetteer of Hua county). 1687.

Huang Foyi 黃佛頤. *Zhujixiang minzu nanqian ji* 珠璣巷民族南遷記 (Southward migration of the Zhujixiang people). Mimeo. Guangzhou: Zhongshan tushuguan, 1957.

Huang Guoqiang 黃國強. "Ming zhongye Jing-Xiang diqu liumin de kenhuang douzheng" 明中葉荊襄地區流民的墾荒鬥爭 (The struggle of the displaced people to open up the wastelands in the Jing-Xiang area in the mid-Ming). In Zhongguo nongmin zhanzheng shi yanjiu hui 中國農民戰爭史研究會, *Zhongguo nongmin zhanzheng shi yanjiu jikan, di si ji* 中國農民戰爭史研究集刊第四輯 (Research on the history of peasant wars in China, fourth collection), pp. 103–8. Shanghai: Shanghai renmin chubanshe, 1985.

Huang Zanfa 黃贊發. "Chao-Shan xianmin chukao" 潮汕先民初考 (A preliminary study of the original inhabitants of the Chaozhou-Shantou area). *Shantou wenshi, di er ji* 汕頭文史第二輯 (Historical materials from Shantou, 2d collection) (Mar. 1985): 90–106.

Huangchao tongzhi 皇朝通志 (General record of the empire). Shanghai, 1935–37.

Hubu zeli 戶部則例 (Precedents of the Board of Revenue). Daoguang edition.

Huichang xian zhi 會昌縣志 (Gazetteer of Huichang county). 1872.

Huizhou fu zhi 徽州府志 (Gazetteer of Huizhou prefecture [Anhui]). 1827.

Huizhou fu zhi 惠州府志 (Gazetteer of Huizhou prefecture [Guangdong]). 1595; 1688; 1881.

Jen Yu-wen. *The Taiping Revolutionary Movement.* New Haven, Conn.: Yale University Press, 1973.

Ji'an fu zhi 吉安府志 (Gazetteer of Ji'an prefecture). 1776; 1876.

Jiang Bingzhao蔣炳釗. "Lun kejia yu dangdi minzu zhu guanxi" 論客家與當地民族諸關系 (On the relations between the Hakkas and other local nationalities). *Xiamen daxue xuebao, zhe she ban* 廈門大學學報哲社版 (Xiamen University journal, philosophy and social sciences) 1992.4 (Oct. 1992): 106–12.

———, comp. *Shezu gudai lishi ziliao huibian* 畲族古代歷史資料匯編 (Materials on the ancient history of the She people). Mimeo. Ethnological Section of the Museum of Anthropology, Xiamen University, June 1979.

Jianghua xian zhi 江華縣志 (Gazetteer of Jianghua county). 1870.

Jiangshan xian zhi 江山縣志 (Gazetteer of Jiangshan county). 1713; 1873.

Jianyang xian zhi 建陽縣志 (Gazetteer of Jianyang county). 1832.

(Xuxiu) Jiashan xian zhi 續修嘉善縣志 (Gazetteer of Jiashan county). 1894.

Jiaying zhou zhi 嘉應州志 (Gazetteer of Jiaying department). 1898.

Jieyang xian zhi 揭陽縣志 (Gazetteer of Jieyang county). 1779.

Jing Junjian 經君健. *Qingdai shehui de jianmin dengji* 清代社會的賤民等級 (The "mean people" strata in Qing society). Hangzhou: Zhejiang renmin chubanshe, 1993.

Jing'an xian zhi 靖安縣志 (Gazetteer of Jing'an county). 1989.

Jingde xian zhi 旌德縣志 (Gazetteer of Jingde county). 1808.

Jingning xian zhi 景寧縣志 (Gazetteer of Jingning county). 1873.

Jixi xian zhi 績溪縣志 (Gazetteer of Jixi county). 1810, Taipei rep.

Jones, Susan Mann, and Philip A. Kuhn. "Dynastic Decline and the Roots of Rebellion." In John K. Fairbank, ed., *The Cambridge History of China.* Vol. 10: *Late Ch'ing, 1800–1911,* Part 1, pp. 107–62. Cambridge, Eng.: Cambridge University Press, 1978.

(Xuzuan) Jurong xian zhi 續纂句容縣志 (Revised gazetteer of Jurong county). 1904.

Kaihua xian zhi 開花縣志 (Gazetter of Kaihua county). 1896.

Kaiping xian zhi 開平縣志 (Gazetter of Kaiping county). 1823.

"Kanton kyakka minzoku no kenkyū" 廣東客家民族の研究 (Research on the Hakkas of Guangdong), alternative title: "Kyakka minzoku konseki gaiko" 客家民族今昔概況 (The past and present of the Hakka people), appendix to Song Wenbing 宋文炳, *Shina minzoku shi* 支那民族史 (A history of the Chinese people). Trans. Oguchi Goro 小口五郎. Tokyo: Daitō shuppansha, 1944.

Klein, Donald W., and Anne B. Clark. *Biographic Dictionary of Chinese Communism 1921–1965*, 2 vols. Cambridge, Mass.: Harvard University Press, 1971.

Kong Yongsong 孔永松, and Qiu Songqing 丘松慶. *Min-xi geming genjudi de jingji jianshe* 閩西革命根據地的經濟建設 (Economic reconstruction of the western Fujian revolutionary base area). Fuzhou: Fujian renmin chubanshe, 1981.

Kuhn, Philip A. "Origins of the Taiping Vision: Cross-Cultural Dimensions of a Chinese Rebellion." *Comparative Studies in Society and History* 19.3 (July 1977): 350–66.

———. *Rebellion and Its Enemies in Late Imperial China: Militarization and Social Structure, 1796–1864*. Cambridge, Mass.: Harvard University Press, 1970.

———. *Soulstealers: The Chinese Sorcery Scare of 1768*. Cambridge, Mass.: Harvard University Press, 1990.

Kusano Yasushi 草野靖. Sōdai no shuko kyakuko tenko" 宋代の主戸客戸佃戸 (Native, immigrant, and tenant households of the Song dynasty). *Tōyō gakuhō* 東洋學報 (Reports of the Oriental Society) 46.2 (Sept. 1963): 89–93.

Laai Yi-faai, Franz Michael, and John C. Sherman. "The Use of Maps in Social Research: A Case Study in South China." *Geographical Review* 52.1 (Jan. 1962): 92–111.

Lai Jiadu 賴家讀. *Mingdai Yunyang nongmin qiyi* 明代鄖陽農民起義 (Uprisings of the peasants of Yunyang in Ming times). Wuhan: Hubei renmin chubanshe, 1956.

Lamley, Harry J. "Subethnic Rivalry in the Ch'ing Period." In Emily M. Ahern and Hill Gates, eds., *The Anthropology of Taiwanese Society*, pp. 282–318. Stanford, Calif.: Stanford University Press, 1981.

Lee, James. "Migration and Expansion in Chinese History." In William H. McNeil and Ruth S. Adams, eds., *Human Migration*, pp. 20–47. Bloomington: Indiana University Press, 1978.

Lee, Robert H. G. *The Manchurian Frontier in Qing History*. Cambridge, Mass.: Harvard University Press, 1970.

Leong, S. T. "The Hakka Chinese of Lingnan: Ethnicity and Social Change in Modern China." In David Pong and Edmund S. K. Fung, eds. *Ideal and Reality: Social and Political Change in Modern China, 1860–1949*, pp. 287–326. Lanham, Md.: University Press of America, 1985.

Li Mo 李默. "Lun kejia de xingcheng ji minzu ronghe" 論客家的形成及民族融合 (On the formation of the Hakkas and the intermingling of nationalities). *Zhongguo shi yanjiu* 中國史研究 (Studies in Chinese history) 1993.4 (Nov. 1993): 117–29.

Li Youning 李又寧, and Zhang Yufa 張玉法, eds. *Jindai Zhongguo nüquan yundong shiliao* 近代中國女權運動史料 (Historical materials on the modern Chinese women's rights movement). Taibei: Zhuanji wenxue she, 1975.

Lian Wenxi 連文希. "Kejia ruken Taiwan diqu kaolüe" 客家入墾台灣地區考略 (A study of Hakka immigrant agriculturalists in Taiwan). *Taiwan wenxian* 台灣文獻 (Documents on Taiwan) 22.3 (1971): 1–25.

Lianhua xian zhi 蓮花縣志 (Gazetteer of Lianhua county). 1989.

Liling xiangtu zhi 醴陵鄉土志 (Local records of Liling county). 1926.

Lin Daquan 林達泉. "Ke shuo" 客說 (Concerning the Hakkas). In Wen Tingjing 溫廷敬, ed., *Chayang sanjia wenchao* 茶陽三家文鈔 (Literary works of three authors of Dabu county), pp. 131–35. Taibei: Wenhai chubanshe, 1966.

Lin Renchuan. "Fukien's Private Sea Trade in the Sixteenth and Seventeenth Centuries." In E. B. Vermeer, ed. *Development and Decline of Fukien Province in the Seventeenth and Eighteenth Centuries,* pp. 163–216. Leiden: E. J. Brill, 1990.

Lin Zaifu 林再複. *Taiwan fazhan shi* 台灣發展史 (History of the development of Taiwan). Taibei: Sanmin shuju, 1990.

Ling xian zhi 酃縣志 (Gazetteer of Ling county). 1766; 1873.

Lishui xian zhi 麗水縣志 (Gazetteer of Lishui county). 1874; 1906.

Liu, Kwang-Ching. "The Military Challenge: The Northwest and the Coast." In John K. Fairbank and Kwang-Ching Liu, eds., *The Cambridge History of China.* Vol. 11, *Late Ch'ing, 1800–1911,* Part 2, pp. 202–73. London: Cambridge University Press, 1980.

Liu Min 劉敏. "Lun Qingdai pengmin de huji wenti" 論淸代棚民的戶籍問題 (On the question of household registration of the Pengmin during the Qing dynasty). *Zhongguo shehui jingji shi yanjiu* 中國社會經濟史研究 (Studies in Chinese social and economic history) 1983.1 (Feb. 1983): 17–29.

———. "Shilun Ming-Qing shiqi huji zhidu de bianhua" 試論明淸時期戶籍制度的變化 (A preliminary study of changes in the household registration system in the Ming and Qing periods). *Zhongguo gudai shi luncong* 中國古代史論叢 (Studies in the history of ancient China) 1981.2 (Sept. 1981): 218–36.

Liu Shengkui 劉繩逵. "Yiren laiyuan ji qi shenghuo xishang" 邑人來源及其生活習尙 (Origins and customs of the people of Ruijin). *Ruijin wenxian* 瑞金文獻 (Documents on Ruijin) 1 (25 Dec. 1974): 16–18.

Liu Xiusheng 劉秀生. "Qingdai Min-Zhe-Gan-Wan de pengmin jingji" 淸代閩浙贛皖的棚民經濟 (The Pengmin economy in Fujian, Zhejiang, Jiangxi, and Anhui during the Qing period). *Zhongguo shehui jingji shi yanjiu* 中國社會經濟史研究 (Studies in Chinese social and economic history) 1988.1 (Feb. 1988): 53–60.

Liuyang xian zhi 瀏陽縣志 (Gazetteer of Liuyang county). 1733; 1873.

Liuyang xiangtu zhi 瀏陽鄉土志 (Local records of Liuyang county). 1907, rep. 1967.

Lo Wan. "Communal Strife in Mid-Nineteenth Century Kwangtung: The Establishment of Ch'ih-ch'i." *Papers on China* 19 (Harvard University, Dec. 1965): 85–119.

Longmen xian zhi 龍門縣志 (Gazetteer of Longmen county). 1936.

Longnan xian zhi 龍南縣志 (Gazetteer of Longnan county). 1709.

Longquan xian zhi 龍泉縣志 (Gazetteer of Longquan county [Jiangxi]). 1824; 1873.

Longquan xian zhi 龍泉縣志 (Gazetteer of Longquan county [Zhejiang]). 1762; 1878.

Longyou xian zhi 龍游縣志 (Gazetteer of Longyou county). 1925.

Luling xian zhi 廬陵縣志 (Gazetteer of Luling county). 1920.

Luo Xianglin 羅香林, comp. *Kejia shiliao huipian* 客家史料匯篇 (Historical sources for the study of the Hakkas). Hong Kong: Zhongguo xueshe, 1965.

———. *Kejia yanjiu daolun* 客家研究導論 (Introduction to the study of the Hakkas). Xinning: Xishan shucang, 1933.

———. "Kejia yuanliu kao" 客家源流考 (A study of the origins of the Hakkas). In *Shijie keshu dierci kenqin dahui shilu* 世界客屬第二次懇親大會實錄 (Proceedings of the Second World Hakka Congress). Taibei: Shijie keshu dierci kenqin dahui shilu bianji weiyuanhui, 1974.

———. *Zhongguo zupu yanjiu* 中國族譜研究 (Studies on Chinese genealogies). Hong Kong: Zhongguo xueshe, 1971.

Luoding zhili zhou zhi 羅定直隸州志 (Gazetteer of Luoding independent department). 1687.

Luonan xian zhi 雒南縣志 (Gazetteer of Luonan county). Guangxu.

MacIver, D. *A Chinese-English Dictionary: Hakka Dialect as Spoken in Kwangtung Province.* 2d ed. n.p. 1926.

Mao Zedong 毛澤東. *Mao Zedong ji* 毛澤東集 (Collected works of Mao Zedong). Takeuchi Minoru 竹內實主 comp. Rep. Hong Kong, 1976.

———. *Mao Zedong xuanji* 毛澤東選集 (Selected works of Mao Zedong). Beijing: Renmin chubanshe, 1969.

Mei Zengliang 梅曾亮. *Pojian shanfang wenchao* 柏根山房文鈔 (Collected works of Mei Zengliang). Preface 1855, rep. 1917.

Meishui shizhuan 梅水詩傳 (An anthology of poetry from the Mei valley). n.p. 1901.

Michael, Franz, with Chung-li Chang. *The Taiping Rebellion: History and Documents.* 3 vols. Seattle: University of Washington Press, 1966–71.

Ming Muzong shilu 明穆宗實錄 (Veritable records of Ming emperor Muzong). Rep. Taibei: Zhongyang yanjiu yuan lishi yuyan yanjiu suo, 1966–68.

Ming-Qing shiliao, yibian 明清史料乙編 (Materials on Ming and Qing history, second series). Rep. Taibei, 1972.

Ming Shenzong shilu 明神宗實錄 (Veritable records of Ming emperor Shenzong). Rep. Taibei: Zhongyang yanjiu yuan lishi yuyan yanjiu suo, 1966–68.

Morita Akira 森田明. "Minmatsu Shinsho no hōmin ni tsuite" 明末清初の棚民について (The Pengmin of the late Ming and early Qing). *Jimbun kenkyū* 人文研究 (Studies in the humanities) (Osaka shiritsu daigaku bungakubu) 28.9 (Dec. 1976): 1–38.

Nakagawa Manabu 中川學. "Chūgoku kyakka shi kenkyū no shin dōkō" 中國客家史研究の動向 (New trends in the study of the Hakkas in China). *Hitotsubashi ronsō* 一橋論叢 (Hitotsubashi papers) 77.4 (1977): 69–81.

———. *Kyakka ron no gendaiteki kōzu* 客家論の現代的構圖 (Modern trends in Hakka studies). Tokyo: Ajia keizai gakkai, 1980.

———. "Kyako to kyakka no shiteki renkan" 客戸と客家の史的連關 (The historical relationship between the "kehu" and the Hakkas). *Hitotsubashi ronsō* 一橋論叢 (Hitotsubashi papers) 72.1 (1974): 45–56.

———. "Studies on the History of the Hakkas: Reconsidered." *The Developing Economies* 13.2 (June 1975): 208–23.

Nan'an fu zhi 南安府志 (Gazetteer of Nan'an prefecture). 1609; 1710; 1768.
Nankang xian zhi 南康縣志 (Gazetteer of Nankang county). 1710; 1823.
Nanping xian zhi 南平縣志 (Gazetteer of Nanping county). 1810.
Nanxiong xian zhi 南雄縣志 (Gazetteer of Nanxiong county). 1991.
(Xuxiu) Nanzheng xian zhi 續修南鄭縣志 (Gazetteer of Nanzheng county). 1794.
Nanzheng xian zhi 南鄭縣志 (Gazetteer of Nanzheng county). 1921.
Ng Chin-keong. *Trade and Society: The Amoy Network on the China Coast, 1683–1735*. Singapore: Singapore University Press, 1983.
Ningdu xian zhi 寧都縣志 (Gazetteer of Ningdu county). 1592.
Ningguo fu zhi 寧國府志 (Gazetteer of Ningguo prefecture). 1815.
Ningguo xian zhi 寧國縣志 (Gazetteer of Ningguo county). 1869; 1936.
Ningqiang zhou xiangtu zhi 寧羌州鄉土志 (Local records of Ningqiang department). Late Qing ed., rep. 1969.
Norman, Jerry. *Chinese*. Cambridge Language Surveys. Cambridge, Eng.: Cambridge University Press, 1988.
Oh Kem-sung 吳金成. "Minmatsu Shinsho Kōsei nambu no shakai to shinshi" 明末清初江西南部の社會と紳士 (Society and gentry in southern Jiangxi in the late Ming and early Qing). In *Yamane kyōju taikyū ki'nen Mindai shi ronsō* 山根教授退休記念明代史論叢 (Essays on Ming history in honor of the retirement of Professor Yamane), pp. 1081–1106. Tokyo: 1990.
Osborne, Anne Rankin. "Barren Mountains, Raging Rivers: The Ecological and Social Effects of Changing Landuse on the Lower Yangzi Periphery in Late Imperial China." Ph. D. diss., Columbia University, 1989.
———. "The Local Politics of Land Reclamation in the Lower Yangzi Highlands." *Late Imperial China* 15.1 (June 1994): 1–46
Ouning ting zhi 甌寧廳志 (Gazetteer of Ouning subprefecture). 1868–71.
Parish, William L. and Martin King Whyte. *Village and Family in Contemporary China*. Chicago: University of Chicago Press, 1978.
Parsons, James B. *Peasant Rebellions of the Late Ming Dynasty*. Tucson: University of Arizona Press, 1970.
Pasternak, Burton. *Guests in the Dragon: Social Demography of a Chinese District 1895–1946*. New York: Columbia University Press, 1983.
Patterson, Orlando. "Context and Choice in Ethnic Allegiance: A Theoretical Framework and Caribbean Case Study." In Nathan Glazer and Daniel P. Moynihan, eds., *Ethnicity: Theory and Experience*, pp. 305–49. Cambridge, Mass.: Harvard University Press, 1975.
Perkins, Dwight H. *Agricultural Development in China, 1368–1968*. Edinburgh: Edinburgh University Press, 1969.
Pinghe xian zhi 平和縣志 (Gazetteer of Pinghe county). 1719.
Pingjiang xian zhi 平江縣志 (Gazetteer of Pingjiang county). 1874.

Pingli xian zhi 平利縣志 (Gazetteer of Pingli county). 1756.

*(Xuxiu) Pingli xian zhi*續修平利縣志 (Revised gazetteer of Pingli county). 1897.

Pingxiang xian zhi 萍鄉縣志 (Gazetteer of Pingxiang county). 1683; 1784; 1872.

Pingxiang xian zhi 萍鄉縣志 (also *Zhaoping zhi lüe*昭萍志略) (Gazetteer of Pingxiang county). 1935.

Piton, Ch. "On the Origin and History of the Hakkas." *China Review*, 2 (July 1873–June 1874): 222–26.

Poyang xian zhi 鄱陽縣志 (Gazetteer of Poyang county). 1824.

Pucheng xian zhi 浦城縣志 (Gazetteer of Pucheng county). 1811.

Qimen xian zhi 祁門縣志 (Gazetteer of Qimen county). 1827; 1873.

Qinding da Qing huidian shili 欽定大清會典事例 (Collected statutes and precedents of the Qing dynasty). Rep. Shanghai: Shangwu yinshuguan, 1909.

Qing shi liezhuan 清史列傳 (Biographies of Qing history). Rep. Taibei, 1962.

Qingtian xian zhi 青田縣志 (Gazetteer of Qingtian county). 1876.

Qu Dajun 屈大均. *Guangdong xinyu* 廣東新語 (A new lexicon of Guangdong). Rep. Hong Kong: Zhonghua shuju, 1974.

Qu Xuanying 瞿宣穎. *Zhongguo shehui shiliao congchao* 中國社會史料叢鈔(Historical materials on Chinese society). Shanghai: Shangwu yinshuguan, 1937.

Quan Hansheng 全漢昇. *Zhongguo jingji shi luncong* 中國經濟史論叢 (Essays on Chinese economic history). Hong Kong: Xinya yanjiu suo, 1972.

———. *Zhongguo jingji shi yanjiu* 中國經濟史研究 (Studies on Chinese economic history). Hong Kong: Xinya yanjiu suo, 1976.

Quanjiao xian zhi 全椒縣志 (Gazetteer of Quanjiao county). 1920.

Rao Zongyi. "The She Settlement in the Han River Delta, Guangdong." In F. S. Drake, ed., *Symposium on Historical, Archaeological, and Linguistic Studies on Southern China, South-East Asia, and the Hong Kong Region*, pp. 101–19. Hong Kong: Hong Kong University Press, 1967.

Rawski, Evelyn Sakakida. *Agricultural Change and the Peasant Economy of South China*. Cambridge, Mass.: Harvard University Press, 1972.

———."Agricultural Development in the Han River Highlands." *Ch'ing-shih wen-t'i* 3.4 (Dec. 1975): 63–81.

Rhoads, Edward J. M. *China's Republican Revolution: The Case of Kwangtung, 1895–1913*. Cambridge, Mass.: Harvard University Press, 1975.

Roberts, J. A. G. "The Hakka-Punti War." D. Phil. diss., Oxford University, 1969.

Rong xian zhi 容縣志 (Gazetteer of Rong county). 1897.

Rowe, William T. *Hankow: Commerce and Society in a Chinese City, 1796–1889*. Stanford, Calif.: Stanford University Press, 1984.

Rucheng xian zhi 汝城縣志 (Gazetteer of Rucheng county). 1870; 1932.

Ruijin xian zhi 瑞金縣志 (Gazetteer of Ruijin county). 1683; 1753.

(Xuxiu) Ruijin xian zhi 續修瑞金縣志 (Gazetteer of Ruijin county). 1710.

Sanjiang xian zhi 三江縣志 (Gazetteer of Sanjiang county). 1946.
Satake Yasuhiko 佐竹靖彥. "Sōdai Kanshū jijō sobyō" 宋代贛州事情素描 (A rough sketch of conditions in Ganzhou during the Song dynasty). In *Sōdai shi ronsō* 宋代史論叢 (Essays in Song history, in honor of Dr. Aoyama's seventieth birthday), pp. 99–122. Tokyo: Shoshin shobo, 1974.
Segawa Masahisa. "The Ethnic Identity of the She and the Cultural Influence of the Hakka: A Study Based on a Survey of She Villages in Chaozhou, Guangdong." In Michio Suenari, J. S. Eades, and Christian Daniels, eds., *Perspectives on Chinese Society: Views from Japan*, pp. 186–98. Tokyo: Tokyo University of Foreign Studies, Institute for the Study of Languages and Cultures of Asia and Africa, 1994.
Shangyou xian zhi 上猶縣志 (Gazetteer of Shangyou county). 1881.
She xian zhi 歙縣志 (Gazetteer of She county). 1812.
Shepherd, John Robert. *Statecraft and Political Economy on the Taiwan Frontier, 1600–1800*. Stanford, Calif.: Stanford University Press, 1993.
Shezu jianshi 畲族簡史 (A short history of the She people). Fuzhou: Fujian renmin chubanshe, 1980.
Shi Runzhang 施閏章. *Shi Yushan wenji* 施愚山文集 (Collected works of Shi Runzhang). Shanghai, 1909.
Shiba Yoshinobu. *Commerce and Society in Sung China*. Trans. Mark Elvin. Michigan Abstracts of Chinese and Japanese Works on Chinese History, no. 2. Ann Arbor: University of Michigan, 1970.
Shicheng xian zhi 石城縣志 (Gazetteer of Shicheng county). 1660;1745; 1990.
Shiquan xian zhi 石泉縣志 (Gazetteer of Shiquan county). 1849.
Shouchang xian zhi 壽昌縣志 (Gazetteer of Shouchang county). 1930.
Skinner, G. William. "Chinese Peasants and the Closed Community: An Open and Shut Case." *Comparative Studies in Society and History* 13.3 (July 1971): 270–81.
———. *Chinese Society in Thailand: An Analytical History*. Ithaca, N.Y.: Cornell University Press, 1957.
———. "Cities and the Hierarchy of Local Systems." In Skinner, ed., *The City in Late Imperial China*, pp. 275–351.
———, ed. *The City in Late Imperial China*. Stanford, Calif.: Stanford University Press, 1977.
———. "Differential Development in Lingnan." In Thomas P. Lyons and Victor Nee, eds. *The Economic Transformation of South China: Reform and Development in the Post-Mao Era*, pp. 17–54. Ithaca, N.Y.: Cornell East Asia Program, 1994.
———. "Introduction: Urban Development in Imperial China." In Skinner, ed., *The City in Late Imperial China*, pp. 17–54.
———. "Presidential Address: The Structure of Chinese History." *Journal of Asian Studies* 44.2 (Feb. 1985): 271–92.
———. "Regional Systems in Late Imperial China." Paper presented at the 2d Annual

Meeting of the Social Science History Association, Ann Arbor, Mich., 1977.
———. "Regional Urbanization in Nineteenth Century China." In Skinner, ed., *The City in Late Imperial China*, pp. 211–49.
Smith, Carol A., ed. *Regional Analysis*. 2 vols. New York: Academic Press, 1976.
Songxi xian zhi 松溪縣志 (Gazetteer of Songxi county). 1700.
Songyang xian zhi 松陽縣志 (Gazetteer of Songyang county). 1926.
Stauffer, Milton T., ed. *The Christian Occupation of China*. Shanghai: China Continuation Committee, 1922.
Stubel, H., and Li Hua-min. *Die Hsia-min vom Tse-mu-shan*. Nanjing: Academia Sinica, 1932.
Suichang xian zhi 遂昌縣志 (Gazetteer of Suichang county). 1765.
Sun Daren 孫達人. "Chuan-Chu-Yu-Wan liumin yu Shaan-nan jingji de shengshuai" 川楚豫皖流民與陝南經濟的盛衰 (Boom and bust in the south Shaanxi economy and the displaced people from Sichuan, Hunan, Hubei, and Anhui). In Zhongguo nongmin zhanzheng shi yanjiu hui 中國農民戰爭史研究會, *Zhongguo nongmin zhanzheng shi yanjiu jikan, di san ji* 中國農民戰爭史研究集刊第三輯 (Research on the history of peasant wars in China, third collection), pp. 134–47. Shanghai: Shanghai renmin chubanshe, 1983.
Sun Lung-kee. "The Background of the Mid-Qing Popular Uprising of the Hupeh, Szechwan, Shensi Border Region." Unpublished seminar paper, Stanford University, June 1979.
Sun Yiwen 孫衣文. *Ouhai yiwen* 甌海軼聞 (Anecdotes from Ouhai). 1886.
Taihe xian zhi 泰和縣志 (Gazetteer of Taihe county). 1826; 1878.
Taishun xian zhi 泰順縣志 (also *Taishun fenjiang lu* 泰順分疆錄) (Gazetteer of Taishun county). 1879.
Taiwan Sōtokufu, Rınji Taiwan Kyūkan chōsakai da ichi bu 台灣總督府臨時台灣舊慣調查會第一部. *Shinkoku gyōseihō* 清國行政法 (Administrative laws of the Qing period). Tokyo: Rinji Taiwan Kyūhan chōsaki, 1910–14.
Tajiri Minoru 田尻利. "Shindai Kōsei ni okeru ransaku no tenkai" 清代江西における藍作の展開 (The development of the indigo industry in Jiangxi during the Qing). In *Chūgoku kankei ronsetsu shiryō* 中國關系論說資料 (Collected articles on China), vol. 15, part 3, sec. 1, pp. 1–35. Tokyo: Chūgoku kankei ronsetsu shiryō hozonkai, 1973.
Tan Bi'an 譚彼岸. "Sun Zhongshan jiashi yuanliu ji qi shangdai jingji zhuangkuang xinzheng" 孫中山家世源流及其上代經濟狀況新證 (New evidence on Sun Yat-sen's ancestry and his ancestors' economic situation). *Xueshu yanjiu* 學術研究 (Academic research) 1963.3 (May 1963): 32–38.
Tan Qixiang 譚其驤, chief ed. *Zhongguo lishi ditu ji: Qing shiqi* 中國歷史地圖集: 清時期 (The historical atlas of China: the Qing dynasty period). Beijing: Ditu chubanshe, 1987.

———, chief ed. *Zhongguo lishi ditu ji: Yuan-Ming shiqi* 中國歷史地圖集: 元明時期 (The historical atlas of China: the Yuan dynasty period, the Ming dynasty period). Beijing: Ditu chubanshe, 1982.

———. "Zhongguo neidi yimin shi: Hunan pian" 中國內地移民史: 湖南篇 (History of internal migrations in China: Hunan). *Shixue nianbao* 史學年報 (Historical yearbook) 1.4 (1932): 47–104.

Tangxi xian zhi 湯溪縣志 (Gazetteer of Tangxi county). 1931.

Tao Zhu 陶澍. *Tao Wenyi gong quanji* 陶文毅公全集 (Complete works of Tao Zhu). Preface 1840.

Terada Takanobu 寺田隆信. "Yōsei tei no semmin kaikō rei ni tsuite" 雍正帝の賤民開放令について (On the decree of emancipation of the "mean" people by the Yongzheng emperor). *Tōyōshi kenkyū* 東洋史研究 (Journal of Oriental Researches) 18.3 (Dec. 1959): 124–41.

Tonggu xian zhi 銅鼓縣志 (Gazetteer of Tonggu county). 1989.

Tongzheng xian zhi 同正縣志 (Gazetteer of Tongzheng county). 1933.

United States, Department of State, Decimal Files.

Wan'an xian zhi 萬安縣志 (Gazetteer of Wan'an county). 1873.

Wang Tianjiang 王天獎. "Qing Tong-Guang shiqi kemin de yiken" 清同光時期客民的移墾 ("Guest people" migration in the Tongzhi and Guangxu periods of the Qing dynasty). *Jindaishi yanjiu* 近代史研究 (Studies in modern history) 1983.2 (Mar. 1983): 224–41.

Wang Yangming 王陽明. *Wang Yangming quanshu* 王陽明全書 (Complete works of Wang Yangming). 4 vols. Rep. Taibei: Zhengzhong shuju, 1955.

Wang Yeh-chien. "Food Supply in Eighteenth Century Fukien." *Late Imperial China* 7.2 (Dec. 1986): 80–117.

———. *Land Taxation in Imperial China, 1750–1911*. Cambridge, Mass.: Harvard University Press, 1973.

Wanzai xian zhi 萬載縣志 (Gazetteer of Wanzai county). 1683; 1733; 1872; 1940; 1988.

Watanabe Osamu 渡邊修. "Kōsei teitoku Kin Shōkan to sono hanran" 江西提督金聲桓とその反亂 (The Jiangxi military commander Jin Shenghuan and his revolt). *Tōyōshi kenkyū* 東洋史研究 (Journal of Oriental Researches) 49.3 (Dec. 1990): 87–113.

Watt, John R. *The District Magistrate in Late Imperial China*. New York: Columbia University Press, 1972.

Wei Li 魏禮. *Wei Jizi wenji* 魏季子文集 (Collected works of Wei Li). n.p. 1679.

Wei Yuan 魏源. *Guweitang waiji* 古微堂外集 (Outer collection from the Guwei Hall). 1878.

Weng Huidong 翁輝東, comp. *Chaozhou wengai* 潮州文概 (Writings from Chaozhou). First printed 1933.

Who's Who in Communist China. Hong Kong: Union Research Institute, 1969–70.

Wolf, Arthur P., and Chieh-shan Huang. *Marriage and Adoption in China, 1845–1945*. Stanford, Calif.: Stanford University Press, 1980.

Wu Rongchi. *Gan-nan fangyin kao* 贛南方音考 (A study of the dialect of southern Jiangxi). n.p. 1926.

Wu Zongci 吳宗慈. *Jiangxi Ming-Qing liangdai de minzu wenti* 江西明清兩代的民族問題 (The question of ethnic minorities in Jiangxi during the Ming and Qing). Nanchang: Jiangxi-sheng wenxian weiyuan hui, Jan. 1949.

Wukang xian zhi 武康縣志 (Gazetteer of Wukang county). 1829.

Wuning xian zhi 武寧縣志 (Gazetteer of Wuning county). 1824; 1870; 1990.

Wurm, S. A. et al., eds. *Language Atlas of China*. Hong Kong: Longman, 1987.

Wuzhou fu zhi 梧州府志 (Gazetteer of Wuzhou prefecture). 1770.

Xi'an xian zhi 西安縣志 (Gazetteer of Xi'an county). 1811.

Xiang zhou zhi 象州志 (Gazetteer of Xiang department). 1870.

*Xiangshan xian zhi*香山縣志 (Gazetteer of Xiangshan county). 1923.

Xiaoyi ting zhi 孝義廳志 (Gazetteer of Xiaoyi subprefecture). 1883.

Xie Guozhen 謝國楨. *Ming-Qing biji tancong* 明清筆記談叢(Commentaries on *biji* of the Ming-Qing period). Beijing: Zhonghua shuju, 1960.

———. *Qingchu nongmin qiyi ziliao jilu* 清初農民起義資料輯錄 (Materials on peasant uprisings in the early Qing). Shanghai: Xin zhishi chubanshe, 1956.

Xijiang zhengyao 西江政要 (Political essentials from Xijiang). n.p., n.d.

Xin'an xian zhi 新安縣志 (Gazetteer of Xin'an county). 1688; 1819.

Xinchang xian zhi 新昌縣志 (Gazetteer of Xinchang county [Zhejiang]). 1671.

Xinchang xian zhi 新昌縣志 (Gazetteer of Xinchang county [Jiangxi]). 1683.

Xinchang xian xu zhi 新昌縣續志 (also *Yansheng* 鹽乘) (Gazetteer of Xinchang county [Jiangxi]). 1917.

Xingguo xian zhi 興國縣志 (Gazetteer of Xingguo county). 1683; 1771; 1872.

Xingguo xian zhi 興國縣志 (also *Lian shui zhi lin* 瀲水志林) (Gazetteer of Xingguo county). 1711.

Xingning xian zhi 興寧縣志 (Gazetteer of Xingning county [Hunan]). 1758.

Xingning zhi 興寧志 (Gazetteer of Xingning county [Guangdong]). 1518.

Xinhui xian xu zhi 新會縣續志 (Gazetteer of Xinhui county). 1870.

Xinning xian zhi 新寧縣志 (Gazetteer of Xinning county). 1738; 1804; 1839; 1893.

Xiong Renlin 熊人霖. *Nanrong ji* 南榮集. (Collected works of Nanrong).

Xixiang xian zhi 西鄉縣志 (Gazetteer of Xixiang county). 1828, rep. 1970.

Xu Dixin 許滌新, and Wu Chengming 吳承明, chief eds. *Zhongguo zibenzhuyi de mengya* 中國資本主義的萌芽 (The sprouts of capitalism in China). Vol. 1 of *Zhongguo zibenzhuyi fazhan shi* 中國資本主義發展史 (History of the development of Chinese capitalism). Beijing: Renmin chubanshe, 1985.

Xu Songshi 徐松石. *Yuejiang liuyu renmin shi* 粵江流域人民史 (History of the peoples of Guangdong). Shanghai: Zhonghua shuju, 1938.

Xu Xuzeng 徐旭曾. "Fenghu zaji" 豐湖雜記 (Miscellaneous notes from Fenghu). In Luo Xianglin 羅香林, comp. *Kejia shiliao huipian* 客家史料匯篇 (Historical sources for the study of the Hakkas), pp. 297–99. Hong Kong: Zhongguo xueshe, 1965.

Xuancheng xian zhi 宣城縣志 (Gazetteer of Xuancheng county). 1888.

Xuanping xian zhi 宣平縣志 (Gazetteer of Xuanping county). 1656; 1753; 1878.

Xunyang xian zhi 洵陽縣志 (Gazetteer of Xunyang county). 1783; 1870; 1902.

Xunzhou fu zhi 潯州府志 (Gazetteer of Xunzhou prefecture). 1874; 1897.

Yan Ruyi 嚴如熤. *Sansheng bianfang beilan* 三省邊防備覽 (Guide to frontier defense in three provinces). Preface 1822.

Yang Chengzhi 楊成志. *Guangdong renmin yu wenhua* 廣東人民與文化 (The people of Guangdong and their culture). Guangzhou: Guoli Zhongshan daxue yanjiu yuan wenke yanjiu suo, 1943.

Yang Kaidao 楊開道. *Zhongguo xiangyue zhidu* 中國鄉約制度 (A history of the *xiangyue* system in China). Shandong: Shandong sheng xiangcun fuwu renyuan xunlian chu, 1937.

Yang Qingping 楊慶平. "Sun Zhongshan de jiashi yu keshu yuanyuan" 孫中山的家世與客屬淵源 (Sun Yat-sen's ancestry and his Hakka origins). *Kejia xue yanjiu* 客家學研究 (Hakka studies) 2 (Dec. 1990): 66–69.

Yang xian zhi 洋縣志 (Gazetteer of Yang county). 1898.

Yangchun xian zhi 陽春縣志 (Gazetteer of Yangchun county). 1821.

Yangjiang xian zhi 陽江縣志 (Gazetteer of Yangjiang county). 1925.

Yanshan xian zhi 鉛山縣志 (Gazetteer of Yanshan county). 1873; 1990.

Yi xian zhi 黟縣志 (Gazetteer of Yi county). 1812.

Yichun shi zhi 宜春市志 (Gazetteer of Yichun city). 1990.

Yichun xian zhi 宜春縣志 (Gazetteer of Yichun county). 1683; 1871.

Yin Zhangyi 尹章義. *Taiwan kaifa shi yanjiu* 台灣開發史研究 (Studies in the development of Taiwan). Taibei: Lianjing chuban shiye gongsi, 1989.

Yining zhou zhi 義寧州志 (Gazetteer of Yining department). 1824; 1873.

Yong'an xian cizhi 永安縣次志 (Gazetteer of Yong'an county). 1687.

Yong'an xian zhi 永安縣志 (Gazetteer of Yong'an county). 1586.

Yongfu xian zhi 永福縣志 (Gazetteer of Yongfu county). 1612; 1748.

Yongle dadian 永樂大典 (Yongle encyclopedia). Photographic rep. Beijing: Zhonghua shuju, 1960.

Yongning xian zhi 永寧縣志 (Gazetteer of Yongning county). 1750.

You xian zhi 攸縣志 (Gazetteer of You county). 1789; 1871.

Yuanzhou fu zhi 袁州府志 (Gazetteer of Yuanzhou prefecture). 1760, rep. 1803; 1874.

Yudu xian zhi 雩都縣志 (Gazetteer of Yudu county). 1662; 1757.

Yuezhou fu zhi 岳州府志 (Gazetteer of Yuezhou prefecture). 1746.

Yuhang xian zhi 餘杭縣志 (Gazetteer of Yuhang county). 1808.

Yunhe xian zhi 雲和縣志 (Gazetteer of Yunhe county). 1864.

Yuqian xian zhi 於潛縣志 (Gazetteer of Yuqian county). 1906.

Yushan xian zhi 玉山縣志 (Gazetteer of Yushan county). 1823;1873.

Zeng Weicai 曾維才. "Tantan xian yu kejia minxi shenghuo yu Min-Yue-Gan san sheng jiaojie diqu tuzhu jumin de chengfen" 談談先于客家民系生活于閩粵贛三省交界地區土著居民的成分 (On the native inhabitants of the border region between the three provinces of Fujian, Guangdong, and Jiangxi before the Hakkas). *Kejia xue yanjiu* 客家學研究 (Hakka studies) 2 (Dec. 1990): 33–36.

Zengcheng xian zhi 增城縣志 (Gazetteer of Zengcheng county). 1686; 1754.

Zhang Jian 張鑒. *Leitang anzhu dizi ji* 雷塘菴主弟子記 (Notes of Juan Yuan's pupils). n.d.

Zhang Jianmin 張建民. "Qingdai Xiang-Gan bian shanqu de pengmin yu jingji shehui" 清代湘贛邊山區的棚民與經濟社會 (The Pengmin of the mountainous areas on the Xiang-Gan border, and their society and economy). *Zhengming* 爭鳴 (Contention) (Nanchang) 1988.3 (Apr. 1988): 67–71.

Zhang Tingyu 張廷玉. *Chenghuaiyuan wencun* 澄懷園文存 (Collected works from the Chenghuai studio). n.p. 1891.

Zhaoping xian zhi 昭平縣志 (Gazetteer of Zhaoping county). 1934.

Zhaoqing fu zhi 肇慶府志 (Gazetteer of Zhaoqing prefecture). 1673.

Zhen'an xian zhi 鎮安縣志 (Gazetteer of Zhen'an county). 1755.

Zhen'an xiangtu zhi 鎮安鄉土志 (Local Records of Zhen'an county). 1908.

Zhenping xian zhi 鎮平縣志 (also *Shiku yizheng* 石窟一徵) (Gazetteer of Zhenping county). 1880.

Zhongguo renmin daxue Qingshi yanjiu suo, Dang'an xi Zhongguo zhengzhi zhidu shi jiaoyan shi 中國人民大學清史研究所檔案系中國政治制度史教研室. *Kang Yong Qian shiqi chengxiang renmin fankang douzheng ziliao* 康雍乾時期城鄉人民反抗鬥爭資料 (Materials on the resistance struggles of town and country dwellers during the Kangxi, Yongzheng, and Qianlong periods). Beijing: Zhonghua shuju, 1979.

Zhu Cishou 祝慈壽. *Zhongguo gudai gongye shi* 中國古代工業史 (History of industry in pre-modern China). Shanghai: Xuelin chubanshe, 1988.

Zhupi yuzhi 硃批諭旨 (Vermilion endorsements and edicts of the Yongzheng emperor), 60 vols. n.p. 1732.

Character List

This character list omits names of counties and other well-known geographical names or common phrases. It also omits reign names and names of secondary authors appearing in the bibliography.

ailiao 狄獠

Bai Huang 白潢
Baiyue 百越
banggong 幫工
bao 保
baojia 保甲
baotou 包頭
Beibu 北埔
Beijiang 北江
bendi 本地
bianfeng 邊俸

Chen Honge 陳宏萼
Chen Jiongming 陳炯明
Chen Jitang 陳濟堂
Chen Mingshu 陳名樞
Chen Weizhou 陳維週
Chen Yanjin 陳延縉
Chen Yinke 陳寅恪
Chen Yundong 陳運棟
Chengxiang 程鄉
chidahu 吃大戶
Chilao 犵獠/佬
chongxiangfen 春香粉
Chongzheng 崇正
Chu Pengling 初澎齡

Dabashan 大巴山
daikyakka shugi 大客家主義
danggui 當歸
daotai 道台
Datong ribao 大同日報
dazhong 大種
Deng Geng 鄧耕
Deng Yanhua 鄧彥華
Ding Richang 丁日昌
Dong Jiaozeng 董敎增
Dongjiang 東江
Duan Congguang 段從光

Erongan 鄂容安

Fan 氾
Fang Chun 方椿
fei 匪
fei wo zulei 非我族類
Fenghu 豐湖

Foping 佛平
Fu Lianzhang 傅連璋
fuji 附籍

Gan 贛
Gao Tingyao 高廷瑤
gelao 哥老
Geng Jingzhong 耿精忠
Gou Jian 勾踐
Gu Yanwu 顧炎武
Gu Zhi 古直
Guangdong xiangtu lishi 廣東鄉土歷史
Guangfuren 廣府人
Guanglao yin 廣佬音
guanxi 關西
Guo Moruo 郭沫若
guolu 過嚕
guoyu 國語

Hakka (kejia) 客家
Han 漢
Hanjiang 韓江
Hanshui 漢水
Hanzu ke fu shi 漢族客福史
He Xing 何興
He Yasi 何亞四
Hekouzhen 河口鎮
Hoklo 鶴佬 / 河老 / 福老 / 學佬
Hong Xiuquan 洪秀全
Hong Zhong 洪鍾
Hongtou 紅頭
Hu Hanmin 胡漢民
Huang Chao 黃巢
Huang Jie 黃節
Huang Linshu 黃麟書
Huang Zhao 黃釗
Huang Zunxian 黃遵憲
Huanghuagang 黃花岡
huanglian 黃連
Huangpu 黃埔
Huangshan 黃山

Jabina 查弼納
jia 甲
Jiang 姜
jianmin 賤民
Jiansheting 建設廳
jieyuan 解元
jike zhidu 給客制度
Jin 金
Jin 晉
Jin Shenghuan 金聲桓
jinshan 禁山
jinshi 進士
Jiulingshan 九岭山
juren 舉人

ke 客
kebian ren 客邊人
kefei 客匪
kegang 客綱
kehu 客戶
kehua 客話
keji 客籍
kejia 客家
Kejia fengsu 客家風俗
Kejia yanjiu daolun 客家研究導論
kejiahua 客家話
kemin 客民
keren 客人
ketu 客圖
Kexi datonghui 客系大同會
kezei 客賊

lai 猍
Lai Jixi 賴際熙
lairen 猍人
Lang 狼 / 俍
Lang Baochen 郎葆辰
Lao 獠
laolin 老林
Lei 耒
li 里
Li Dexian 李德先
Li Gou 李覯
Li Jingquan 李井泉
Li Jishen 李濟深
Li Wei 李衛

Li Yangjing 李揚敬
Li Zhenfang 李振芳
Li Zicheng 李自成
Liang Jin'ao 梁金鰲
Liangjiang 兩江
Liao Zhongkai 廖仲愷
liaomin 寮民
liaozhu 寮主
Lin Daquan 林達泉
Lin Jizhen 林激眞
Lin Yizhong 林翼中
Lin Yungai 林云陔
ling'an 領岸
Lingnan 嶺南
Liu Min 劉敏
Liu Yalou 劉亞樓
Liu Yongfu 劉永福
Liu Yongsheng 劉永生
Liu Zhenru 劉振儒
liumin 流民
liu-ngai 流狖
liuxi 流徙
liuyu 流寓
Long Jiguang 龍濟光
Longjiang 龍江
Lushui 淥水
Luo Rong 羅榮
Luo Xianglin 羅香林
Luoxiao 羅霄

ma-gai 㔾个 / 末介 / 麼個 / 麻介
mamin 痲民
mapeng 痲棚
Mazu 媽祖
Mei 梅
Mei Zengliang 梅曾亮
Meishui shizhuan 梅水詩傳
Miao 苗
Miao Peinan 繆培南
Min 閩
Min-Chao liuren 閩潮流人
minnanhua 閩南話
Min-Yue 閩粵
mu 畝
muer 木耳
muzi 木子

Nan-Gan xunfu 南贛巡撫
ngai 涯
ngai 狖
ngai-lou 狖佬
Ninghua 寧化

Ou 甌
Ouning 甌寧
Ouyang Xiu 歐陽修

pai 牌
Pei Shuaidu 裴率度
peng 棚
pengmin 棚民
pengtou 棚頭
pengzhang 棚長
Punti (bendi) 本也

qing 頃
qingke 箐客
qingmin 箐民
Qiu Chuangcheng 邱創成
Qiu Fengjia 邱逢甲
Qiu Yanghuan 邱仰寰
Qu Dajun 屈大均

Rao Qingzhong 饒清中
Ruan Yuan 阮元
ruji 入籍

San Shan Guo Wang 三山國王
Sansheng bianfang beilan 三省邊防備覽
shan duo tian shao 山多田少
Shang Zhixin 尙之信
shanke 山客
shanpeng 山棚
shanzhu 山主
She 畲
shexue 社學
Shen Daihe 沈戴和

shengyuan 生員
shi 石
Shi Dakai 石達開
Shi Lang 施瑯
Shi Runzhang 施閏章
Shibicun 石壁村
Shilu 實錄
shizu 氏祖
shuban 書辦
shuiyuan 水源
Song Xiang 宋湘
Su Yapo 蘇丫婆
Sun Yat-sen 孫逸仙 / 孫中山 / 孫文

Taihu 太湖
Tan 蜑 / 疍
Tan Qixiang 譚其驤
Tangren 唐人
Tao Shilin 陶士霖
Tao Zhengzhong 陶正中
Tao Zhu 陶澍
taohu 逃戶
Taowu 桃塢
ti 題
tianche 天車
Tiandi 天也
Tianheng 天橫
Tianjingwo 天井窩
Tianmushan 天目山
Tianqi 天啓
ting 廳
Ting 渟
tong 桐
Tong Kangnian 佟康年
Tonggu 銅鼓
Tongmenghui 同盟會
tongzi 桐子
tu 土
tu 圖
Tuhua bao 圖畫報
tuzhu 土著

Wako (wokou) 倭蔻
Wang Anshi 王安石
Wang Haiyang 汪海洋
Wang Ping 王平
Wang Yangming 王陽明
Wanyang 萬洋
Wei Li 魏禮
Wei Yuan 魏源
Wen Shanggui 溫上貴
Wen Zhonghe 溫仲和
Wu 吳
Wu Peifu 吳佩孚
Wu Sangui 吳三桂
Wu Xiangda 吳祥達
Wu Zongci 吳宗慈
Wucheng 吳城
Wuyi 武夷

xiahebang 下河幫
xian 縣
xiandalang 閒打浪
Xiang 湘
xiang 鄉
Xiang Hanping 香翰屏
xianghua 向化
xiangyue 鄉約
xiaozhong 小種
Xing-Chang Yue 興長約
Xinjiang 信江
xinmin 新民
Xinzhuang 新莊
Xiong Renlin 熊人霖
Xu Xuzeng 徐旭曾

Yan Ruyi 嚴如熠
Yang Chengwu 楊成武
Yang Maotian 楊懋恬
Yang Xiuqing 楊秀淸
yangyu 洋芋
Yangzhou 揚州
Yanwangzong 閻王總
Yao 猺/傜
Yao Yuping 姚雨平
yaoque 要缺
Ye Chucang 葉楚傖

Ye Jianying 葉劍英
yiguan zhi zu 衣冠之族
Yin Zhangyi 尹章義
Yingqian 螢前
yingxun 螢迅
you ming wu shi 有名無實
Yu Xian 余賢
Yuan Shikai 袁世凱
Yuanshui 袁水
yue 粵
Yugui 雩桂

Zhang Dingcheng 張鼎丞
Zhang Fakui 張發奎
Zhang Jian 張鑒
Zhang Licun 張立村
Zhang Tingyu 張廷玉
Zhang Xianzhong 張獻忠
Zhang Xuan 張煊
zhanggui 掌櫃
Zhang-Long hui 漳龍會
Zhangshuzhen 樟樹鎮
Zhao Hongen 趙宏恩
zhaolai 招徠
zhaozhu 招主
zhenbei 榛杯
Zheng Chenggong 鄭成功
Zhong Yonghe 鐘用貉
Zhonghua xinbao 中華新報
zhongyuan 中原
Zhou Baoheng 周寶衡
Zhou Huifu 周輝甫
Zhou Shenxuan 周慎軒
zhu 主
Zhu De 朱德
Zhu Peide 朱培德
Zhu Yigui 朱一貴
Zhu Yiwu 朱益吾
Zhuang 僮
Zhuanping 磚坪
zhuhu 主戶
Zhujixiang 珠璣巷
Zhuo Bingtian 桌秉恬
Zou Lu 鄒魯
zudang zhi yi 族黨之誼
zuoza 佐雜

Index

In this index an "f" after a number indicates a separate reference on the next page, and an "ff" indicates separate references on the next two pages. A continuous discussion over two or more pages is indicated by a span of page numbers, e.g., "57–59." *Passim* is used for a cluster of references in close but not consecutive sequence.

Library of Congress Cataloging-in-Publication Data

Leong, Sow-Theng.

Migration and ethnicity in Chinese history: Hakkas, Pengmin, and their neighbors / Sow-Theng Leong ; edited by Tim Wright, with an introduction and maps by G. William Skinner.

p. cm.

Includes bibliographical references and index.

ISBN 0-8047-2857-7 (cloth)

1. Hakka (Chinese people)—Ethnic identity—History. 2. Migration, Internal—China—History. 3. China—Economic conditions—To 1644—Regional disparities. 4. China—Economic conditions—1644–1912—Regional disparities. I. Wright, Tim. II. Skinner, G. William (George William), 1925–. III. Title.

DS731.H3L46 1997

305.895'1—dc21 97-413

CIP

Original printing 1997

Last figure below indicates year of this printing:

06 05 04 03 02 01 00 99 98 97

Kolibri 360 GmbH
Ferdinand-Jühlke-Straße 7
99095 Erfurt, Deutschland
produktsicherheit@kolibri360.de